DISCOURSES ON SOCIAL SOFTWARE

T·L·G
Texts in Logic and Games
Volume 5

Discourses on Social Software

EDITED BY
JAN VAN EIJCK
RINEKE VERBRUGGE

Texts in Logic and Games
Volume 5

AMSTERDAM UNIVERSITY PRESS

Cover illustration and four full page illustrations: © Marco Swaen

Cover design: Maedium, Utrecht

ISBN   978 90 8964 123 6
e-ISBN   978 90 4851 041 2
NUR   918 / 980

Table of Contents

Preface

This book has its genesis in a multi-disciplinary project "Games, Action and Social Software", which was carried out at the Netherlands Institute for Advanced Studies in the Humanities and Social Sciences (NIAS) in Wassenaar, from September 2006 through January 2007. This project brought together a group of creative researchers from philosophy, logic, computer science, cognitive science and economics, to investigate the logical, computational and strategic aspects of social mechanisms. The aim was to arrive at a multi-disciplinary perspective, and help create an active community with a more definite agenda. One of the deliverables of the project was to be an overview of this emerging new field, and with an agenda for further research, with the contents of the book to be shaped by discussions and interaction at NIAS.

Even though we had promised just one book as a collective deliverable of the project, it soon turned that it would also be worthwhile to publish two books. The present book is meant as an overview aimed at a wider audience. A second volume collects a set of chapters presenting the research that the group of affiliated researchers carried out as part of the NIAS project, individually and in small interdisciplinary subgroups. This second book, which has a more conventional flavour than the present volume, will appear in the "Studies in Logic" series published under the editorship of Dov Gabbay by College Publications in London, under the title *Games, Actions and Social Software*.

The core theme group of the "Games, Action and Social Software" project was led by Jan van Eijck, from CWI, Amsterdam and Uil-OTS, Utrecht, and Rineke Verbrugge, from the Institute for Artificial Intelligence of the University of Groningen. The other team members were Barbara Dunin-Kęplicz, from the Institute of Informatics, of Warsaw University and the Polish Academy of Sciences, Martin van Hees, from the Philosophy Department of the University of Groningen, and Krister Segerberg, from the Institute of Philosophy at the University of Uppsala. In the course of the project several scholars joined this core group for shorter or longer visits: Johan van Benthem from the University of Amsterdam, Marc Pauly from Stanford University, Barteld Kooi from the University of Groningen, Keith

Dowding then of the London School of Economics, now at the Australian National University, Canberra, Rohit Parikh from the City University of New York (CUNY), Hans van Ditmarsch from the University of Otago, New Zealand, Peter Gärdenfors from Lund University, Andrzej Szalas from Linköping University, and Nicola Dimitri from the University of Siena. They all contributed in one way or another to this volume, even if not all their names show up as chapter authors.

Computer science, philosophy and logic have witnessed a shift of interest from the study of *individual rational action* to the study of *rational interaction*. Examples of the first are computation of an output from a given input in computer science, individual rationality in philosophy, inference systems modelling a single idealized reasoner in logic. Examples of rational interaction are communicating systems in computer science, rational communities in philosophy, interactive proof systems and multi-modal logics modeling interaction of agents in logic. As we hope to show in these discourses, the study of intelligent interaction is highly relevant for society as a whole. It is certainly true in the case of social software that a new field is emerging.

When the project actually started in September 2006, we soon discovered that all of us had embarrassing gaps in our understanding of what the other disciplines in the project had on offer for our common enterprise. So we decided to make a virtue out of a necessity, by elevating the achievement of common understanding to the status of one of the project goals, and by making it our aim to write in-depth overviews of a number of core topics, in the literary form that was also used by Galileo Galilei in 1632 for his *Dialogue Concerning the Two Chief World Systems*, his famous comparison of the Copernican world view with that of Ptolemy. Heyting's introduction to intuitionistic mathematics [120] comes to mind as a more recent example. This book was written in the form of a discussion between a classical mathematician, a formalist, an intuitionistic mathematician, a finitistic nominalist, a pragmatist, and a significist. Other sources of inspiration for this format were the dialogues on theoretical computer science which often appear in the *EATCS Bulletin*, the delightful dialogues by Raymond Smullyan ("Is God a Taoist?", in *The Tao is Silent* [218]), and the dialogues in Hofstadter's *Gödel, Escher, Bach* [122].

Given the broad scope of our project, the adoption of the discourse format was a natural way to start our quest for an overview of rational interaction. The present volume can be viewed as a first step towards a more unified picture of the emerging field of social software and of the different factors generating social complexity. Providing such a picture was among the original project goals.

More specific issues mentioned in the project description, such as the development and refinement of general theories of intelligent interaction, or the analysis of specific social mechanisms for voting, decision making, exchange of goods and services, auctioning, and so on, will be dealt with in the other project book.

The intended readership of the present volume is quite broad: we hope the book will appeal to a wide range of scientifically minded readers willing to look beyond the borders of their own specialisms. Anyone to which this description applies, and who has a bit of knowledge of mathematics and logic, should be able to grasp what goes on in the discourses. We have tried to make sure that specific expertise in any of the fields contributing to "Games, Action and Social Software" is not required.

A few words about the intellectual genesis of the chapters are in order. Two of the discourses in this volume are directly connected to NIAS seminars organized by our project. The NIAS Seminar series given by fellows of the current research group is a sequence of lectures set up each academic year by the Rector of the Institute. The lectures are meant to appeal to interested parties from a wide range of backgrounds, and are highlights of the intellectual life at NIAS. "Social Software" was a guest seminar delivered by project visitor Rohit Parikh on 19 October 2006. This is the topic of *A Guest Lecture on Social Software* in Chapter 4. "Eating from the Tree of Ignorance", the NIAS seminar on 25 January 2007 that marked the end of the project, is the topic of Chapter 13. The feedback from NIAS fellows and staff that these lectures generated has been invaluable for shaping the discourses. The chapter *On Social Choice Theory* was inspired by an overview of social choice theory presented by Martin van Hees during the first project month.

The Lorentz workshop *Games, Action and Social Software* that took place at the Lorentz Centre in Leiden on October 30–November 3, 2006, has also been important for the creation of this book. In the break between lectures by international speakers, an hour was scheduled each afternoon after lunch for structured discussion. Themes for these discussions were *Social software: what is it?*, *Protocol analysis*, *Battle of the logics* and *The role of logic in game theory*. The results from these discussions were used in the discourses in the book.

The discourse on *Game Theory, Logic and Rational Choice* (Chapter 9) is based on a hand-out from Johan van Benthem for a talk in Beijing in Summer 2006. The discourse *On Collective Rational Action* (Chapter 14) has its genesis in a *Maagdenhuis lecture* organized by Johan van Benthem and delivered by Jan van Eijck (19 February 2007), where Abram de Swaan was among the audience; the text benefited from many perceptive comments by de Swaan. The discourse on *Social Software and the Ills of Society* (Chapter 15) was inspired by an extended email conversation between its four authors in early 2007.

Marco Swaen created four page-size drawings that illustrate themes from the book, on pp. 48, 122, 146 and 217.

The way the book came into being owes much to the general cultural atmosphere at NIAS, and we very much hope that some of the pleasure that we derived from putting the dialogues together shows through in the finished product.

Acknowledgements

We are grateful to the NIAS staff, in particular to NIAS rector Wim Blockmans and to NIAS head of research planning and support Jos Hooghuis, for their open-mindedness in welcoming our rather unusual project team at NIAS, and for making us feel genuinely at home. Our project operated in a rather different fashion from the rest of NIAS. While the individual fellows quietly carried out their learned studies, drafting their papers and writing their books in the splendid isolation of their comfortable NIAS offices, our group's first demand was for whiteboards, so that we could scribble formulas and discuss them in unruly meetings and impromptu workshops. The project gatherings also drew unusually large groups of PhD students from around the Netherlands, often hungry and arriving just in time for lunch. Also, we had new project visitors almost every week. Still, the NIAS staff never complained, and all practical matters were handled very smoothly, with generous help from Rita Buis, Rink van den Bosch, Annette Bottema, Ruud Nolte and Saskia van der Holst-Pels.

We gratefully acknowledge NWO, the Netherlands Organization for Scientific Research, for enabling the thematic NIAS group 'Games, Action and Social Software' both by Advanced Studies grants 051-04-120 for the project group and by Replacement grant 400-05-710 covering a lecturer at the University of Groningen during Rineke Verbrugge's stay at NIAS. Thanks also to the Centre for Mathematics and Computer Science (CWI) for allowing Jan van Eijck to take part in the NIAS project.

We thank the Lorentz Center in Leiden for a generous grant, supporting the workshop at which four of the discussions leading to this book took place. The relaxed atmosphere and the unique facilities at the Lorentz Centre fostered lively discussions during the workshop on *Games, Action and Social Software*, which sometimes went on into the late evening. We would like to thank Martje Kruk, Wim van Saarloos, Gerda Filippo and Henriette Jensenius for their wonderful enthusiasm and highly professional support.

Several people helped and stimulated us with their feedback on the discourses. Floor Sietsma made us understand that a preface could not be missing from a book like this. Rob Economopoulos wrote a long commentary on the discourse on collective rational action. Kathy van Vliet-Leigh helped with editing the first dialogue (which also appeared in a NIAS newsletter [83]). Heleen Verleur's reaction to her husband's growing concern and agitation while he was reading up on climate change led to the discourse on social software and the ills of society. Abram de Swaan sent us his detailed and perceptive comments on the discourse on collective rational action. Alan Taylor and Don Saari answered questions about issues in the discourse on social choice theory. Davide Grossi assisted with the proofreading, and Krzysztof Apt made a helpful suggestion for the first discourse. Donald Light, NIAS fellow during the academic year 2006–2007, participated in many discussions about collective rationality and ethics. Paul van den Broek, Lorentz fellow 2006–2007, discussed issues in cognitive science with us. NIAS fellows Dick van Lente and Peter Kroes stimulated us with their interest in what our project was up to. With Mohammad Bagheri, Lorentz fellow, we talked about puzzles of knowledge and social interaction; Mohammad also introduced us to wonderful Persian music. All other fellows stimulated us with their attitudes ranging from genuine interest, pleasant skepticism, eagerness to understand, and willingness to consider connections with broader issues.

The editors of the new series *Texts in Logic and Games* which started to appear with Amsterdam University Press at the end of 2007, Johan van Benthem, Wiebe van der Hoek, Bernhard von Stengel, Robert van Rooij and Benedikt Löwe, were almost immediately enthusiastic about our plans, and they were invariably encouraging and helpful. Benedikt Löwe has managed to find competent and thorough reviewers for the individual chapters. The reports that this generated were of great help to us, and we thank all referees for their much appreciated efforts. We are proud that this volume is appearing as a *Text in Logic and Games*. Joel Uckelman helped us with the LATEX formatting.

Our final thanks go to Paul Nolte for cooking the delicious NIAS lunchtime meals that are referred to in the text.

Amsterdam & Groningen   J.v.E R.V.

List of Authors

Johan van Benthem, Institute for Logic, Language & Computation (ILLC), University of Amsterdam, Plantage Muidergracht 24, 1018 TV Amsterdam, The Netherlands, johan@science.uva.nl

Francien Dechesne, Formal Methods Group, Department of Mathematics & Computer Science, Eindhoven University of Technology, P.O. Box 513, 5600 MB Eindhoven, The Netherlands, f.dechesne@tue.nl

Hans van Ditmarsch, Computing Science, University of Aberdeen, Aberdeen AB24 3UE, Scotland, hans@cs.otago.ac.nz

Keith Dowding, Political Science Program, Research School of Social Sciences, ANU College of Arts and Social Sciences, Australian National University, Canberra ACT 0200, Australia

Jan van Eijck, Centre for Mathematics and Computer Science (CWI), P.O. Box 94079, 1090 GB Amsterdam, The Netherlands, jve@cwi.nl

Martin van Hees, Faculty of Philosophy, University of Groningen, Oude Boteringestraat 52, 9712 GL Groningen, The Netherlands, Martin.van.hees@rug.nl

Barteld Kooi, Faculty of Philosophy, University of Groningen, Oude Boteringestraat 52, 9712 GL Groningen, The Netherlands, B.P.Kooi@rug.nl

Rohit Parikh, Department of Computer Science, CUNY Graduate Center, 365 Fifth Avenue, New York NY 10016-4309, USA, rparikh@gc.cuny.edu, rohitcuny@juno.com

Marc Pauly, Faculty of Philosophy, University of Groningen, Oude Boteringestraat 52, 9712 GL Groningen, The Netherlands, m.pauly@rug.nl

Krister Segerberg, Filosofiska institutionen, Uppsala Universitet, P.O. Box 627, 751 26 Uppsala, Sweden, Krister.Segerberg@filosofi.uu.se

Wouter Teepe, Faculty of Science, University of Nijmegen, P.O. Box 9010, 6500 GL Nijmegen, The Netherlands, w.teepe@cs.ru.nl

Rineke Verbrugge, Institute of Artificial Intelligence, Faculty of Mathematics and the Natural Sciences, University of Groningen, P.O. Box 407, 9700 AK Groningen, The Netherlands, rineke@ai.rug.nl

Yanjing Wang, Centre for Mathematics and Computer Science (CWI), P.O. Box 94079, 1090 GB Amsterdam, The Netherlands, y.wang@cwi.nl

Chapter 1
Introductory Conversation

Krister Segerberg

The scene is a corridor outside a lecture hall. Students are discussing a lecture they have just heard. Among them is a group of three students: a good student (Star), an angry young student (Angry), and a more pragmatic student (Prag).

STAR: Oh, what an interesting lecture! The Professor is so knowledgeable, so entertaining! All those clever examples, all those interesting little anecdotes!

ANGRY: Anecdotes is right. Entertaining, sure. But is there anything beyond anecdotes and entertainment in social software? I may be in a computer science department, but I like to think of myself as a philosopher. In philosophy, the fundament of human culture, what do you think we are after?

PRAG: Tenure?

ANGRY: No: understanding, you dummy. Understanding—understanding with a capital U! That's what it's all about. And I don't think social software does anything for understanding. I think old Dotty is off on a wild goose chase.

PRAG: By old Dotty you mean the Professor, do you?

ANGRY: You bet I do.

STAR: I don't think the Professor is any dottier than you are.

PRAG: Claims like that are notoriously difficult to settle.

(The Professor emerges from the lecture hall.)

STAR: In any case, to me social software seems like an extremely important and fruitful concept. I really liked the lecture.

PROFESSOR: *(Having overheard the last remark, he is surprised.)* I couldn't help hearing that. Thank you!

STAR: *(Embarrassed, having failed to notice the arrival of the Professor:)* Oh, I didn't hear you coming.

PROFESSOR: It is all right, I am really pleased. My student evaluations are the worst in the department, so any encouragement is welcome.

(The students make sympathetic noises.)

PROFESSOR: Funny thing is, it is only really good students that ever like my lectures.

STAR: *(Even more embarrassed:)* Oh, ...

PRAG: That figures! Angry, you did not like the Professor's lecture. Why don't you tell him why?

ANGRY: *(Feeling awkward:)* It is not that I didn't like the lecture, I just don't think that social software is such a big deal.

PROFESSOR: Would you care to elaborate?

ANGRY: It's very simple. I have just two complaints. One is that the term "social software" is meaningless. The other one is that such a term is not needed anyway.

PROFESSOR: All right, let us begin with the first complaint. You think the term "social software" lacks meaning?

ANGRY: I do. At any rate, if there is a meaning, no one has been able to say what it is. The only examples given are very pedestrian. Not to say trivial. No wonder Star refers to them as anecdotes! And no wonder people outside the small circle of social software fanatics won't take "social software" seriously. If 'social software' is such an important concept, why can't you say what it is?

PROFESSOR: Well, let me begin with what I think Professor Parikh would say.

PRAG: Who is Professor Parikh?

STAR: Oh Prag, everyone knows that!

PROFESSOR: Rohit Parikh is a university professor of computer science and philosophy—and perhaps mathematics, I don't remember—at CUNY. He is one of the world's leading logicians. It was he who coined the term "social software". *(To Prag:)* I did mention this in my lecture, you know.

PRAG: Sorry to have missed it, Professor.

PROFESSOR: Now, interestingly, Parikh does not give a precise definition of the term.

STAR: Why should he? There are many important concepts we can't do without, and yet are not able to define. Take 'love' and 'justice', for example. People from Plato and on have failed to capture what love really is, yet we all use that concept.

ANGRY: 'Love' is not a scientific concept.

STAR: All right, take 'truth' and 'knowledge' and 'intelligence'. Same thing: they are used all the time, both privately and scientifically. We all know what they are, yet none of us can say exactly what they are. That is, if by "exactly" you mean 'exactly'.

PRAG: In fact it is difficult to say even what "exactly" means. At least it is difficult to say exactly what it means.

ANGRY: *(Paying no attention to Prag:)* When such concepts are used scientifically, respectable writers are careful to define their understanding of them. Why can't you do the same with 'social software'?

STAR: Perhaps it is a good thing to have an umbrella sort of concept— when you need to use it in a particular situation, you define it. In between it may be useful to have a vague, general notion of social software. Think of Wittgenstein's family resemblance!

PRAG: I wonder if the problems some people have with 'social software' are the same as some people have with 'social capital'? That has also been much criticized but seems to be here to stay.

PROFESSOR: If you want to hear my view ...

STAR: *(Absorbed in her own thought, she does not hear the Professor.)* Perhaps social software is a cluster name for algorithmic methods in social science.

PRAG: What's a cluster name? What's an algorithmic method?

ANGRY: Well, if that's what it is, why not say so. But then, why a new name?

STAR: Let me quote a passage from an article by Professor van Benthem that may be relevant [22, p. 6]:

Computers are no longer autistic devices striving (in delusional spells of grandeur) to emulate humans with the techniques of AI. They communicate, collaborate and compete for scarce resources in multi-agent societies, all very much like us. Accordingly, computer scientists have developed a rich arsenal of new techniques to model information flow in such interactive settings.

PRAG: I like that! It makes sense.

ANGRY: Sure it makes sense, but what about understanding?

PRAG: You mean, with a capital U?

ANGRY: I can see that computer scientists are thrilled by the formation of computer societies, but what do they tell us about human societies? Simulation may be good for some purposes, but what does it do for understanding?

PROFESSOR: If I may make a suggestion ...

ANGRY: *(Interrupting:)* Don't interrupt! Oh, I am sorry, Professor, I didn't mean to be rude. But this is important! What I mean is, may I please finish? Simulation is fine for some purposes, but surely it can't be the ultimate goal in science.

PRAG: Not even in science with a small s? Not even in the social sciences (with two small s's)?

ANGRY: Not even in the social sciences. Not ultimately. Simulation is fine for some purposes, but any simulation leaves out—must leave out—innumerable features of reality.

STAR: *(With heavy sarcasm:)* And I who had thought that that was the very point of abstraction!

PROFESSOR: Angry, your first claim was that 'social software' is a meaningless concept. Now you seem prepared to accept that social software is something that can be used to simulate certain social phenomena.

ANGRY: If you want to put it that way, why not? But that idea is not new. Take Turing and his famous test. Suppose computer people become so clever that they can build robots that fool us—robots that pass the Turing test. What would that tell us about *la condition humaine*?

PRAG: Wow, French! I can hear you are a real philosopher, Angry. *La condition humaine*, that would be "the human condition", wouldn't it?

ANGRY: *(Patiently:)* Yes, Prag.

PRAG: Turing did discuss that. And so have philosophers after him. It's a big topic, you know.

STAR: But could it be that we are dealing with two different cases here, and that there is an important difference between them? On the one hand, one computer is offered as a model of a human being. On the other hand, a network of computers is offered as a model of a human society. With a human being there are so many immaterial aspects—metaphysical, if you wish—that are essential to humanhood and seemingly beyond rational analysis, at least for now. But with society it is harder to think of such aspects. There does not seem to be a "social condition" on a par with the human condition. I mean, it seems to me that talking about social software makes a lot of sense in connection with societies.

PRAG: "The social condition", what would that be in French?—*la condition sociale* or *la condition de la société*?

ANGRY: Oh, Prag!

STAR: *La condition sociale or la condition de la société.*

PRAG: OK, but which?

ANGRY: Prag, really!

PRAG: But those two are different, you know! Seriously! The condition of being an individual in a society is different from the condition of being a society. *(Bitterly, when no one pays attention to his observation:)* Why is Star allowed to make distinctions if I am not?

STAR: *(Disregarding Prag:)* As Angry says, things will be left out, whether you model a human being or a society. But perhaps fewer essential features are left out in the latter case. Here is another passage in van Benthem's article [22, p. 8] that I think supports this view:

> Logical and computational tools do not supplant our natural sense of interaction, they rather offer new ways of looking at its structure—and new perspectives, on what is, after all, a highly mysterious, complex, and difficult feat that we humans perform. Moreover, our lives are filled with procedures that have been designed for regulating interactions, be they laws, supermarket queues, or rules of debate.

PRAG: I like that! It makes sense.

ANGRY: It is important to note that what van Benthem talks about here is behavior. The behavior of complex societies has of course evolved over innumerable generations. It would not be in the least surprising if computer scientists were able to write programs that simulate the evolution of societies. Probably they already have.

PRAG: But don't you think that also the human mind has evolved? So how great is the difference between Star's two cases really? *(No one takes notice of his remark.)* Why doesn't anybody ever listen to me?

PROFESSOR: I wonder if we must not leave these questions to the philosophers. What I would like to ask is whether any of all this does anything for Angry's understanding.

PRAG: With a capital U.

ANGRY: *(With dignity:)* I concede that it may engender an illusion of understanding.

PRAG: Probably with a capital I.

PROFESSOR: Very well. What was your second complaint about social software?

ANGRY: That there is no need for a new term. You may need it for political reasons: a banner under which to gather your followers. It might be good if you want to apply for funds or organize conferences. But if you are serious you have to agree that there are already methods in the social sciences that cover everything you are talking about. Take Schelling's work in micro-economics as an example [206]. One example among many.

STAR: Schelling, the Nobel prize winner?

ANGRY: That very Schelling. Harvard economist. He showed how the actions of individuals, acting on their own private, local preferences, may lead to (and explain!) the emergence of global patterns of change in society that no one might have predicted and perhaps not even wanted. Racial segregation, for example. Schelling shows how individual preferences and actions of fair-minded and rational people can translate into changes that are surprising to all involved and even deplored by them.

PRAG: Why is this relevant?

ANGRY: Because Schelling describes processes that are constructive—processes that can in principle be implemented on a computer. His were early examples of evolutionary game theory, I guess. When I try to understand what social software might be, examples like this one come to mind. But Schelling never called them social software.

STAR: The term did not exist in his day, you know.

ANGRY: Right. And now we have the term. But have we got anything else that is new beside that term?

PROFESSOR: At this point, may I say something.

PRAG: I am sure you can say anything you wish, Professor.

ANGRY: *(Too absorbed by his own argument to hear the Professor:)* So let me try this on you. Some sociologists are dissatisfied with the explanations traditionally offered in sociology, which are usually either covering-law explanations or statistical explanations. What we need, they say, is explanations that uncover what they call underlying mechanisms. In their view, to explain a phenomenon in sociology is to identify a mechanism. See Peter Hedström's recent book [117], for example.

PRAG: Who is Peter Hedström?

ANGRY: Peter Hedström is a professor of sociology at Oxford.

PRAG: What is a mechanism?

ANGRY: They are a little vague on that. At least their definitions are not like those you find in logic. For example, one characterization of mechanism-based explanation is that there are three core features: minimize the gap between input and output ("the principle of direct causality"), don't prematurely try to establish universal social laws (which are unlikely to exist anyway) ("the principle of limited scope"), and accept that in the social sciences it is actors, not variables, that do the acting ("the principle of methodological individualism") [118, p. 30]. In another place they say that mechanisms are "theoretical constructs that provide possible hypothetical links between observable events" [118, p. 16]. Yet another characterization, attributed to Jon Elster is this:

> A mechanism explains by opening up a black box and showing the cogs and wheels of the internal machinery. A mechanism provides a continuous and contiguous chain of causal or intentional links between the explanans and the explanandum [117, p. 25].

This is vague by our standards, but I find it suggestive. Mechanisms (which are sometimes called generative mechanisms) seem to be something like procedures.

PRAG: Who is Jon Elster?

STAR: Everybody knows that, Prag!

ANGRY: Consider one of their stock examples, the run-on-the-bank. One day someone says, I will withdraw all my money today. Someone else hearing this tells his friends about it, saying perhaps he, too, will withdraw his money. This is the beginning of a process consisting in the repetition of this element: one customer tells other customers he is going to withdraw his money from the bank. As a result more and more people withdraw their money. The bank goes out with a statement saying there is no need to worry. This of course induces even more people to withdraw their money. In the end, the bank crashes. How could this happen?

PRAG: You want to understand this with a capital U.

ANGRY: Yes, we want an explanation: we want to understand the "mechanism" that led to the demise of the bank.

PRAG: A mechanism with a capital M. I am catching on to your way of thinking.

ANGRY: *(Patiently:)* Just a mechanism, Prag. An explanation could be a narrative, a story; but a constructive story, if you know what I mean.

PRAG: I don't know what you mean.

ANGRY: Well, it should be something concrete: a mechanism depending on the beliefs, desires and opportunities of the individuals involved in the example. Something that could be re-enacted. That is, under the same circumstances it would be re-enacted. My own view is that what they call a mechanism is something that could be translated into a computer program.

STAR: Probably allowing for non-deterministic computers?

ANGRY: What I want to say is, here is a connection between what those sociologists are doing and social software. *(Sarcastically:)* I guess Hedström and his colleagues have been involved in social software for years without knowing it.

PROFESSOR: I have a comment.

ANGRY: Could it wait? I am sorry to take so long, but this is important.

PRAG: Angry will be happy to take questions after his talk, Professor.

PROFESSOR: *(Apologetically:)* It is only a brief comment. The original example is even more interesting than you say. The *locus classicus* is a 1948 paper by Robert K. Merton, called "The self-fulfilling prophecy". In Merton's version, everything starts with a rumor that the bank is insolvent. The interesting thing is that, although the initial rumor is unfounded, nevertheless the bank goes under. This was really the point of Merton's example and the reason why this example is such a big topic in sociology. The rumor is false to begin with, but in time it becomes true. Sorry for the interruption.

ANGRY: That's right, I had forgotten that.

PRAG: You don't remember the name of the bank, do you?

STAR: Professor, that is very interesting!

ANGRY: *(Having collected himself he is resolved to get back to his agenda.)* Now let me tell you about boids.

PRAG: You mean birds, don't you?

ANGRY: No, I mean boids. But they are related to birds. How is it possible that dumb animals like birds can behave in such a seemingly well-organized way they do? Some fly in formation, some in flocks, and even flock behavior seems in some sense to be well-organized. Craig Reynolds showed how you can simulate the behavior of the group by assuming that each boid (member of the group) behaves in accordance with a very small number of rules [195].

STAR: It is like Schelling you just told us about.

PRAG: What kind of rules?

ANGRY: In one particularly simple case there are three main rules: Steer to avoid crowding local flockmates. Steer towards the average heading of local flockmates. Steer to move toward the average position of local flockmates. It is actually very entertaining to see this implemented on a computer screen.

PRAG: There must be additional auxiliary rules, of course. To handle terms like "average" and "local".

STAR: The initial conditions must be extremely important. Those systems might be chaotic, mightn't they?

ANGRY: My point is that if by social software you mean something like this, then fine. But to me it is old hat.

PROFESSOR: So you do approve of simulation after all?

PRAG: There is no point in trying to get him to contradict himself, Professor, even if you succeed. He is a philosopher, remember!

ANGRY: *(Defensively:)* I never said I was against simulation. Being able to simulate something may well be an indication that there is something that you have comprehended. (Remember that the Latin *prehendere* means 'grasp'!)

PRAG: Fancy that! I wonder what *prehendere* is in French? Or in any other language?

ANGRY: Oh, Prag!

STAR: Angry keeps talking about understanding, but the way he does it makes it sound like something entirely passive. Professor Van Benthem has pointed out that there is also an active dimension to understanding [22, p. 7]:

> Two different aspects are involved in understanding formal structures in interaction. One is the formal *analysis* of given social phenomena, modelling them, and trying to understand what makes them tick. But there is also the activist and more ambitious stance of *designing* new and better forms of interaction, using ideas from logic, computer science, game theory and so on. Both aspects, especially the latter, come under the heading 'Social Software'.

And he goes on to say, a little further on:

> And who is to say we cannot improve our daily procedures [...] for debate, or decision, or divorce, by applying some mathematical clarity and formal tools from disciplines that have developed to great maturity?

ANGRY: O.K., so I have been arguing that there is nothing new about social software when it comes to trying to analyze what happens. But I am also happy to argue that there is nothing really new about social software when it comes to design. It was a great step forward when sometime in the mid-nineteenth century Anthony Trollope invented the mail box: from then on people had a place to go to when they wanted to send a letter, and that made it so much easier for the postal services to collect letters. Or when some hundred years later someone came up with the idea of zip codes, which made sorting letters so much more feasible and hence to deliver them. I suppose that you would call those examples instances of social software? Fine, but there is already a discipline that concerns itself with providing solutions to exactly problems of this kind: O.R., operations research. People in O.R. have developed queuing theory, optimization theory, linear programming, and I don't know what. Computer science may of course contribute to this kind of research, but why insist on this new term "social software"?

(The professor's cell phone rings.)

PROFESSOR: *(Into the phone:)* Yes? Yes. Yes! Yes!! Yes!!! *(Puts away the phone.)* My wife. I have got to go.

STAR: We have got to go, too. Thanks for talking to us, Professor! It has been really interesting.

PRAG: I don't know. We have been talking about social software for hours, and by my lights we have got absolutely nowhere. What a waste of time!

STAR: I don't agree. I think our discussion has been worthwhile. We have been reviewing a number of possibilities all of which deserve consideration. Before we go, let me try to summarize our discussion and say where I stand. First about meaning. There were three alternatives: The term 'social software' has no meaning; it has a meaning that is fixed; it has a meaning that varies. I personally dismiss the first alternative. And I already told you what I think about the other two: a little of each!

PRAG: A little of p and a little of not-p. Bingo! Contradiction! Star, you are as bad as Angry!

STAR: Then there was the disagreement over novelty: Is social software something radically new, or has it been studied before under other names? Again I think, both of those, in a way. Angry is very persuasive. I think he is right about citing the work done by those sociologists. But I think he is missing something when he rejects the new term "social software". Having a new term will sometimes let us say things we might not have said as easily without it. It might make us see things we might not have seen otherwise. It has to do with focusing, I think. Social software has always been around, but with this new concept we can focus on structures and actually see them in a way we couldn't before. Does this make sense?

PRAG: *(Getting bored:)* Who is to say?

STAR: Then the question is whether social software is of interest only to specialists in computer science, or whether it is of general concern. Here I am definitely for the latter alternative. And finally Professor van Benthem's distinction between analysis and design becomes obvious as soon as you hear it: analysis with the help of social software versus design of social software. *(Summarizing her position:)* I think all of this is extremely exciting!

ANGRY: Excuse me, but why do you think it is so exciting?

STAR: Because I feel that we are on to something deep and important. I think we shall hear a lot more about this in the future, and I am excited to be in on it from the beginning.

ANGRY: I could summarize our discussion much more quickly. Star and the Professor think they know what social software is, and they like it. I, on the other hand, have no idea of what social software is.

PRAG: But nevertheless do not like it. (How can one dislike something if one has no idea of what it is?)

ANGRY: What I mean is, you may talk about social software all you want, but it only means introducing a new jargon. As if we didn't have jargon enough!

STAR: What about you, Prag? Do you know what social software is?

PRAG: No, I don't know what social software is. But then I don't care.

STAR: And why don't you care?

PRAG: Because I have decided to go into business, and in business we have no use for social software.

STAR AND ANGRY AND THE PROFESSOR: *(Looking at Prag in horror:)* Business!

(Their joint exclamation is on the loud side. A policeman nearby looks at them with suspicion.)

PRAG: *(Virtuously:)* I will go into business because I want to make a real contribution to society.

STAR: *(Hairs bristling:)* And you don't think academics do that?

PRAG: Just joking. Do you know what I am really after?

ANGRY: Tenure?

PRAG: *(Good-humoredly:)* Silly, in business there is no tenure. No, I want to earn a lot of money quickly so I can retire while I am still young and have my wits about me. No offense, Professor.

PROFESSOR: I am sure we all wish you well in retirement, dear Prag, and perhaps in your case early retirement is a good idea. But I am not sure you are right in thinking that social software is irrelevant to business. In business you care about efficiency, and that is definitely one place where social software comes in. Under whatever name.

PRAG: Yeah, yeah. If social software is so important, I am sure they will tell me what I need to know in business school. *(Makes an extravagant gesture.)*

(The policeman decides to intervene.)

POLICEMAN: What is going on here?

PROFESSOR: We are just having a friendly disagreement on what is social software. Have you got any ideas?

POLICEMAN: Don't you get smart with me! *(To the students:)* Now get lost, or I will show you some social hardware you will never forget.

(The students disperse. The policeman examines the professor's ID.)

POLICEMAN: So you're a professor. What do you teach?

PROFESSOR: Philosophy.

POLICEMAN: Philosophy? Social software sounds more like computer science.

PROFESSOR: Well, it is important to philosophy as well. Perhaps even more important. There is social philosophy, you know. And political philosophy. Even ethics.

POLICEMAN: Ethics?

PROFESSOR: Ethics. And don't forget justice!

POLICEMAN: Don't forget justice? You're telling me! *(To himself:)* Completely harmless.

(The policeman gives back the professor's ID and departs. A dean approaches.)

DEAN: What was that? A policeman on campus? Did he arrest them?

PROFESSOR: No no, he just wanted to know what we were doing.

DEAN: What were you doing?

PROFESSOR: We were discussing social software. The students could not agree on what it is.

DEAN: I know—social software, your new obsession. I have to say that I sympathize with your students. I have heard you explain social software a number of times, but I, too, don't know what it is. So if I had been here, I guess I would have been arrested too!

PROFESSOR: *(With some irritation:)* There were no arrests!

DEAN: Never mind, just make sure it doesn't happen again. *(Departs.)*

PROFESSOR: *(To himself:)* I had no idea that 'social software' would be such a controversial concept. And those three are among my best students. If they have difficulties, then what about the others? I know I am not very good at explaining things. What am I to do?

PRAG: *(Passing by on a skateboard:)* Why don't you ask the bigshot at CUNY? If he invented the word, he should know what it means. *(Disappears.)*

PROFESSOR: But that's a brilliant idea! Why didn't I think of that myself? Only I wonder if he will bother to answer. He must be a very busy man. But it is worth a try. What should I say? "Dear Professor Parikh, I am having a difficult time explaining to my students what social software is, and I wonder if you would be so kind and help me. In particular there is an aggressive young man, I would almost say iconoclastic, called Angry. Angry does not think there is anything new to social software. And, he asks, what *is* social software anyway? One of my difficulties is that I don't actually know the answer to that question myself. That's to say, the full answer. I am sure social software is important, but what is it? I mean, really? If you had time to answer me I would be very grateful. Or send me a letter I could pass on to Angry. He is a lot of trouble. Yours sincerely, etc." Would that do? *(His cell phone rings. He answers.)* Yes? Yes. Yes! Yes!! Yes!!! *(Departs.)*

Chapter 2
Replies to Angry, Prag and Star

Rohit Parikh

During the discourse, Angry raised several questions. I thought that Star's answers were very good, but perhaps a slight feeling of incompleteness remained.

Two questions raised by Angry were, "Why do we need a new term for something old?" and "Is *Social Software* of any use anyway?"[1]

Rather than address these questions directly, perhaps I should say something about how I see social software myself.

But before that, let me cite, with approval, two comments made in the dialogue, one by Star and the other by Angry, who, while angry, had some insights.

Star says, "Perhaps it is a good thing to have an umbrella concept—when you need to use it in a particular situation, you define it."

This is indeed quite similar to the notion of *language game* in Wittgenstein's *Philosophical Investigations (PI)*; it was published posthumously in 1953, but my friend Juliet Floyd assures me that some of the ideas go back to his *Philosophical Grammar* (1932–34). Wittgenstein intended these language games to illustrate certain philosophical problems arising in the philosophy of language. But it is clear from the *PI* that they can also serve as inspiration for social software. And an important thing about language games is that Wittgenstein does *not* think of them as all being the same or similar. In paragraph 67 of *PI* he says,

> I can think of no better expression to characterize these similarities

---

[1] Actually Angry's language was a bit more forthright. He said, "I have just two complaints. One is that the term 'social software' is meaningless. The other one is that such a term is not needed anyway."

than "family resemblances"; for the various resemblances between the members of a family: build, features, colour of eyes, gait, temperament, etc. etc. overlap and criss-cross in the same way.

So we would be asking too much of social software to expect it to be more precise than an umbrella concept. But umbrella concepts can also be very useful and one *can* loosely define social software as, *thinking of social procedures as analogous to computer algorithms—both for a single computer and for a system of computers—and to study these algorithms using techniques from mathematics and logic.*

Angry also says something which is useful as an answer to his own questions. "That there is no need for a new term. You may need it for political reasons: a banner under which to gather your followers." Perhaps so, but are banners *useless*? Somewhere at the end of the movie *Wizard of Oz* the wizard says to the (supposedly) cowardly lion, "You have already proved that you are brave. What you need is a medal."

And what the wizard might say to us is, "You already have a program. What you need is a name for it."

Social choice theory, game theory, implementation theory, deontic logic, judgment aggregation, fair division, are all parts of social software. And perhaps the existence of a term will help all the people working in these fields to see that they have something in common. And this commonality can lead to cross-fertilization.

Here is the famous "Five red apples" example from *PI*.

> Now think of the following use of language: I send someone shopping. I give him a slip marked 'five red apples'. He takes the slip to the shopkeeper, who opens the drawer marked 'apples', then he looks up the word 'red' in a table and finds a colour sample opposite it; then he says the series of cardinal numbers–I assume that he knows them by heart–up to the word 'five' and for each number he takes an apple of the same colour as the sample out of the drawer.–It is in this and similar ways that one operates with words–"But how does he know where and how he is to look up the word 'red' and what he is to do with the word 'five'?" —Well, I assume that he 'acts' as I have described. Explanations come to an end somewhere.–But what is the meaning of the word 'five'? –No such thing was in question here, only how the word 'five' is used.

Very little of the literature in economics reaches this level of sophistication. The apples are surely a commodity, but what is the role of the 'someone' who takes the slip to the shopkeeper, or the shopkeeper's knowledge of counting? These things cannot be counted as 'goods' except by stretching the meaning of the term 'good'. So what sense can we give to the idea of an equilibrium where 'the markets have cleared'? Do the markets clearing include the situation where someone needs to know how to count, someone else knows how to teach arithmetic and these two have got together? Perhaps so, but the existing theory does not address such issues directly. It will address the cost of hiring an arithmetic teacher, and what will happen to the rates if there are many teachers and few pupils. But it will have more trouble addressing the issue why we want to learn to count in the first place.

My point is that much of the literature in economics takes buying and selling as its model for social activity, but social activity is much more varied and rich. Wittgenstein's 'five' and 'red' are data types, and these do not occur in economics, although somewhat similar data types, like number or stack or queue do occur in computer science.

Thus if an analysis of what happens in society is to be carried out at a level where it can have an impact on *life* beyond mere trading, then tools from computer science are likely to come out to be useful. This is part of the reason why the word 'software' occurs in 'social software.'

We do of course have other parts of existing and old social software. For instance *social choice theory*, which started with Condorcet and acquired momentum through the results of people like Arrow and Sen.

Social choice theory considers the issue of combining preference orderings. Arrow's theorem points to some difficulties here since Condorcet cycles can, for instance, arise. Thus the notion of *the* social preference ordering does not really make sense. We do of course have some methods of conducting elections, which at least we theoreticians know cannot be perfect. We all know this, so I won't go into details.

But now consider the question of why campaigning takes place before elections. What has *that* got to do with combining preferences?

The voters already have preferences, don't they? So why don't we just combine these preferences using some aggregation method? The answer is actually quite simple. Many voters already *have* a preference ordering, but not one among the candidates. A voter may put high value on honesty, or competence, perhaps on knowledge of foreign policy, perhaps less on the tax rate. So if honesty, competence, knowledge of foreign policy, and tax policy are four dimensions, then the voter may decide that $(1, 0.5, 0.5, 0.2)$ rates higher than $(0.3, 0.5, 0.5, 0.9)$.

In any case a typical voter *already* has a (rough) preference ordering on what I will call the space $\mathcal{V}$ of vectors of virtues. And a voter may already know what weight she wants to put on various virtues so she has already made up her mind that honesty is important and a low tax rate is less so.

But she *doesn't know* how the candidates are going to measure up in terms of virtues. If $\mathcal{C}$ is the space of candidates, and $\mathcal{V}$ is the space of virtue vectors, then she wants to construct the map φ from $\mathcal{C}$ to $\mathcal{V}$ and that will enable her to transfer her ordering backwards from $\mathcal{V}$ to $\mathcal{C}$. She will prefer candidate c to candidate c' iff $\varphi(c) > \varphi(c')$.

Candidates campaign in order to affect the values of φ. In particular, if c, c' are candidates, then c will try to raise the value (as the voter sees it) of $\varphi(c)$ and *lower* the value of $\varphi(c')$. Thus McCain or his supporters will try to raise the value of $\varphi(m)$ in the voter's mind, and lower the value of $\varphi(o)$ in the voter's mind. Obama supporters will try to convince the voters that Palin (if she ever becomes president) could not possibly stand up to Putin i.e., lower the value of $\varphi(p)$.

Now that I have pointed this out, many readers will see at once that this is a main purpose of campaigns, but it is *not* addressed in social choice theory as it stands. It takes logicians and philosophers to think of such things, and this is why it is important that these groups participate much more than they have in the past. An umbrella term (like 'social software') which says, *This area is for everyone and not just for economists* can be very beneficial in bringing about this state of affairs.

A second point I want to make is the role of knowledge—which is more than bare information as it also includes knowledge of other people's knowledge and beliefs. The importance of knowledge in society is made vivid in a paragraph by Umberto Eco in "Towards a Semiological Guerrilla Warfare":

> Not long ago, if you wanted to seize political power in a country, you had merely to control the army and the police. Today it is only in the most backward countries that fascist generals, in carrying out a coup d'état, still use tanks. If a country has reached a high level of industrialization, the whole scene changes. The day after the fall of Khruschev, the editors of *Pravda*, *Izvestiia*, the heads of the radio and television were replaced; the army wasn't called out. Today, a country belongs to the person who controls communications [81].

Michael Chwe's *Rational Ritual* [47] makes a similar point. Whether it is a peacock's tail, or a royal procession with elephants and drums, the point is made, "I am powerful". The peacock's tail plays the role of convincing peahens, and the royal procession does the same with subjects.

The notion of knowledge (and common knowledge) does occur in game theory, introduced by the classical paper of Aumann [8] and followed up in [101, 178]. But it is not sufficiently developed so as to capture all aspects of knowledge in society. For instance, a large public building needs restrooms, of course, but it also needs signs saying where these are. This is of course a trite observation, but once one is used to think of knowledge as an essential part of the theory, one can look to see where some procedure is failing to work because the actors do not have adequate knowledge (and sometimes the opposite, that actors up to some mischief do have knowledge, like that of your social security number, which they should not have).

Cryptographic protocols do study how to transmit information from A to B, while preventing a snooper S from learning the information. But they do not consider *why* we don't want the snooper to snoop and what would be the algorithmic effects if the snooper did find out something she should not know. Perhaps the snooper only finds out that you bought that dress used at Goodwill and you are embarrassed, or the snooper finds out where to get plutonium, which is much worse.

The following dialogue from Yule's book [244] illustrates this point. Two women return from a trip to find that the desk of one of them has been piled up with work.

> LEILA: Whoa, has your boss gone crazy?
> MARY: Let's go get some coffee.

Mary does not reply directly to Leila's question but wants to change the knowledge situation to one where the boss cannot hear them.

Other examples abound. For instance a lecture setting, where the students can see the teacher but not each other, and a seminar setting around a round table where all students can see each other in addition to the teacher allow different kinds of transmission of information. In a seminar, if the teacher says something foolish, one of the students may smile, and other students will see her smile as a subtle comment on the teacher. In a lecture theater, such transmission from student to student is impossible, and the teacher may feel more safe. At the same time, the seminar also has advantages for both sides.

In the movie *The Messenger*, Joan of Arc, in addition to a sword and a war horse, asks also for a banner. But why a banner? The banner allows the troops to see where Joan is and that she is alive.

Having a social software view would alert us to such considerations.

Contrary to what Angry says, people working on mathematical models of society have rarely thought about such matters. Whether they *could* have thought of these things without leaving their field is beside the point—it hasn't been done.

I want to say something about recursion, a useful tool in computer algorithms, but less frequently used or analyzed in Economics. The Banach-Knaster algorithm for a fair cake division uses a double recursion, and its surface complexity is $o(n^2)$. Its correctness is analyzed in [175] using Game logic, a sort of modal logic. Should such tools be used in analyzing other social algorithms?

I should think so because what people do tends to depend on the conditionals they believe in. "If I do α then the other agent (who might be a person, or nature) will do β," is the sort of reasoning we all use. If I like the outcome β, then I will do α and if I don't like β then I won't do α. This kind of reasoning is implicit in analyzing notions in game theory like iterative elimination of dominated strategies, but again, tends not to be used so much outside a narrow context. To analyze such reasoning, some sort of possible world analysis will be needed. This again is not a tool which has been used very much in the past.

I will close with one last comment. Work on signaling has two sources. One source is the signaling games of the philosopher David Lewis [140]. Another is work on signaling by people like Crawford and Sobel [52], both economists. Until very recently the two groups have never known of, much less referred to, each other's work. That has changed with contributions by Jäger and Stalnaker [29]. Having an umbrella term like social software will surely make such encounters more likely.

Setting

A computer scientist, a logician and a philosopher have found shelter at NIAS, an institute for advanced studies in the humanities and social sciences, situated in a couple of luxurious villas in the most prosperous part of Wassenaar, a Dutch place of residence for the affluent near The Hague. The spacious rooms look out on wooded dunes. NIAS provides a quiet atmosphere for reflection, and it is also renowned for the quality of its lunchtime meals. What follows is a digest of some mealtime conversations.

Chapter 3
What is Social Software?

Jan van Eijck and Rohit Parikh

It is a sunny autumn day, and our protagonists have taken their meals outside, to enjoy the mild rays of the September sun. The NIAS cook Paul Nolte, as always glowing with pride while serving out his delicious food, has prepared a traditional Dutch meal today with sausage, red cabbage and pieces of apple.

COMPUTER SCIENTIST: Hmmm, very tasty. Do you all realize that for the first time NIAS has opened its gates to the likes of us? Logic and computer science used to be outside the compass of NIAS. Moreover, all of our other colleagues are pursuing goals of their own. They can devote themselves exclusively to their individual academic projects, as the NIAS website puts it, and I must say: I envy them. We are the only ones who are supposed to perform a *collective* task. We have to come up with new ideas in an area that hardly exists, but that is supposed to bridge a gap between the humanities and science. A rather tall order, if you ask me.

LOGICIAN: Yes, but you cannot deny that it is very pleasant here. I enjoyed yesterday evening's concert very much, for instance. One can get used to the ways of NIAS; humanities research is carried out here in a very civilized fashion, indeed. The only thing that worries me right now is the vagueness and vastness of our topic. We are supposed to come up with something we can show after our "Games, Action and Social Software" project here finishes. The trouble is that I have only the vaguest of ideas of what social software actually is or might be.

PHILOSOPHER: The term "Social Software" was coined by Rohit Parikh, in a paper which appeared in *Synthese* [177]. It had been circulating as a manuscript for some years. Parikh does not give a precise definition but he lists a series of evocative examples, rather in the manner of Wittgenstein in *Philosophical Investigations*. What Parikh has in mind is procedures that structure social reality, in a very broad sense. He makes a plea for investigating these with the tools of mathematics, logic and computer science. This was taken up by various people. See for instance the PhD thesis of Marc Pauly [180] or that of Eric Pacuit [172].

LOGICIAN: Now that the term has caught on, I suppose there is little reason for Parikh to come up with a precise definition. Such a definition will cost him the support of people who like his examples but might dislike the way he draws demarcation lines.

COMPUTER SCIENTIST: Yes, I think it is wise not to rely too much on Rohit for a definition. In trying to understand what the term "Social Software" might mean, why not take our cue from computer science? Software is what you feed a computer to make it do something useful. Feeding it with appropriate software turns a computer into a text processor, or into a digital entertainment center. As we all know, the dividing line between hardware (the machine) and software (the programs running on the machine) is blurred by the fact that an increasing number of system tasks are carried out by hardware.

PHILOSOPHER: I suppose that drawing the precise line between hardware and software is not that easy, indeed. But couldn't we agree on the following: what can be changed without changing the machine itself is called software?

LOGICIAN: Yes, that will do for now. Computer software is roughly divided into *system software*, namely, the software that is needed to make other software run, and *application software*, the software that turns the computer into a tool for a specific task. Taking our lead from computer science, we get the following distinction between social hardware and social software: Social hardware consists of institutions such as schools, churches, law courts, parliaments, banks, newspapers, supermarkets and prisons, while social software consists of the *more specific procedures* followed in these institutions.

COMPUTER SCIENTIST: Most computer software is designed, although if you look at large software systems such as the Linux operating system, then these can certainly be viewed as products of evolution of a certain kind. Genetic algorithms are another example. These are search techniques for finding programs for specific tasks by a process of genesis and natural selection, so programs resulting from a genetic algorithm are not designed.

PHILOSOPHER: There is a large class of social practices that have evolved in the course of development of a civilization. Our practice of eating with knife and fork while observing certain rules is one of many examples [86, 87]. Other social practices were designed and redesigned over a long period of time, e.g., the principles of common law.

COMPUTER SCIENTIST: The division of software in two broad categories carries over to the case of social software too, I suppose. Let us call *social system software* the rules of social interaction that make a society civilized. The rule of law, and the rules of civic behavior that engender mutual trust among social agents.

PHILOSOPHER: How did Thomas Hobbes say it? Without social system software our lives would be 'solitary, poor, nasty, brutish, and short.' The theme of *trust* as a quintessential product of social system software has been taken up in our times by Francis Fukuyama [98] and others [50, 209]. No doubt the general principles that constitute aspects of the so-called 'rule of law' [229] would fall under social system software.

LOGICIAN: What is it you have in mind?

PHILOSOPHER: Let me give some examples. *Nemo judex in sua causa.* This describes the principle of natural justice that no person can judge a case in which he or she is a party. It seems fairly obvious to us, but then again our societies are partly a product of the Roman law system where this principle evolved. Or take *Nulla poena sine lege*, or *Lex retro non agit*. One cannot be penalized for doing something that is not prohibited by law.

LOGICIAN: A key principle of law, I suppose, is that nobody shall be judged unheard, which means reasonable opportunity must be given to an accused to defend his side of the case. Without such a principle it is hardly thinkable that a fair jurisprudence could evolve at all.

COMPUTER SCIENTIST: Yes, and other principles no doubt have the purpose of ensuring that court cases can terminate. *Ne bis in idem* is an example of this: no legal action can be instituted twice for the same cause of action.

PHILOSOPHER: Another one, one that I have memorized, is *Volenti non fit injuria*. Someone who knowingly and willingly puts himself in a dangerous situation will be unable to sue for his resulting injuries. Comes in handy quite often as an erudite way of saying 'serves him right'. If you go bungee jumping and get injured, you cannot sue the one who supplied the elastic cord.

COMPUTER SCIENTIST: Not everywhere. Some countries require bungee sites to have liability insurance.

LOGICIAN: Bungee jumping was just an example, remember. I think we got the point. The main perspective on the law in Dutch society, by the way, seems to be that other basic principle from Roman law: *De minimis non curat lex.* This is taken to mean that the law is not interested in trivial matters. In Dutch society there are many things which are thought not worthy of the law's attention. Possessing less than ten grams of cannabis, for example.

PHILOSOPHER: I am afraid we are getting side-tracked here. It is obvious that the foundations and principles of legislation are part and parcel of the broad field of social software. But it is not so clear what *we* have to contribute here. I propose we concentrate instead on the social procedures and protocols geared towards specific tasks, such as division of goods, voting, reaching agreement, negotiation, settling disputes, that kind of thing. Let us focus on what one might call *social application software*.

COMPUTER SCIENTIST: Fair division of goods is an excellent example. For the fair division between two people we have what in English is called *I cut, you choose*. In Dutch this is called *kiezen of delen*. This is the procedure where one person makes the division, and the other person has the right to choose one of the pieces. Apparently, this is known from antiquity. It appears in a famous medieval story, 'Charlemagne and the Elbegast' [72, 71].

PHILOSOPHER: A rather peculiar version of this was used by King Solomon in the Old Testament. He took the 'I cut' quite literally, in his proposal to settle a dispute between two women about a baby. He threatened to cut the child in half.

COMPUTER SCIENTIST: The case of Solomon and the two women is interesting, for it has been noticed that Solomon's procedure hinges on the surprise element. Suppose Solomon has to settle a second dispute about a child between two women, while his first judgment is well known. Surely, the second pair of women would *both* say that they prefer the other to have the child than for him to die.

PHILOSOPHER: Yes, the surprise element is crucial for Solomon's procedure to work. If the impostor knows the procedure, she will be able to play strategically, by pretending she is also willing to give up the child. Almost all social procedures are susceptible to strategic behavior, where it pays not to act according to your real preferences.

COMPUTER SCIENTIST: If you ask people to invest real money, you can always force them to reveal their real interests, I suppose. In a second dispute about a child, Solomon would simply propose to sell the baby to the highest bidder, knowing that she had to be the real mother.

LOGICIAN: Beforehand he should offer them both a generous loan from the Temple funds, to be paid back in monthly installments plus interest. And this time the rules can be publicly announced: bids in closed papyri, highest bidder gets the baby at the offered price, loser pays a fee into the Temple funds to cover court expenses.

PHILOSOPHER: This might not work if the pretender has more money than the true mother. Better to ask them how many times their annual income they are willing to bid for the child.

COMPUTER SCIENTIST: If the bids are in closed papyri, and the first mother offers A times her annual income and the second mother B times her annual income, with $A > B$, then the child should go to the first mother for B times *her* annual income. For this is what she would have paid in an open auction, with the second mother (the 'fake' mother) dropping out at B times annual income.

PHILOSOPHER: This is called a *sealed bid second price auction*, isn't it? Such auctions are strategy-proof, in the sense that it is never in the interest of the bidders to put in a lower bid than what they believe is the true value.

LOGICIAN: Yes, such an auction would work in this case. In fact, a variation on this solution was proposed in the literature: see Moore [159] (and also [181]). Suppose the child is worth A times her annual income for the real mother, and B times her annual income for the pretender, with $A > B$. Now the women make their bids in sealed papyri, and Solomon collects the papyri without looking at who handed them in. He announces his procedure to the women. If one of them gives the child to the other, he will consider the case settled. If not, then he will toss a coin to decide who gets the child, and (looking at the bids) rule that that woman will have to pay M times her annual income, with $A > M > B$, and the other woman will have to pay a small fine.

PHILOSOPHER: Court expenses again.

LOGICIAN: Yes. Solomon then asks the first woman whether she is willing to give the child to the second woman. If so, all is over and done with. If not, he asks the second woman whether she is willing to give the child to the first woman. If so, all is over and done with. If not, he tosses his coin, decides who gets the child, and both women pay expenses as stipulated: the woman who gets the child pays M times her annual income, and the other woman pays the fine.

COMPUTER SCIENTIST: Ah, I see how this works. If the first woman is not the true mother, she knows she is running the risk of having to pay more than the child is worth to her. She has offered B times her annual income, but if she gets the child she will have to pay more than that, and if she does not get the child she will have to pay a fine. So she will give it up. If the first woman is the true mother, the second woman will know that she is running the risk of ending up with the child at a price she does not want to pay, or ending up with nothing and having to pay a fine. So then *she* will give it up. If both act rationally, the true mother gets the child, at no cost at all. How brilliant!

PHILOSOPHER: I suppose it is essential that Solomon announces the price M for the winner and the small fine for the loser beforehand. Then both women know that the other one knows what might happen.

LOGICIAN: Yes, and note that the procedure assumes that the women are both rational, and know of each other that they are rational. If the pretender acts irrationally by refusing to give up the child—'I will never part with my darling, I just can't, and to hell with the cost'—then she could end up having the child after all.

COMPUTER SCIENTIST: The Solomon case is special because the goods are non-divisible. With divisible goods, real money always makes for smoother fair division, I suppose. Here is a procedure for dividing an inheritance between n inheritors: first auction the goods among the n inheritors, next divide the auction revenue in n equal shares.

PHILOSOPHER: This may not be a fair procedure if some of the inheritors are much poorer than the others.

COMPUTER SCIENTIST: OK, but how about the following procedure. This is a simple generalization of *I cut, you choose* to the case of n participants.

> I cut out a piece of the inheritance that I know I am satisfied with and offer it to the others. If someone else wants it, I give it to him, and we continue with $n - 1$ players. If no-one else wants it, I take it myself and let the other players continue.

Doesn't this guarantee that everyone gets his fair share? So what's the big deal about cake cutting algorithms?

PHILOSOPHER: In the literature [36, 37] it is common practice to use cake cutting as a metaphor for a *division of a single heterogeneous good*. Dividing a piece of land at inheritance would be an example. The cake has different toppings that cannot all be cut into pieces with the same composition: it may have Turkish delight cherries on top that someone likes but another person abhors, and so on. A cake division is *simply fair* if each of n players feels she received at least $\frac{1}{n}$ of the cake, according to her individual valuation of its parts, that is. I agree that the procedure you propose is simply fair, but your procedure does not rule out the possibility of hard feelings. A cake division is called *envy-free* if each person feels that nobody else received a larger piece. A sure sign of a division being envy-free is that nobody wishes to trade pieces with anyone else. The procedure you propose is not envy-free.

COMPUTER SCIENTIST: Ah, I see what you mean. The procedure guarantees that I get what I consider a fair share, but it does not rule out that someone else gets a share that I consider excessive. This explains, by the way, why fair, envy-free division between two is simpler than fair, envy-free division among many. If I have received my fair $\frac{1}{n}$ share, I can still be envious because I feel that some of the other $n-1$ pieces are larger than mine. The *I cut, you choose* procedure is fair, and it is envy-free simply because the rest of the cake is a single piece, so there is no possibility for envy.

LOGICIAN: If the preferences of the players are not the same, then I suppose the typical result of fair division will be that all players feel they have received *more* than their fair share. In fair division there is no objectivity, remember.

COMPUTER SCIENTIST: And if the division is also envy-free then each player will feel that she has done at least as well as each of the others. A very satisfactory outcome indeed.

PHILOSOPHER: Yes, but it is surprisingly difficult to generalize *I cut, you choose*. One of the difficulties, by the way, is that preferences might change while the division is in progress. Consider the case of a land inheritance where you have picked your piece of land. Then the piece of land next to yours has increased in value for me, because of the attractive prospect of having you as my neighbor.

COMPUTER SCIENTIST: You are teasing me, but I take your point. But wait, didn't Rohit's social software paper [177] have a discussion of cake cutting?

LOGICIAN: Ah, you mean the Banach and Knaster cake cutting algorithm? That is indeed a good example. It goes like this.

> I cut a piece intended for myself. All others consider it. If nobody objects, I get my piece. If someone raises an objection, she has the right to cut off a slice and put that back with the rest of the cake. She then asks if she can have the reduced piece. If nobody objects, she gets it, otherwise someone else takes the knife and reduces the piece a bit further, and so on, until someone gets the trimmed piece. Then on to the next round, with $n-1$ players.

COMPUTER SCIENTIST: A nice feature about Parikh's discussion is that he shows how the methods of computer science can be used to argue that the procedure is fair. The key ingredient of the procedure is a loop operation:

> continue to trim the piece until there are no further objections about the size.

If r stands for the action of trimming, and if $F(m, k)$ is the proposition that the main part of the cake is large enough for k people, then we can see that $F(m, k)$ is invariant under the action r. If $F(m, k)$ is true before r, then it will still be true after r has occurred. Clearly, if one can show that $F(m, k)$ continues to hold through the algorithm, for k running through $n, \ldots, 1$, then this establishes that the division is fair, for surely $F(m, n)$ holds at the beginning: the whole cake is large enough for the whole group to begin with.

LOGICIAN: Yes, and if I remember well, Parikh proposes a game logic to carry out the verification. Don't you think, by the way, that an additional argument would be needed for envy-freeness?

PHILOSOPHER: Yes, I think you are right. But what I don't like about the algorithm is the way it spoils the cake. You were looking forward to a treat, and you end up with an unappetizing mush of cake, cream and topping.

LOGICIAN: There is also a version with a continuously moving knife. This leaves the cake intact. See [127].

PHILOSOPHER: Ah, I take that to mean that we, as social software designers, are allowed to propose improvements on social division procedures. Then how about the following?

> I start by cutting off a piece intended for myself. All others consider it, and are allowed to make money offers on it. If nobody does, I get the piece, without paying for it. Otherwise, it is auctioned to the highest bidder among those who have not yet been served cake, and the money is put in a pile. And so on, until everybody has been served. After that, the pile of money is split evenly among the participants.

Note that it is assumed here that cake cutting is difficult, but splitting an amount of money is easy. What do you guys think: is this a fair and envy-free procedure?

LOGICIAN: We should be able to tackle this with Parikh's logic, I suppose. But before we do that, it might be wise to have a look at the vast literature on this matter [36, 37, 38, 198, 212].

PHILOSOPHER: Yes, and let's not forget that rational action and the investigation of rationality is a classical theme in philosophy. Let me tell you a wonderful Indian story about the Mughal emperor Akbar and his minister Birbal [204] about the way in which knowledge and incentives affect a social algorithm. Birbal had asserted to the emperor that all wise (or clever) people think alike.

LOGICIAN: And then the emperor challenged him, right?

PHILOSOPHER: Right, so he suggested the emperor to order all men in Agra, the capital, to come at night to the palace grounds, and pour one potful of milk in the pool there, which was covered by a white sheet. The punishment for not doing so was severe, so one by one, all the residents of Agra came at night and poured a potful in the pool. And when the sheet was removed in the morning, it turned out that the pool was entirely full of water.

LOGICIAN: Of course.

PHILOSOPHER: Yes, and Birbal could explain to the emperor how this had to come about. "Your majesty, each man thought that if he, and he alone, would pour water instead of milk, it would not make much difference, and no one would notice. So they all did just that, for all your subjects are rational. And that's why your pool is full of water."

COMPUTER SCIENTIST: How wonderful!

PHILOSOPHER: By the way, there also is a story where Birbal acts exactly like Solomon. In the Hindu version, Ramu and Shamu claimed ownership of the same mango tree, and decided to ask Birbal to settle the dispute. Birbal's verdict: "Pick all the fruits on the tree and divide them equally. Then cut down the tree and divide the wood." Ramu thought this was fair but Shamu was horrified, and Birbal declared Shamu the true owner.

COMPUTER SCIENTIST: It may interest you that Birbal's milk-pouring experiment was repeated by the psychologist Dan Batson, and with the same outcome. What Batson and his co-workers did [16] was set up a Birbal-like situation, where the subject was asked to flip a coin in private. The outcome of the coin toss was supposed to decide whether she herself or her team-member was scheduled for some unpleasant task. In collecting the results it turned out that these contradicted the laws of probability: more than 90 per cent of the subjects allotted the unpleasant task to their team member.

PHILOSOPHER: Why am I not surprised?

COMPUTER SCIENTIST: But the interesting thing was that all these cheating subjects duly reported that they had reached their decision in a fair way. Batson then tried to find out what incentive was needed to force the subjects to behave more honestly. It turned out that giving firm instructions about fairness and next placing them in front of a mirror was the only way to enforce ethical behavior. Mind you, the subjects were psychology students, no doubt familiar with the one way mirror.

LOGICIAN: So what Batson was studying was not rational behavior but the phenomenon of moral hypocrisy: our common tendency to believe ourselves to be more ethical than we truly are.

COMPUTER SCIENTIST: What still puzzles me about the Akbar and Birbal story is this: why did each of the cheating water pourers believe that he was the only cheater?

LOGICIAN: Well, they did as we all do, I suppose. They knew it didn't matter as long as they were not found out, so they gave it no further thought.

COMPUTER SCIENTIST: In any case, the story illustrates that reflection on social algorithms has a long history.

PHILOSOPHER: There is no doubt that the Akbar and Birbal stories go back a long time: emperor Akbar the Great ruled the Mughal Empire in the second half of the sixteenth century.

COMPUTER SCIENTIST: We talked briefly about auctions in connection with the Solomon verdict. The study of auctions and their properties is part of an discipline called *mechanism design*. Surely, this also belongs to social software. You can find an overview in economics textbooks. See, e.g., Chapter 23 of [146]. Mechanism design deals with the problem of aligning agents' preferences so that the decision taken by the central authority is beneficial for the society. The best known example of a mechanism is that of a Vickrey auction, according to which the winner in a sealed-bid auction has to pay a price equal to the second highest bid.

LOGICIAN: Yes, we talked about that before.

COMPUTER SCIENTIST: Another area in social software where there is already a long and established tradition is voting theory. The mathematical study of voting procedures was started by Condorcet in the eighteenth century [49], and the literature has grown ever since. We surely know a lot about the advantages and disadvantages of different voting schemes.

PHILOSOPHER: It is interesting to reflect upon what motivated Condorcet to study voting procedures in the first place. He was struck by the fact that majority voting does not always lead to results that represent what the voters truly wish. A dangerous concept, by the way, but we will let that pass for now. In one and the same election, it is possible that a majority prefers A over B, another majority prefers B over C, and a third majority prefers C over A. Majority preference is not transitive, and this is a flaw. Therefore, Condorcet proposes to start from pairwise comparisons between all alternatives. The Condorcet winner is the choice that beats all alternatives in pairwise comparisons.

COMPUTER SCIENTIST: Condorcet proposed organizing elections like chess tournaments. Not a very practical way to elect the president of France or the United States, if you ask me. Also, it is unfortunate that a Condorcet winner need not exist.

PHILOSOPHER: Not very practical for large-scale elections, indeed. And you are right that there is not always a Condorcet winner. Condorcet was aware of these facts, of course. But it is getting a bit chilly. May I propose we go inside and try to get some work done? Tomorrow, or at some later time, we can continue our discussion. Maybe we should try to come up with areas of social software where our combined expertise might make a difference.

COMPUTER SCIENTIST AND LOGICIAN: Good idea. Let's think about it, and continue some other time.

Chapter 4
A Guest Lecture on Social Software

Jan van Eijck

Rohit Parikh, visitor to the project, has delivered a NIAS lecture on social software. On the next day, the project members discuss the contents and the reception of his talk. An ethicist (professor of ethics) has joined the project team, and a visiting political scientist is also present.

LOGICIAN: It is such a pity I had to miss Rohit's lecture. And Rohit himself has dashed off now, to a conference in Paris. On the day before the talk, one of the NIAS fellows asked me with a worried look on his face what the word "algorithm" meant that he had seen in the lecture announcement, and could we please make sure that our guest lecturer knew that part of the audience was unfamiliar—even uncomfortable—with the jargon of computer science and logic? So we forewarned Rohit, of course. Now you all understand why I am curious how it went. Can anyone tell me?

PHILOSOPHER: Yes, I did get the impression that part of the audience was a bit suspicious of logicians and computer scientists taking on problems in humanities. The NIAS audience consists of highly articulate opinion leaders in the field of humanities and social sciences, but some of them seemed wary about the methods of the exact sciences.

LOGICIAN: It seems to me that it is quite important to articulate our answers to the typical questions and worries of such an audience. The kind of objections that were raised on this particular occasion will no doubt be raised again and again when one tries to outline the task and goals of the social software enterprise.

COMPUTER SCIENTIST: Let's recall what went on, then. I will start, and maybe the others can all comment, so that we get at a reasonable reconstruction. The main theme of the talk, of course, was an outline of the conception of social software as an interrelation of (i) logical structure, (ii) incentive structure, and (iii) knowledge transfer. By the choice of his examples, Rohit made clear that improving a social process involves analysis of what goes on (logical structure), understanding what makes the participants in the process "tick" (incentive structure), and understanding the flow of knowledge that takes place during the process (knowledge transfer).

PHILOSOPHER: Rohit took great care to explain his terminology and conceptual tool set, by the way. His explanation of what an algorithm is, for instance, used the example of Euclid's recipe for calculating the greatest common divisor of two positive whole numbers.

COMPUTER SCIENTIST: Yes, a nice illustration indeed. The calculation is based on the insight that if you have two positive whole numbers, A and B, with A larger than B, then replacing the larger number by $A - B$ does not affect the set of common divisors of the pair. As soon as this is clear, it is also clear that Euclid's procedure for finding the greatest common divisor has to be correct.

LOGICIAN: Yes, yes, but I suppose we can skip all that for now. How was the talk received? What were the questions?

PHILOSOPHER: The talk itself was very well attuned to the audience, it seemed to me. As for the questions, well, various people expressed doubts about the use of formal methods in trying to capture aspects of human interaction. Their main worry seemed to be that the essence of what goes on in the ways human beings behave towards one another and give meaning to their interactions might get lost in the mathematical analysis.

COMPUTER SCIENTIST: As I remember, Rohit had various things to say about this. One of the points he made was about the virtue of idealization and abstraction. Analysis of the trajectories of moving bodies like flying cannon balls always starts by making some unwarranted but very useful assumptions: that there is no air resistance, or that there is no drag from the rotation of the earth. These assumptions are necessary to get started. Indeed, it takes great skill to find the right abstractions; this is what progress of the natural sciences is all about. In our understanding of the movement of cannon balls it turns out to be illuminating to disregard earth rotation, but for understanding the emergence of cyclones the drag from the rotation of the earth is an essential element.

PHILOSOPHER: Another thing that could be said—and if I remember well Rohit touched on this too—is that there is no pretense that the abstractions fit the aspects of reality one tries to understand in every detail. Same for social software. A social software analysis might be useful despite the fact that it does not explain and is not meant to explain *all* that there is to explain about what goes on when human beings interact in institutions.

COMPUTER SCIENTIST: Can we elaborate on this still further? A related question was asked by Donald Light. He questioned the main paradigm of many mathematical approaches to economy, where the starting axiom is that human beings are always maximizing their interest. What is it that warrants this assumption? Selfish individuals surely are not the only possible paradigm? I cannot remember how Rohit handled this.

POLITICAL SCIENTIST: For one thing, Rohit agreed that *homo sapiens* is not the same animal as *homo economicus*. As a matter of fact, the abstractions of economics were borrowed from a psychological fashion called behaviorism. Fortunately, psychologists have now abandoned this, and it is to be hoped that economics will follow suit. You might want to have a look at [45] if you are interested.

COGNITIVE SCIENTIST: Unfortunately, this was only mentioned in passing, for the death blow to psychological behaviorism was dealt by cognitive science. An important development in our field is that subjective feelings of happiness and despair can be correlated to objective happenings in the brain. 'Feeling good' turns out to have a physical basis, and what is more, the way people report on how they feel corresponds quite well with the findings of fMRI scans [59, 60].

POLITICAL SCIENTIST: A recent plea to take these findings into account in public policy making was made by economist Richard Layard [137, 138]. Layard argues that the key question economists should ask themselves is this. How can we explain that since 1950, despite a huge increase in income, average happiness among people in the West has not increased? For more information I can recommend the World Database of Happiness on the web [237].

COMPUTER SCIENTIST: Ah, the site maintained by our Dutch happiness professor Ruut Veenhoven, right? Yes, a visit to his website always cheers me up. At the very least such information makes clear that money is not everything.

PHILOSOPHER: None of this came up in yesterday's discussion, but Rohit mentioned the fact that social procedures often have parameters that can be adjusted to reflect participant attitude. For instance, Steven Brams and his co-workers have developed algorithms for mediating the property settlement in a divorce. Suppose you and your ex-partner want to use this software. Then the starting point is for each of you to divide 100 points over the common property items, reflecting your individual valuation of the items. Next, use the algorithm to decide what is the agreement that will maximize happiness of each of you, and is most fair. Now suppose you want to do your ex-partner a good turn. Then you can decide that she is allowed to divide 150 points, and you are content with 50 points. This shows that the social software algorithm is really just a tool; it is completely up to you to decide just how greedy you want to be.

LOGICIAN: A topic that strikes me as relevant in this context are the game-theoretical paradoxes, such as the Allais paradox, the Elsberg paradox, or the St. Petersburg betting paradox. Were any of those mentioned?

COMPUTER SCIENTIST: I don't think so.

PHILOSOPHER: Can anyone explain, please?

LOGICIAN: Rohit and I discussed the St. Petersburg paradox at some other occasion. The St. Petersburg game is played by flipping a fair coin until it comes up tails, and the total number of flips, n, determines the prize, which equals 2^n euros. If the coin comes up tails the first time, the prize is $2^1 = 2$ euros, and the game ends. If the coin comes up heads, it is flipped again until it shows tails. So if the coin comes up heads the first and the second time, and tails the third time, the prize is $2^3 = 8$ euros, and so on. The relevant events are sequences of head flips followed by a tail flip, and the probability of the sequence of $n - 1$ head flips followed by a tail flip is 1 over 2^n. The prize for this event is 2^n euros, so the expected payoff (prize times likelihood) is 1 euro. Now the space of possible events is infinite, and each of these has an expected payoff of 1 euro. So the value of the game is infinite. A rational gambler would enter the game if the price of entry was less than the value. Still, most people would be reluctant to offer even 25 euros for playing the game.

COMPUTER SCIENTIST: What does this show? That most people are irrational? Or that there is something wrong with the underlying concept of rationality?

LOGICIAN: Daniel Bernoulli, who invented the paradox—he was a mathematics professor in St. Petersburg for some time—believed the latter. He observed that the calculation of expected value does not take into account that money has a decreasing marginal utility: money means less to the rich than it does to the poor. However greedy an individual is, an extra assumption of diminishing marginal utility will explain why human beings tend to reject the bet.

COMPUTER SCIENTIST: But it is well known that this does not resolve the paradox. For if you give me a function for calculating the decrease in utility, then I can use that function for constructing a new version of the game, and the paradox reappears.

PHILOSOPHER: I can think of a different and very rational reason for refusing to play the game. Ask yourself who is supposed to act as bank, if the game is played? The problem is that it takes infinite wealth to underwrite it. If Yukos or Gazprom invite offers to play the St. Petersburg game, I will abstain. Chances are they are not rich enough to pay up just when I am about to collect real money.

COMPUTER SCIENTIST: Let's get back to the discussion after Rohit's lecture. A completely different issue was brought up by Gül Ozyegin. Is the attempt to describe human behavior in abstract (and maybe quantified) terms in any way related to the attempts of damage insurance lawyers who tried to *calculate* the monetary value of their clients who were killed in the 9/11 disaster, for use by the heirs of the life insurance policy owners? The dishwashers in the WTC restaurants were worth much less than the high profile chief executives that were killed. Gül described these lawyers as a kind of vultures, I remember, and expressed moral qualms about any attempts to describe the worth of a human life in terms of money.

PHILOSOPHER: I have no notes of how the actual discussion went on this point, and I must admit I got lost.

POLITICAL SCIENTIST: The fact that people make money because others have died is a fact of life. That cannot be the moral issue. The same holds for the fact that some life insurance policies are worth more than others.

ETHICIST: If these damage insurance lawyers work on a 'no win no fee' basis then there is a moral issue, I suppose. For then they may induce their clients to engage in endless litigation, and this—it has been argued—generates a claims culture that is clearly not in the interest of the community. In many countries of the European Union—including the Netherlands—'no win no fee' is against the law.

POLITICAL SCIENTIST: The case is not clear cut. Other countries allow what is known as conditional fee agreements (cfas). Under such agreements, if you win your case, you must pay your solicitor's fees and any expenses for items such as experts' reports, so-called disbursements. If you lose, you need pay no fees to your solicitor. However, you may have to pay your opponent's legal costs and both sides' disbursements. So also in these cases there is a mechanism to discourage pursuing weak cases. Conditional fees are subject to regulations which set out what a solicitor must tell the client. A solicitor who does not abide by the regulations runs the risk of not getting paid at all, win or lose.

COMPUTER SCIENTIST: I suppose that finding out what is the effect of the fee structure for attorneys on patterns of litigation in a country is also social software analysis?

PHILOSOPHER: But it seems to me that we need have no qualms about expressing what someone's life is worth in quantitative terms. Quality Adjusted Life Year (QALY) has been proposed in the medical profession as a measure for combined quantity and quality of life. QALY calculations are useful for measuring efficacy of medical treatment. QALY calculation takes one year of perfect health-life expectancy to be worth 1, but regards one year of less than perfect life expectancy as less than 1. Suppose the prognosis for a patient is to die within one year, with quality of life fallen from 1 to 0.4. Then an intervention which keeps the patient alive for an additional four years rather than die within the year, and where quality of life falls from 1 to 0.6 on the continuum will generate 2.0 QALYs: 4×0.6 for the extra life years at quality 0.6, minus 1 year at quality 0.4 which would have been the result of no intervention. The definition is in any medical dictionary, or you can look it up in Wikipedia. What is the moral worry?

COMPUTER SCIENTIST: In my notes, there is also an entry on how to take the non-rational into account in rational analysis of human behavior. In this context, Michael Suk-Young Chwe's *Rational Ritual* was mentioned [47].

PHILOSOPHER: Yes, that is a beautiful book. I happen to have it with me. It illustrates that rituals that appear at first sight to be completely non-rational turn out to have a strong rational element. The rationale of many public rituals comes to light if one views them as procedures for creating common knowledge.

POLITICAL SCIENTIST: Ah, common knowledge is what is generated when I send out emails with long `cc:` lists. I only use those for invitations, when I want to generate common knowledge of who is also invited, so that everybody who gets invited knows what kind of party to expect.

PHILOSOPHER: Chwe argues that the wish to create common knowledge is behind many social rituals. It explains Apple's decision to introduce their (then) new Macintosh computer during the 1984 Super Bowl TV show. Look here: *(quotes from Chapter 1 of the book [47])*

> By airing the commercial during the Super Bowl, Apple did not simply inform each viewer about the Macintosh; Apple also told each viewer that many other viewers were informed about the Macintosh.

Creating common knowledge in this case was important, for prospective buyers knew that getting a Macintosh was a good investment only in case the Macintosh would turn out a success. The book has many more examples, of course.

COMPUTER SCIENTIST: The issue of common knowledge and how it is created is a topic in its own right. Let's get back to it at another occasion (see p. 99).

PHILOSOPHER: At some point the discussion also touched on cultural relativism. One of Rohit's examples was about queueing for buses. He had noticed that shelters at bus stops near Wassenaar have advertisements on all sides except for the side where you see the bus approaching if you are inside the shelter, and where the driver sees you, of course. Also, in his talk he had mentioned signs in London with 'queue this side please,' as examples of social software. In connection with this, Sadik Al-Azm remarked that boarding a bus in Cairo or Damascus is rather different than boarding a bus in London or Wassenaar. It involves different skills: London bus boarding habits would simply fail to get you a place. If social software designers were hoping to come up with proposals to improve bus boarding procedures for Cairo or Damascus, he wished them good luck.

ETHICIST: Here Rohit's reply was that social software analysis should always take how people actually behave and what they actually believe as given, and propose small adjustments to improve a given situation.

COMPUTER SCIENTIST: Another thing that raised questions was the issue of strategic behavior. What is it? Is it good, is it bad, or are moral qualifications of it beside the point? Should social software be designed in such a way that possibilities for strategic behavior get minimized? If so, why?

PHILOSOPHER: Yes, this issue came up in an amusing way during the discussion. At the start of the discussion many hands were raised, and someone proposed to chairman Wim Blockmans that people who wanted to ask follow-up questions should raise a single finger, while people who wanted to address a different aspect of the lecture should raise their whole hand.

COMPUTER SCIENTIST: Yes, and someone then remarked that when Sadik Al-Azm raised a single finger and asked a question about something completely different, this was a nice example of strategic behavior. Sadik was only mildly amused, it seemed. Others thought his reaction was quite funny.

PHILOSOPHER: Maybe we should try to make explicit—or at least say something illuminating about—how social software relates to moral debate. The moral aspects of some of Rohit's examples seemed to baffle the audience.

COMPUTER SCIENTIST: One of Rohit's examples during the lecture revolved around the notions of agency, ability, and responsibility. Rohit asked us to imagine a trolley moving downhill along a track, with malfunctioning brakes. You are standing beside the track. The only way you can prevent it to kill five people standing on the track is by switching a lever, to divert the trolley to a different track. The trouble is that there is also a person standing on that other track, who will certainly get killed as a result of the diversion. The point of the example is the distinction between moral responsibility for one's action and moral responsibility for one's inaction. Not touching the lever makes one guilty through inaction, switching the lever makes one guilty through active involvement. Guilt through inaction presupposes the ability to act, of course.

POLITICAL SCIENTIST: I can see why this made the audience uneasy. If fine metaphysical distinctions like the difference between sins of commission and sins of omission are relevant for a 'science' of social software, one might reasonably ask whether one is doing exact science at all. Science can only flourish where one has learned ways to put metaphysical worries on hold.

PHILOSOPHER: Anyway, when time was up, there were still many questions left unanswered. Is analysis of how procedures are incorporated in social institutions also part of the task of social software? What does social software have to say about how we interact with banks, schools and churches? Does social software provide analysis, or does it make recommendations? And if both: how do the two relate? Does social software take a moral stance? If so, what is the foundation? If not, how can it still make recommendations? I seem to remember that some part of the audience thought that it was strange that value judgments like "order is better than chaos", or "it is better if less people get hurt" seemed to play a role.

ETHICIST: Questions, questions. Does anyone care for a coffee?

Chapter 5
Social Software and the Social Sciences

Keith Dowding and Rineke Verbrugge

Our Philosopher, Political Scientist, Logician and Ethicist meet yet again at a conference after lunch, and are joined by some new discussants: a Computer Programmer and a Cognitive Scientist, and the discussion is moderated by a Chair.

CHAIR: So we are here today at the Lorentz Center in Leiden to discuss precisely what it is that is the subject of this conference *Games, Action and Social Software*. What is social software? And how is it related to the social sciences?

LOGICIAN: We have already discussed the question of demarcating social software from several angles in the first few discourses. For the new participants in this discussion, let me give a short reminder. The most obvious place to start to answer that question is to look at the original articles by Rohit Parikh [176, 177] that introduced the term into our language. He suggested, I recall, that the issue of constructing and verifying social procedures in as systematic a manner as verifying computer software is pursued by computer scientists, be called "social software". And such a process requires theories of program correctness; an analysis of programs and checks to see that different programs do not frustrate each other.

PHILOSOPHER: That is all very well but are social processes really like computer programs in that way? Computer software makes applications run; but in social life people make things run.

LOGICIAN: As Parikh first suggested people must want to carry out the program. Their aims and the algorithm used must work together. The algorithm must be set in such a way that it somehow conforms to their wishes. We can see that we need to set some optimizing conditions, and then see the algorithm as something that allows that optimizing.

PHILOSOPHER: One problem is that people have different sets of interests. And we know from Arrow's Theorem [6], which we will extensively discuss at another occasion (p. 71), we cannot have a means of aggregating any set of interests into a social welfare function. One implication is that there is always the possibility that there will be no agreement on an efficient algorithm.

LOGICIAN: One direction we can go in is the following. We can agree that in many areas of social life there will be disagreement over the most desirable outcomes. However, it does not follow from the ever-present possibility of disagreement that there will *always* be disagreement. Very often a small group of people, or even a whole society, will agree on what the optimal outcome will be. Under those conditions we can study in a systematic way what the best algorithm might be for attaining their desires.

COGNITIVE SCIENTIST: We could make distinctions between different sorts of problems. At one level there is no disagreement about what people want. The only difficulty is attaining that outcome. These are pure coordination problems. Dunin-Kęplicz and Verbrugge show that once a certain level of collective beliefs, intentions and commitments is established, there is no difficulty in attaining cooperation [63, 75, 76]. It is in everyone's interests to coordinate their activities according to the algorithm.

POLITICAL SCIENTIST: Then there are what we might call "collective action problems". Here there might be general agreement about the best outcome so part of the problem is a coordination game, but there are also conflicts of interest. In a pure coordination game for example, everyone might need to act to attain some outcome that is in everyone's interests. In a collective action game, fewer than 100 per cent need to act for the outcome to be achieved. Here there is the possibility of free riders and so each person wants the outcome, but also knows that the outcome can be optimally achieved without their input. For example, the famous analogy in Hume's *Treatise of Human Nature* [124] was that two farmers might agree to meet the following morning to dig a ditch between their fields. They are both needed so both have the incentive to turn up. But a hundred villagers find it harder to all agree to turn up to drain a field, since not all 100 are required. But if all try to free ride then none turn up and the field is not drained.

PHILOSOPHER: Yes I see that. But is that not a problem of assuring compliance: with the 100 villagers it is simply that we cannot tell who has turned up or not. We might not see our neighbor and complain to him that he did not help, but he replies he was there, but in a different corner of the field.

POLITICAL SCIENTIST: It might be perceptibility that is the problem, but not necessarily. Think of shortcuts across the grass. If we all take the shortcut the grass becomes worn and mud patches appear. But if only a few take a shortcut occasionally the grass is not affected at all. We might be able to see who takes the shortcut. And as long as it is not always the same people there is no problem. Optimality suggests that people should only take the shortcut if there is an emergency. In other words, there might be good reasons to allow a few free riders. But my point is that for collective action problems, as I am defining them, there is an added problem of conflict as well as cooperation. With pure coordination games the element of conflict is absent.

LOGICIAN: I see that.

COGNITIVE SCIENTIST: Negotiation is a prime example of such a mixed situation of 'co-opetition' [187, 39].

POLITICAL SCIENTIST: Then we have games which involve conflict over the outcomes as well. Here we might all agree that we should coordinate on some outcome, but we disagree over which. That is, we all want to play an equilibrium strategy, but which equilibrium strategy? Then of course, we have pure conflict games.

PHILOSOPHER: Okay, we can see different types of problems, but I thought social software was about finding solutions.

LOGICIAN: The point as I see it is that different types of algorithms might be necessary for different types of problems. Economists might be best at constructing answers in some fields, for example about market relations. Logicians are better at solving other problems, for example those concerning belief, knowledge or common knowledge. Political scientists are good at yet other questions, for example about voting procedures. The social software program is not about taking over the social sciences, it is rather an umbrella term to bring people from different disciplines together. Rather as this conference is trying to do.

COMPUTER PROGRAMMER: Economists themselves seem to believe that they are best equipped to deal with all domains. One sometimes gets the impression that they want to take over the social sciences. There was a course at Harvard run by two political scientists last year called "The Economists are Coming".

PHILOSOPHER: The big thing is game theory, you know. Logicians have just discovered game theory, and game theorists are just discovering the issues surrounding knowledge and the problems of common knowledge, and they are becoming interested in language interpretation. Each side is aware of the other like the rhino and the elephant in the jungle. Each knows how big they are themselves but can only see a little bit of the other. They are about to come into the open and find out. Will the elephant push the rhino over, or the rhino the elephant?

POLITICAL SCIENTIST: Which is the elephant and which the rhino?

PHILOSOPHER: We shall see.

LOGICIAN: Actually both are grassland animals and don't live in the jungle. And logicians and economists do not have to fight.

POLITICAL SCIENTIST: I think we are getting off the point. I am sure that logicians can learn from game theorists and vice versa. My point is that both do social software. They both examine social interactions using algorithmic processes.

COMPUTER PROGRAMMER: I am afraid we have gone too quickly for me. We are talking about what social software is, and now I learn it is what logicians and game theorists do. So game theory is social software? Are you saying that everyone who acts in society is a game theorist?

LOGICIAN: Of course not everyone is a game *theorist*, but everyone is playing games. Games of coordination, cooperation and conflict. Every social exchange is part of a game, and each game is part of the overall game of life. The point is that we can model those games and see whether they are being played well, or could be played better. We can model the structures and then examine all the strategies available within those structures, and see if there are better strategies we can play; or better structures we can evolve that will help us reach the outcomes we desire.

COMPUTER PROGRAMMER: It seems to me that "social software" as you describe it is just a metaphor for modeling. In agent-based social simulations, which can be seen as a part of Artificial Intelligence, we put in all the parameters and the program tells you what to do. This is a micro-level and this is where social software should concentrate. If we find out what is going on in the human mind by modeling it in terms of Artificial Intelligence then that will give us our social software. After all, social software has to exist somewhere, and where better than in the mind. The mind has been programmed to deal with its environment. We program the cognitively plausible simulated agents, place them in a simulated social environment and model their behavior. In that way social software is not a metaphor or analogy anymore. It is the real thing. Social software will be software in a programmed agent-based social simulation [227]. We will be modeling the real thing with a real thing.

PHILOSOPHER: It will not be exactly the same thing. Artificial Intelligence is programmed on hardware and the human mind is programmed on a biological organism which does not operate in the same way as computers. The brain is not a parallel processor for one thing. I am not putting down Artificial Intelligence, it can teach us much, but it is not yet a good model of the human mind. And what it does is less analogical than the mathematical modeling we are discussing.

COMPUTER PROGRAMMER: Is a neural net software? We may not know what is going on, we just have outcomes that we can discuss. Or do we have to be able to understand and represent the action mathematically? A lot of agent-based models are designed to examine situations that we cannot yet model mathematically. The math gets too horrendous so we set up automata and they play a set of games within parameters and we see the sorts of outcomes that occur. Sometimes the same beginning states can lead to very different outcomes. We can of course start to understand why the different outcomes occur, but we do not know in the kind of detail that a computer programmer needs to know to ensure his program does what he wants it to do.

LOGICIAN: And I think this misses the point. We do not have to model social software in terms of a representation of the human mind. Rather we can look at processes which occur at a different level.

COMPUTER PROGRAMMER: We can model things at all sorts of levels. If we adopt Dennett's intentional stance [61], we do not need to worry about what is "really" going on in actors' minds. We have a set of institutional processes—algorithms—that lead to sets of outcomes and we interpret these in ways that make sense. We interpret behavior as being rational. Actors do not have to be consciously following the rules that our algorithms model. We explain their behavior by the algorithms no matter what is "really" going on. Dennett would say, indeed, that if our algorithms are better predictors of behavior than what the actors say they are doing, then it is the algorithms that are "real".

LOGICIAN: We can perhaps predict what people will do in certain situations in terms of the intentional stance. But to improve their situation we need to set up new algorithmic processes which appeal to their interests and beliefs and lead them to better solutions.

COMPUTER PROGRAMMER: That is something I am not sure about. Is social software a positive or a normative exercise? Is it about explaining social processes or is it about improving them?

LOGICIAN: It could be either. We use our algorithms to explain the processes we see, and then interrogate those processes to see if they can be improved. That is the example of the airport luggage carousel in Parikh's

[177, p. 193]. Let me quote Parikh:

> Then on arrival one has to wait at a moving carousel which brings
> all pieces of luggage one after another. If we are lucky, ours is among
> these. However, a curious phenomenon takes place which resembles
> the problems of the Prisoners' Dilemma, or The Tragedy of the Com-
> mons. One gets a better view of the approaching suitcases if one goes
> closer to the carousel. But by doing this, one inevitably blocks the
> view of one's neighbour who then also proceeds forward towards the
> carousel. When this process is finished, all passengers are right at
> the carousel, blocking each other's view, and every one is worse off
> than if no one had walked up to the carousel. [...] And the airline
> does have a solution to the carousel problem. All they need to do
> is to paint a line about 18 inches from the carousel and post signs
> saying "Do not cross the line until you actually see your own suitcase
> approaching". Then social pressure would keep people from crossing
> the line unnecessarily, and everyone would enjoy a better view of the
> oncoming luggage. Subways routinely do something similar at plat-
> forms to prevent passengers from falling onto the tracks or being hit
> by an incoming train.

We can see why everyone presses forward to find their bags, but can think
of a simple institution—based on social hardware, if you like—that is in
everyone's interests to improve the situation for all.

COGNITIVE SCIENTIST: But if it is about explaining what really happens,
then game theory is not a good tool. What really happens in people's
minds is not the equilibrium selection strategies of classical game theory.
According to some cognitive scientists and behavioral economists, human
beings use decision heuristics. They see a situation within one frame of
reference and then use the appropriate decision heuristic for that frame.
Sometimes what we might see as the objective frame is different from the
frame of reference chosen by the human subject. And that is why we get
sub-optimality; or we find that people are inconsistent or contradictory—
they are choosing different frames of reference for what is essentially the
same decision process.

LOGICIAN: I assume you are referring to the work of Cosmides and Tooby
[233, 14], and some of the results of experimental psychologists such as
Kahneman and Tversky [128]. And you are right, we might understand
how evolution has fitted us for working out some kinds of problems within
certain contexts and not for doing so within others.

COGNITIVE SCIENTIST: Such as the Wason selection test?

LOGICIAN: Exactly.

POLITICAL SCIENTIST: What is the Wason selection test?

COGNITIVE SCIENTIST: Experimental subjects are shown the four cards, A, K, 4, 7, and are told that each card contains a numeral on one side and a letter on the other. They are asked to evaluate the truth of the statement "If there is a vowel on one side, then there is an even number on the other side" by turning the minimum needed number of cards.

LOGICIAN: Based on the truth table for the material implication, they should of course turn around only A and 7.

COGNITIVE SCIENTIST: Exactly. But in reality, only around 4% of the subjects correctly take these two cards. Around 33% takes only the A, while around 46% take the A and the 4, and around 17% take still other combinations. On the other hand, experimental psychologists have given subjects isomorphic problems in a concrete setting. For example, subjects are shown the four cards: "beer", "cola", "16 years", and "22 years", and are told that on one side of each card is the name of a drink; on the other side is the age of the drinker. They are asked to put themselves into the shoes of the barman, and are asked what card(s) they must turn over to determine whether the following statement is false: "If a person is drinking beer, then that person must be over 19 years old." And lo and behold, almost all subjects correctly turn over the cards "16 years" and "beer". You see, they cannot solve the problem when given as a logical exercise, but they can solve exactly the same problem when framed as a social exercise. Cosmides and Tooby draw the conclusion that humans do not have a general capacity for abstract logic, but must have developed a specialized module for detecting cheaters [51, 233].

LOGICIAN: Objection! As Van Lambalgen and Stenning showed, these two problems are not at all isomorphic, let alone "exactly the same" [222, 221, 223]! In the barman version, the subjects are asked to evaluate a *deontic* conditional, containing the word "must" in the consequent, and they can do that *per drinker*. It is highly likely that such a deontic conditional is much easier to process for subjects than a descriptive conditional, such as the one with the vowels and the even numbers, which is to be interpreted as a kind of general statements about all cards. So, in her analysis of the Wason card selection task [51], Cosmides wrongly conflates two logically different kinds of propositions to be of the same logical form but to differ only in content. Still, we can understand why we are able to solve the Wason selection test if it is framed right, but not otherwise. The social software program, in its normative guise, might ask us to frame important issues—where solving the Wason selection really matters—in such a way that people can solve them more precisely.

POLITICAL SCIENTIST: Perhaps logicians can solve it when it is posed as a logical problem on cards, but not when they serve behind the bar and try to find out who is an underage drinker.

LOGICIAN: Not funny.

PHILOSOPHER: But I do not precisely see the point here. Solving the Wason selection test is not exactly an algorithm, is it? I mean, in computing you write a program and if you get it right, it does what you want it to. Here you are trying to set up a problem in such a way that ordinary people can solve it.

POLITICAL SCIENTIST: And if they can solve it then you have written the right algorithm. But what interests me is the evolutionary point. It was suggested that what goes on in the mind is not the same as game theory. People do not solve games as game theorists do. They just bumble along somehow. And this is important. One could have two entirely different causal explanations of some outcome, that have the same game-theoretic explanation.

COGNITIVE SCIENTIST: That's right! In evolutionary biology, Maynard Smith and Price devised a simple conflict model, where members of a species fight over some resource [150]. Winning the resource is worth 50 points. Individuals have access to two strategies. As a "hawk" they fight over the resource, and as a "dove", they merely threaten and posture. If both play hawk, they will fight until one is injured (-100 points) and the other gets the resource. The pay-offs are computed as expected values, so for example for hawk-hawk we have $\frac{1}{2}(50) + \frac{1}{2}(-100) = -25$. If two doves meet, one will eventually get the resource of 50 points, but they will both get -10 for wasted time. Here's the pay-off matrix [225]:

	hawk	dove
hawk	$(-25, -25)$	$(50, \ 0)$
dove	$(0, \ 50)$	$(15, 15)$

It turns out that in populations with pure hawks and doves, if there are almost entirely doves, the doves would expect an average of 15 points per game. In that situation, the hawks are genetically advantaged because they would expect an average of 50 points and their population would rise: the hawk minority would invade the dove population. Similarly, a population of almost entirely hawks would be unstable: then the doves are the guys with an advantage, winning an average of 0 points against -25 points for hawks. Maynard Smith and Price introduced the concept of *evolutionary stable strategy*. It turns out that a population of $\frac{7}{12}$ hawks and $\frac{5}{12}$ doves is stable, and the proportion stays fixed. In such a population, the expected pay-offs for both hawks and doves are $\frac{25}{4}$.

POLITICAL SCIENTIST: That's right. But notice that there is an interesting aspect here. The same equilibrium as in the case with the pure strategies would be attained if every individual played a *mixed strategy* of $\frac{7}{12}$ hawk and $\frac{5}{12}$ dove. Or indeed, one could have some mix of strategies in between. All that matters is that the process maps on to the equilibrium mixed strategy at the macro-level. Now if we wanted to write social software to reach that equilibrium we could write it for all to play mixed strategies or for some to play pure dove and some pure hawk.

COMPUTER PROGRAMMER: Now it seems that you are saying that social software is something for the brain. Some loaded with pure dove, some with pure hawk and some maybe with a mixed strategy. That is what agent-based modeling can help us solve. We can write programs that map onto cognitive processes and see where that gets us.

POLITICAL SCIENTIST: No, I meant the opposite really. We don't need to look into the brains—or minds better—of the players. We can explain the outcomes we get through the macro-level equilibrium. How that equilibrium arises is another question. An interesting one perhaps, but the game-theoretic or social software explanation does not concern itself with the causal explanation. It simply notes the macro-level algorithms that map onto the outcomes. The analogy is that we don't care how the electric circuits carry our information in computer software (unless there are systematic problems perhaps which can mean that some programs do not run as well as others) and we don't care how people actually behave or think about what they are doing. We just care about the outcomes, and the general processes—the way institutions structure or channel human behavior into the optimal paths.

ETHICIST: I would like to come in here. I've not spoken yet, because I was not sure I could offer anything. But I have been a little concerned about the direction of the conversation from the start. And now I am most concerned. You all seem to think that whilst there might be disagreement about outcomes, once a group of people agree on an outcome, all that matters is coordinating activity so the outcome occurs. Now first, surely even if everyone in a group agreed on an outcome then it might still be wrong. I mean a group of people might all agree that human sacrifice once a year is okay, as long, say, as the victim is chosen by lot. But surely such outcomes are wrong.

LOGICIAN: I'm not sure we can say that it is "wrong". Should we judge a community on what they believe if all are in unison?

ETHICIST: Okay, look I don't want to get into a debate about objective and subjective values and about cultural relativism, that is not my main point. I just wanted to emphasize that we should not simply accept outcomes as given. It was merely a preface to my main point. I can't accept that once there is agreement on outcomes, the only social software point is the macro-level equilibrium that sustains the outcome. I mean even if we all agree on the outcome, even if the outcome is objectively the right one in some sense, the process by which we get there is important. For example, it matters if some play pure hawk and some play pure dove, rather than all play the same mixed strategy. The one playing pure hawk might be better off than the one playing pure dove. It is all right saying that we can carry some free riders but if some ride free and some do not, then that matters. Some gain and some lose. I mean after all, optimality is one thing, but equality another. We might want an equal society even if it is not socially optimal because some could free ride, say, with no material loss to others. And, after all, there are individual rights as well as socially optimal outcomes in a welfare sense. Can social software model rights? Or another way round, are rights constraints on the kinds of algorithms that are socially acceptable?

LOGICIAN: Those are good points. I think we can see rights as constraints on what sorts of algorithms we would want to introduce into a society. I am not sure how rights can be modeled in social software terms. Did Sen not have a proof that welfare maximization and rights are incompatible?

POLITICAL SCIENTIST: His impossibility of the Paretian liberal [210]. Sen's result can be seen as viewing society as a social decision function, that is, as a function F that defines possible combinations of individual preference orderings $P_1, \ldots, P_n$ to a "social preference" $P = F(P_1, \ldots, P_n)$. Whatever the feasibility constraints on the alternatives open to society, F provides the answer to the question of what is best for society by generating the social preference relation R. For any situation the best social state relative to R is chosen from the set of feasible social states.

LOGICIAN: Obviously, it is thereby assumed that the social preference relation always contains a best element, right?

POLITICAL SCIENTIST: Indeed. Sen defines a condition of minimal liberalism (ML) that is supposed to be a necessary but not a sufficient condition for rights. ML states that there are at least two individuals such that for each of them there is at least one pair of alternatives over which each is decisive. An individual is decisive over a pair of social states (x, y) if it is always the case that if the person strictly prefers x to y, then society should strictly prefer x to y, and conversely, if that person strictly prefers y to x, then society should strictly prefer y to x.

LOGICIAN: Okay, so the condition of minimal liberalism, ML, now states that there are at least two individuals who are decisive for some pair of distinct alternatives, that is, there are individuals i and j and distinct pairs of alternatives (x, y) and (z, v) such that $[yP_ix \rightarrow yPx$ and $xP_iy \rightarrow xPy]$ and $[zP_jv \rightarrow zPv$ and $vP_jz \rightarrow vPz]$.

POLITICAL SCIENTIST: Indeed. Sen's liberal paradox states that condition ML cannot be satisfied simultaneously with the (weak) Pareto-condition (P) and the condition of Universal Domain (U). According to the Pareto-condition, a strict preference that is shared by all individuals should also be represented in the social preference relation: if all individuals strictly prefer some alternative x to some other alternative y, then society should also strictly prefer x to y. The condition of Universal Domain demands that a social preference relation is generated for any logically possible configuration of individual orderings: no individual preference orderings are excluded a priori. The incompatibility of the three conditions is easy to demonstrate. Take the simple case in which there are only three alternatives x, y, z and two individuals. Assume the two individuals, i and j, have rights over x and y, and over y and z, respectively. Given U, suppose that individual i strictly prefers y to x and x to z, whilst j strictly prefers x to z and z to y. We then see that i's rights over x and y implies that yPx and that j's rights over y and z implies zPy. The Pareto principle yields xPz, which means that we have $xPzPyPx$: the social preference relation is cyclic and hence does not contain a best alternative.

LOGICIAN: So what is the upshot of all this?

POLITICAL SCIENTIST: Sen's results show that, under the conditions U and P, a person's decisiveness over one pair of alternatives is incompatible with other persons having any rights at all. To see rights in terms of decisiveness over pairs of alternatives means that, in a very strong sense, individual rights are incompatible.

LOGICIAN: The incompatibility of rights only follows if the social decision function satisfies U and P. It can easily be shown that if one of these conditions is dropped rights can be made compatible with each other.

ETHICIST: I think Dowding and Van Hees [70] showed that for any set of compossible rights the rights are, in their words 'vanishingly small'. Compossibility is the condition that rights can always be satisfied—all rights are "co-possible". But one might see that the acceptance of a set of individual rights is a convention that people abide by, and so the conventional behavior within that society is composed of algorithms that have rights built into them. We might learn from Sen that respect for such rights might not always be socially optimal in some other welfare sense; but such rights might allow a society to run more smoothly. After all, one cannot even run a market system without some respect for property rights.

COMPUTER PROGRAMMER: Can we get back to the levels of analysis discussion? I mean there is nothing incompatible with saying that there are various micro-causal processes that could lead to the same macro-outcome, and then deciding that one is preferable to other. One might even think one preferable to another, but the latter is the one we are stuck with. We simply cannot move to a better equilibrium from the one we are at.

POLITICAL SCIENTIST: Kenneth Shepsle, a Harvard political scientist introduced the notion of structure-induced equilibrium into political science [213]. He introduced it in the context of legislatures but it might be generalized. Do you know the McKelvey-Schofield type results [152, 208], where in an n-dimensional issue space with many agents there could be a constant cycling of majority preferred outcomes? Well, Shepsle argued that in those situations one can have equilibria institutionally generated. One just needs to make alterations in the equilibrium costly by having legal constraints and costly actions in order to change them.

LOGICIAN: Oh, yes?

POLITICAL SCIENTIST: Well, he suggested that the rules by which legislatures are run—the committee systems that are set up; the closure motions on bills, the rules governing how different bills might be bundled together and so on—constitute a set of structures which constrain the space of possible outcomes. Committees for example, can reduce policy space from n dimensions to one dimension, as policy space is carved up into individual issue spaces, so education policy is not bargained over with defense policy. Any bargains struck are struck in the same issue space. He argues that in that way certain equilibria are chosen rather than other ones. There is nothing inherently superior about those equilibria, it is merely that the rules as laid down constrain the possible set [213]. And that is, at least in the short run, of advantage to the whole legislature. Well we might generalize the idea of structure-induced equilibrium to the whole society. And suggest that property rights, welfare rights and so on, are all structures that constrain outcomes.

PHILOSOPHER: Didn't Shepsle's mentor Bill Riker point out that the particular rules chosen were probably chosen for the advantage of the majority at the time they were chosen [196]? But as that majority interest changes then so should the rules. You just get a new cycle.

POLITICAL SCIENTIST: Yes, but such a cycle might be better in the much longer run; and there are much greater transaction costs of changing rules.

I mean, changing a rule like a seniority rule for chair of committees might be against your advantage now, so you want to change it, but you never know it might be to your advantage later.

LOGICIAN: Well, it must be to your advantage in the long run, when you get older and more senior!

POLITICAL SCIENTIST: Exactly! But even if there is uncertainty over how the rules will operate to your advantage or disadvantage, it might be easier for you to play by the current rules, than try to change them. You know how the current rules operate. With new rules you might not be aware of all the strategic possibilities.

PHILOSOPHER: So again, reasoning about belief and knowledge becomes an important aspect of social software.

ETHICIST: And some equilibria might be chosen simply for cultural reasons. I mean some cultures do things one way and others another way.

LOGICIAN: But saying it is for cultural reasons does not explain the differences. Saying it is our culture to pick the red pencil and your culture to pick the blue might explain why a particular coordination problem is solved through common knowledge, but it does not explain why those conventions started in the first place [140].

ETHICIST: No, but I mean, it does explain the transmission of the coordination. And moreover, it can generate interests. Because it is our culture to pick the red pencils, red pencils are *our* interest, and we will fight you if you say there have to be blue pencils for note-taking at the UN Assembly.

LOGICIAN: So both blue and red pencils are provided, and maybe that is more expensive and socially sub-optimal.

ETHICIST: But, I mean, such a rule does recognize culturally specific interests and rights. It might be more egalitarian, and that is another consideration. Optimality is not the only thing.

POLITICAL SCIENTIST: Sure. Though depending on how you define utility, you might be able to build in those concerns into your social welfare function. But let us not talk about that. I want to get back to the earlier point. Even if everyone knows that some rules might be better than others, getting there could be costly. For example, say property rights are set up so that the members of a small aristocracy own everything. Then it might be advantageous to the vast majority to have a revolution and re-allocate property. But two things. The day after the revolution everyone might be worse off than the day before the revolution. During the re-allocation process, property has been destroyed; crops have been burnt, trade disrupted.

Even if the majority are better off in the long- or even medium run, in the short run the revolution has made them worse off. Second, the re-allocation then has to stick. If you have revolutions, too often there is a commitment problem. I won't invest, or lend, or even trade, if I think that next week everything is going to be re-allocated. So rules are important for governing our behavior. We might realize the ones we've got are not ideal, but if we are going to change them we had better be careful because the new ones do need to be better; changing them is costly; and we can't keep changing them.

PHILOSOPHER: Adam Pzeworski had an argument a bit like that [186]. He wondered why democratic socialist parties never ended up being socialist when they got into power. In the end they always end up supporting capital. He argued that transforming property rights would disrupt capital accumulation in the short run making everyone worse off, even though the vast majority (the working class) would be better off in the long run. The problem for democratic socialist parties is that the short run is longer than the electoral cycle. So if socialist governments pursue such socialist policies they make everyone worse off by the time of the next election, so they lose that election! The leaders then realize this, so in order to stay in power they don't follow socialist policies of re-allocating property rights. Thus social-democratic parties end up supporting capitalism just as much as capitalist parties.

POLITICAL SCIENTIST: There is a similar argument in urban political economy over so-called growth coalitions. The argument there is that local politicians always support development for re-election purposes as it gives a buoyant local economy even though a majority of local people would prefer that their communities have stricter zoning laws and not so much development.

ETHICIST: These seem to be problems that political scientists have identified. Can social software provide solutions?

LOGICIAN: I am not so sure about that. I will not claim that all our problems can be solved by our approach. Just that it can help us examine the issues and evaluate possible solutions.

CHAIR: Revolutions as the re-allocation of property! I am reminded that when Gordon Tullock was mugged in Rio he described it the next day as "an occasion of the re-allocation of private property." However, this has all been very interesting, but I am afraid we must stop now, or we will miss the presentation of the next paper.

PHILOSOPHER: Goodness! That is me, I must dash.

Chapter 6
On Social Choice Theory

Jan van Eijck

An economist is visiting the project. The weather continues to be excellent, permitting the project members and their guest to eat their meals outside on the NIAS terrace again. This time the computer scientist has brought a laptop.

ECONOMIST: Your project on Games, Action and Social Software is intriguing, and this is certainly a splendid environment for carrying it out. But I wonder if what you guys intend to develop doesn't already exist. The field that is called *Social Choice Theory*, isn't that what Social Software is all about?

PHILOSOPHER: Oh, you mean the branch of welfare economics that was founded following the celebrated impossibility results that Kenneth Arrow proved in his thesis (later published in [6])? That work is certainly very relevant to us. You could say that Arrow, like Condorcet, is a founding father of our field of study.

COMPUTER SCIENTIST: Can anyone give me a brief sketch of what Arrow's result is about?

LOGICIAN: OK, I will give it a try. Suppose you have three voters $1, 2, 3$ and three states x, y, z that represent the things they want to achieve in casting their votes. The states could represent preferences for which game to play: hide-and-seek, kick-the-can or I-spy. Or they could represent the range of choice of candidates for leader of the nation. It does not really matter. Suppose each voter has a ranking of the states. We do not allow ties, so there are six possible rankings:

$$x < y < z \quad x < z < y \quad y < x < z$$
$$y < z < x \quad z < x < y \quad z < y < x.$$

PHILOSOPHER: I see that you list all the orderings of the set $\{x, y, z\}$ that are linear and transitive. Linearity presumably reflects the condition that a voter has to make up her mind about how she values the outcomes. Fair enough. Transitivity imposes a kind of consistency requirement: if I prefer x over y and y over z then it is only natural that I prefer x over y. Why are ties not allowed?

ECONOMIST: Formally it does not matter much, but it makes sense to rule them out in the preferences. The preferences are established by voting. It is natural to assume that a valid vote expresses a definite preference one way or the other. The challenge is to combine the wishes of the voters in a single outcome, and in this outcome, ties are allowed. So in the outcome there are thirteen possible rankings: six rankings where the preferences are all different as before, six rankings where the voter is indifferent between two of the three options:

$$x, y < z \quad z < x, y \quad x < y, z$$
$$y, z < x \quad y < x, z \quad x, z < y;$$

and finally the don't care case x, y, z.

LOGICIAN: That is right. Now processing the votes boils down to mapping the preference orderings of the voters to an outcome. In our example case, there are thirteen possible outcomes. Arrow calls such an outcome a social ordering.

COMPUTER SCIENTIST: Arrow sets out to study social welfare functions by imposing reasonable conditions on them, isn't that right?

LOGICIAN: Yes, indeed. There are four conditions. In the first place, there is the condition of *universal* or *unrestricted domain*, call it U. What it says is that every possible set of individual voter preferences should be in the domain of the social welfare function.

COMPUTER SCIENTIST: Let us see. Taking the example case, there are six linear orderings and three voters, which means there are 6^3 sets of preference orderings for the three voters. That is $6 \times 36 = 216$ preference orderings. According to condition U, all of these should be in the domain of the welfare function. But this means that even in this simple example case the number of possible welfare functions is truly enormous: 13^{216}. *(Consults his laptop.)* This is larger than 10^{240}, so it is a number with more than 240 digits.

LOGICIAN: The second condition is what Arrow calls *independence of irrelevant alternatives*. If x and y are social choices, and if voters are allowed to change their preferences about other choices than x and y, then this change should have no effect on what the social welfare function says about the relation between x and y. Let us call this condition I.

COMPUTER SCIENTIST: I suppose that this is a severe restriction.

LOGICIAN: The third condition is the so-called *Pareto principle*, call it P. If x and y are possible choices, and all voters prefer x over y, then the social welfare function should prefer x over y.

COMPUTER SCIENTIST: Why is this called the Pareto principle?

ECONOMIST: Because it has to do with a method of optimization proposed by the economist Vilfredo Pareto. According to Pareto, if a situation can be changed so as to make one individual better off without making anybody else worse off, then the change is an improvement. A situation is Pareto optimal if no such improvement is possible.

COMPUTER SCIENTIST: Clearly, if everyone prefers x over y then outcomes that rank x above y are Pareto optimal, with respect to x and y at least.

LOGICIAN: The final principle says that there should be no dictator. Call this ND, for 'not D'. There should be no voter such that for every set of orderings in the domain of the social welfare function and every pair of distinct social states x and y, if that particular voter strictly prefers x over y, then the social welfare function ranks x above y.

COMPUTER SCIENTIST: I suppose a social welfare function would be dictatorial if it is a projection function, a function that projects the preference vector to a particular component of the vector. So ND rules out that the social welfare function is a projection function?

LOGICIAN: Yes, that's another way of putting it.

PHILOSOPHER: Sounds reasonable enough, all of it.

ECONOMIST: Yes, one would think so. But here is the snag. Arrow's theorem states that no such social welfare function exists. In other words the four principles U, I, P and ND, taken together, are inconsistent.

LOGICIAN: Put otherwise, principles U, I, P together imply D. So in our example case, imposing U, I and P cuts down the number of possible social welfare functions from 13^{216} to just three: projection of the first input component, projection of the second input component, and projection of the third input component.

PHILOSOPHER: I object to the word *dictator* for a voter who happens to have preferences that agree with the social welfare function.

ECONOMIST: You are missing the point. Let me try to explain this in a different way. A social welfare function would be democratic (in social choice theory this is called *anonymous*) if it assigns every individual vote the same weight. In other words, in the case of three voters with preference orderings L_1, L_2 and L_3, the value $F(L_1, L_2, L_3)$ should be identical to $F(L_2, L_1, L_3)$, which again should be identical to $F(L_2, L_3, L_1)$, and so on. Now the point is that not only is a social welfare function F satisfying U, I and P not democratic, but it is much worse than that ...

PHILOSOPHER: I see. I take it, then, that the only way to get around these results is by relaxing some conditions. Suppose we allow the input preferences to be weak orderings, with ties allowed?

COMPUTER SCIENTIST: This would give an initial domain of 13^3 possibilities *(consults his laptop again)* which gives 2197 possible inputs, and 13^{2197} possible welfare functions. Wow, that is a number with more than 2400 digits.

ECONOMIST: Yes, but Arrow's result still holds for this case.

PHILOSOPHER: How about relaxing the conditions on the input preferences still further? Many American voters may in retrospect prefer both Gore and Kerry to Bush, without feeling any need whatsoever to compare Gore to Kerry.

ECONOMIST: Well, a way to think about Arrow's theorem is that there exist situations where a conflict among the assumptions occurs. Note that the theorem does not assert that the assumptions always are in conflict. For instance, the plurality vote is included in his theorem, but there are many profiles where everything is perfectly fine.

PHILOSOPHER: What do you mean by a profile?

ECONOMIST: A vector giving the individual preferences over a set of options for a set of voters, the mathematically explicit version of "what the voters want". So if we require the conditions U, I and P to *always hold for all possible profiles*, then we need a dictator.

PHILOSOPHER: So when the preferences are partially ordered, are there democratic social welfare functions satisfying U, I and P?

LOGICIAN: Since partial orderings include linear orders, there exist settings where a conflict arises among his assumptions, so Arrow's result still applies.

ECONOMIST: One of the other cornerstones of social choice theory is a famous theorem of Gibbard and Satterthwaite [102, 205].

PHILOSOPHER: Isn't this a theorem about manipulability?

ECONOMIST: Well, I guess you could call it that. It has to do with the non-existence of certain social choice functions. A social choice function is like a social welfare function, except that the outputs are social states. Recall that social states represent anything voters may want to achieve. So if x, y, z are social states, a function that picks one of these is a social choice. A social choice function is *strategy-proof* if no voter can improve the social choice by voting against his true preferences.

LOGICIAN: Suppose the social choice for a preference vector $L_1 \ldots L_N$ is x, and i changes his preference from L_i to L_i'. If the social choice for preference vector $L_1 \ldots L_i' \ldots L_N$ is y (different from x), then y should be ranked above x in L_i'.

PHILOSOPHER: So if a preference change for i has as a result that the social choice changes, then the change should reflect the new preference of i. But then it holds by symmetry that x should be ranked above y in L_i, isn't that right?

LOGICIAN: Yes, right indeed.

ECONOMIST: A choice function is dictatorial if there is a voter i such that it holds for every input vector $L_1 \ldots L_N$ that the social choice is x if and only if x is at the top of i's preference ranking L_i. What the theorem of Gibbard and Satterthwaite says is that if there are at least three social goods, then any social choice function that is strategy-proof and has the property that for each social good there should be a voting profile that results in the choice of that good, then the function is dictatorial.

PHILOSOPHER: In other words, if the function is strategy-proof and onto (or: surjective), then it is dictatorial.

ECONOMIST: That's what the theorem implies, indeed.

LOGICIAN: In a paper I have just read there is a claim that a single proof yields both results [193]. In other words, the logical underpinnings of Arrow's theorem and the theorem of Gibbard-Satterthwaite are identical.

ECONOMIST: It is well known that there are close connections between the two theorems. They are pointed out in a textbook by Alan Taylor [230]. As a matter of fact, I discussed the matter once over a glass of wine with Don Saari, who filled me in on historical details. Gibbard and Satterthwaite proved the theorem at essentially the same time. But, Satterthwaite was a graduate student—and this result was part of his University of Wisconsin thesis—so there was a delay in his publishing it. By the time he submitted his paper, Gibbard's paper was in the works, which meant that Mark's paper was not publishable. Hugo Sonnenschein, however, suggested to Mark that he show the connection of his result to Arrow's result, so he did. As such, the real person to show that the logical underpinnings of Arrow's result and the Gibbard-Satterthwaite result are the same is Mark Satterthwaite.

PHILOSOPHER: *(To the logician:)* Do you still remember the structure of the proof you just mentioned? Do you think you can present it to us?

LOGICIAN: If I am allowed to use pencil and paper, yes. As a matter of fact, I reread the paper yesterday, in preparation for our discussion. I will give you a proof of the fact that any Pareto efficient and monotonic social choice function is dictatorial. From this the Gilbert-Satterthwaite result easily follows.

COMPUTER SCIENTIST: But first you have to explain to us what it means for a social choice function to be Pareto efficient and monotonic. Pareto efficiency, I can guess: a social choice function f is Pareto efficient if whenever social good x is at the top of every voter's preference list, then f yields value x.

LOGICIAN: That's right. Monotonicity is also straightforward. If social choice function f yields choice x for preference vector $L_1 \ldots L_N$, then the choice does not change if we adjust the preferences of all the voters, provided in each new preference L_i' no social good y that was ranked below x in L_i is promoted to rank above x.

PHILOSOPHER: So only lowering the position of x in the voter preferences might effect a change from x to a different choice. This is the Gibbard-Satterthwaite counterpart of *independence of irrelevant alternatives*, I suppose.

LOGICIAN: Indeed, it is. Now here is the theorem: if there are at least three social goods, and f is a social choice function that is Pareto efficient and monotonic, then f is dictatorial.

PHILOSOPHER: Fine. Let's go for the proof.

LOGICIAN: Suppose x, y are distinct social goods. Assume a voter profile with x top of the list and y bottom of the list in every voter's ranking. What should the outcome of f be?

PHILOSOPHER: Well, x, of course. This follows from the fact that f is Pareto efficient.

LOGICIAN: That's right. Remember that y was bottom of the list for every voter. Now suppose that I take the preference list of the first voter, and start moving y upward on the list. What will happen?

COMPUTER SCIENTIST: As long as y stays below x, nothing I suppose.

LOGICIAN: And if I move y above x?

COMPUTER SCIENTIST: Either nothing, or the value changes to y. This follows by monotonicity of f, doesn't it?

LOGICIAN: Correct. Now suppose I am going through the voter list, and for each voter move y from the bottom position to the top position. What will happen?

PHILOSOPHER: Then for some voter i, at the point where y gets raised past x, the choice will change from x to y. For suppose it does not. Then we end up with a preference list where y is above x in every voter's preference, while the choice is still x. This contradicts Pareto efficiency.

LOGICIAN: That's right. So we get the following two pictures. Let's call these Figure 1 and Figure 2. *(Draws two pictures for them to look at:)*

$$
\begin{array}{cccccccc}
L_1 & \cdots & L_{i-1} & L_i & L_{i+1} & \cdots & L_N & \\
y & \cdots & y & x & x & \cdots & x & \\
x & \cdots & x & y & \cdot & \cdots & \cdot & \\
\cdot & \cdots & \cdot & \cdot & \cdot & \cdots & \cdot & \mapsto \quad x \\
\cdot & \cdots & \cdot & \cdot & \cdot & \cdots & \cdot & \\
\cdot & \cdots & \cdot & \cdot & \cdot & \cdots & \cdot & \\
\cdot & \cdots & \cdot & \cdot & y & \cdots & y & \\
\end{array}
$$

This first picture shows the situation just before the value flips from x to y.

$$
\begin{array}{cccccccc}
L_1 & \cdots & L_{i-1} & L_i & L_{i+1} & \cdots & L_N & \\
y & \cdots & y & y & x & \cdots & x & \\
x & \cdots & x & x & \cdot & \cdots & \cdot & \\
\cdot & \cdots & \cdot & \cdot & \cdot & \cdots & \cdot & \mapsto \quad y \\
\cdot & \cdots & \cdot & \cdot & \cdot & \cdots & \cdot & \\
\cdot & \cdots & \cdot & \cdot & \cdot & \cdots & \cdot & \\
\cdot & \cdots & \cdot & \cdot & y & \cdots & y & \\
\end{array}
$$

This second picture shows the situation just after the value has flipped from x to y.

PHILOSOPHER: Fair enough. And now I suppose further on in the proof the patterns in these pictures get manipulated a bit more?

LOGICIAN: That's exactly right. Let us study what would happen if in the first picture and the second picture we were to move x down to the bottom for all voters below i, and move x down to the second last position for all voters above i.

COMPUTER SCIENTIST: Nothing, I suppose.

LOGICIAN: That's right, the situations would be as pictured in the following figures. Let us call these Figures 3 and 4.

L_1	$\cdots$	L_{i-1}	L_i	L_{i+1}	$\cdots$	L_N		
y	$\cdots$	y	x	$\cdot$	$\cdots$	$\cdot$		
$\cdot$	$\cdots$	$\cdot$	y	$\cdot$	$\cdots$	$\cdot$		
$\cdot$	$\cdots$	$\cdot$	$\cdot$	$\cdot$	$\cdots$	$\cdot$	$\mapsto$	x
$\cdot$	$\cdots$	$\cdot$	$\cdot$	$\cdot$	$\cdots$	$\cdot$		
$\cdot$	$\cdots$	$\cdot$	$\cdot$	x	$\cdots$	x		
x	$\cdots$	x	$\cdot$	y	$\cdots$	y		

This is Figure 3. It is the result of taking Figure 1 and moving x down to the bottom for voters below i and moving x to the second last position for voters above i.

L_1	$\cdots$	L_{i-1}	L_i	L_{i+1}	$\cdots$	L_N		
y	$\cdots$	y	y	$\cdot$	$\cdots$	$\cdot$		
$\cdot$	$\cdots$	$\cdot$	x	$\cdot$	$\cdots$	$\cdot$		
$\cdot$	$\cdots$	$\cdot$	$\cdot$	$\cdot$	$\cdots$	$\cdot$	$\mapsto$	y
$\cdot$	$\cdots$	$\cdot$	$\cdot$	$\cdot$	$\cdots$	$\cdot$		
$\cdot$	$\cdots$	$\cdot$	$\cdot$	x	$\cdots$	x		
x	$\cdots$	x	$\cdot$	y	$\cdots$	y		

This is Figure 4. It is the result of making similar changes to Figure 2.

PHILOSOPHER: For Figure 4, I can see why the value does not change. In Figure 2 the value was y, and it must remain y in Figure 4 by monotonicity.

COMPUTER SCIENTIST: OK, so Figure 4 has value y. But the Figures 3 and 4 differ only in the order of x, y in the ranking of i. It follows by monotonicity that the value in Figure 3 must be either y or x.

PHILOSOPHER: And it cannot be y, because then by monotonicity the value in Figure 1 would have to be y as well, and it is not. So the value in Figure 3 has to be x.

LOGICIAN: Just as I told you. Now suppose I take Figure 3 and move y down to the one but last position for all voters below i. This would not change the choice from x to a different value, would it?

PHILOSOPHER: I suppose it would not, by monotonicity again. The relative position of y with respect to x does not change.

LOGICIAN: So we get the following picture:

L_1	$\cdots$	L_{i-1}	L_i	L_{i+1}	$\cdots$	L_N		
.	$\cdots$	.	x	.	$\cdots$	.		
.	$\cdots$	.	y	.	$\cdots$	.		
.	$\cdots$	.	.	.	$\cdots$	.	$\mapsto$	x
.	$\cdots$	.	.	.	$\cdots$	.		
y	$\cdots$	y	.	x	$\cdots$	x		
x	$\cdots$	x	.	y	$\cdots$	y		

Call this Figure 5. Now consider a social good z different from x and y. By moving z through the preference orderings without letting z move past x we can obtain the following situation without changing the value of the choice function:

L_1	$\cdots$	L_{i-1}	L_i	L_{i+1}	$\cdots$	L_N		
.	$\cdots$	.	x	.	$\cdots$	.		
.	$\cdots$	.	z	.	$\cdots$	.		
.	$\cdots$	.	y	.	$\cdots$	.	$\mapsto$	x
z	$\cdots$	z	.	z	$\cdots$	z		
y	$\cdots$	y	.	x	$\cdots$	x		
x	$\cdots$	x	.	y	$\cdots$	y		

Call this Figure 6.

PHILOSOPHER: I suppose monotonicity ensures that the value of the function does not change by the transition from 5 to 6?

LOGICIAN: That's correct. Now swap the rankings of x and y for all voters above i. By monotonicity, the choice value for the result must be either x or y.

COMPUTER SCIENTIST: But it cannot be y. For suppose it is, and consider the effect of moving z to the top in every preference. Since this would nowhere effect a swap with y, the value would have to remain y, by monotonicity. But then a profile with everywhere z on top would have value y, which contradicts Pareto efficiency.

LOGICIAN: So the value has to remain x, and we get the following picture:

$$
\begin{array}{ccccccc}
L_1 & \cdots & L_{i-1} & L_i & L_{i+1} & \cdots & L_N \\
\cdot & \cdots & \cdot & x & \cdot & \cdots & \cdot \\
\cdot & \cdots & \cdot & z & \cdot & \cdots & \cdot \\
\cdot & \cdots & \cdot & y & \cdot & \cdots & \cdot \quad\mapsto\; x \\
z & \cdots & z & \cdot & z & \cdots & z \\
y & \cdots & y & \cdot & y & \cdots & y \\
x & \cdots & x & \cdot & x & \cdots & x
\end{array}
$$

Now we are done, for observe that monotonicity ensures that making changes in the preferences of i while making sure that x remains on top will have no effect on the outcome. This means that the social choice will be x whenever x is at the top of i's ranking.

PHILOSOPHER: So i is a dictator for social good x. But since x was arbitrary, there must also be a dictator j for social good z as well. Clearly if i dictates whether x is on top, and j whether z is on top, then, to paraphrase Henk Wesseling, i and j have to be the same guy. Hence i must be a dictator for all alternatives.

LOGICIAN: Why do you quote Henk Wesseling?

COMPUTER SCIENTIST: *(To the economist:)* Henk Wesseling is an honorary NIAS fellow. You met him yesterday at dinner.

PHILOSOPHER: In a column in a Dutch newspaper Wesseling once commented on the lack of historical knowledge of modern students. His juiciest example was the following anecdote. After an undergraduate history seminar, a student came up to him with bright eyes. "Professor, now I suddenly got it. This Jesus and this Christ that they are all talking about, that must be the same fellow."

ECONOMIST: Yes, I was introduced to Wesseling during yesterday's NIAS Banquet Dinner in Leiden. "May I introduce you to the teacher of Alexander"? I didn't get the joke, and nobody explained it to me.

PHILOSOPHER: Because it was no joke. Wesseling is professor emeritus of History from Leiden University, and he was the master's thesis supervisor of the Crown Prince of the Netherlands, Willem Alexander, or Alexander for short.

LOGICIAN: Not the same guy as the student from the seminar, I should hope.

COMPUTER SCIENTIST: I suppose it is shown in [193] that the proof of Arrow's theorem follows exactly the same pattern? And deriving the theorem of Gibbard and Satterthwaite from the above is just a matter of showing that any function that is strategy-proof and surjective has to be Pareto efficient and monotonic?

LOGICIAN: Right on both counts.

ECONOMIST: There is still an issue of how to interpret Arrow's results. Don Saari has written eloquently on that in two books that appeared in 2001 [200, 201]. Arrow's theorem hinges on the fact that the principle I of independence of irrelevant alternatives, or the principle of binary independence, as Saari calls it, allows one to hide the rationality of the voters.

LOGICIAN: That's right. In his investigation of positional voting procedures, Saari proposed a modification of I. His proposal is to replace I by what he calls the principle of *intensity of binary independence*. Let's call it II. This principle states that also the *intensity* of a voter's preference of one alternative over another should be taken into account.

ECONOMIST: In particular, it matters not only that x is preferred over y, but also how many candidates there are between x and y.

PHILOSOPHER: Aha, I can see how that would break steps in the reasoning above. The manipulations of the preference vectors in the proof rely heavily on monotonicity. But what is a positional voting method?

ECONOMIST: Positional voting methods are methods that score candidates by allotting numbers of points to them to reflect their position in the preference ordering of a voter. The paradigm of this is the so-called Borda count. This was proposed in 1770 by Jean-Charles de Borda. Suppose there are n candidates. Then the Borda count assigns $n - j$ points to a voter's jth ranking candidate.

PHILOSOPHER: So in the case of three candidates, my first choice gets 2 points, my second candidate 1 point, and my least preferred candidate 0 points?

ECONOMIST: That's right. In the case of three candidates ordered $x < y < z$, the Borda count has the form $x : 2$, $y : 1$, $z : 0$. When this was proposed as voting method for the *Académie Française*, of which Borda was a member, another member, the mathematician Laplace, proposed to compare this to other ways of assigning points to a candidate depending on position in the preference ordering.

LOGICIAN: The mind of a true mathematician at work.

ECONOMIST: Such methods are positional methods. Plurality voting, where each voter votes for one candidate assigns points $(1, 0, \ldots, 0)$. Antiplurality voting, where each voter object to one candidate assigns points $(1, \ldots, 1, 0)$.

The Borda count assigns points $(n - 1, n - 2, \ldots, 1, 0)$. Saari has a theorem stating that the only positional social welfare function satisfying U, P and II is the Borda count. All other positional methods fail.

PHILOSOPHER: It looks like Saari turns his analysis of Arrow's result into a plea for adopting voting procedures for rational voters that reflect transitivity of preferences.

ECONOMIST: That's right. The Borda count voting procedure does so. All kinds of pairwise comparison procedures are dangerous, is what he claims.

PHILOSOPHER: But wait. I seem to remember that Condorcet, also a French Academy member, made his proposal for pairwise run-off voting procedures precisely because he did not agree with the Borda method. We have talked about Condorcet before (see p. 46). Condorcet objected to positional methods generally because they do not always select the candidate that would be victorious in a pairwise voting contest against *any* of the other candidates.

ECONOMIST: Surely, the Borda count does not always pick what has come to be known as the Condorcet winner. But the point Saari is trying to make is that this may not be as bad as Condorcet thought it was. Saari analyzes Condorcet's original example of a selection procedure with three candidates.

PHILOSOPHER: You have me intrigued. Why don't you look it up?

ECONOMIST: *(Leafs through Saari's* Chaotic Elections.*)* Right, here it is. In the case of three candidates x, y, z there are six voting profiles: $x < y < z$, $x < z < y, y < x < z, y < z < x, z < x < y, z < y < x$. Call these profiles 1 through 6. Condorcet's example was as follows: *(Draws a table on a sheet of paper:)*

1	$x < y < z$	30
2	$x < z < y$	1
3	$y < x < z$	29
4	$y < z < x$	10
5	$z < x < y$	10
6	$z < y < x$	1

Condorcet reasoned that a positional voting scheme will elect y: 39 voters put y in first place, 30 put y in second place, 31 voters put x in first place and 39 put x in second place, and 11 voters put z in first place, and 11 put z in second place. So any reasonable positional voting scheme would yield profile 3, the profile with $y < x < z$, as outcome of the voting procedure. According to Condorcet, this is counterintuitive: x would have beaten y

with 41 to 40 votes, and x would have beaten z with 60 to 21 votes.

PHILOSOPHER: Wait, wait, not so quick. No-one will be able to work out these numbers on the fly.

ECONOMIST: Well, after reading Saari's books you will be. Saari presents beautiful geometric representations. Let me draw the one for the Condorcet example. *(Draws on the paper:)*

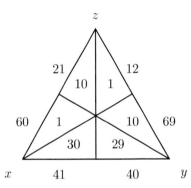

PHILOSOPHER: Let me figure this out ... The vertices in the equilateral triangle represent the three candidates x, y, z, right? Presumably closeness to a vertex indicates preference. Then each region in the triangle corresponds to a profile. Yes, that's right. The region with 30 written in it corresponds to profile $x < y < z$. And the numbers to the side of the triangle indicate the results of pairwise run-offs. Now I can see how you can say so quickly that x beats z with 60 votes to 21.

ECONOMIST: You are quick. *(With a smile:)* I will never underestimate a philosopher again. Saari, by the way, draws a completely different conclusion from the example than Condorcet did. He argues in favor of y as winner, as follows. He is looking for profiles that cancel out. For instance, let me ask you the following question. Is it reasonable to assume that opposite profiles cancel out, in the sense that if one voter with preference $x < y < z$ and one voter with preference $z < y < x$ stay home, this should not affect the voting result? Or put otherwise, can we tally ballots by counting the votes of these two voters as a tie?

PHILOSOPHER: Are you asking me? Well, I think it should make a difference. After all, the two voters agree that y is not so bad, and that information gets lost if they don't vote.

COMPUTER SCIENTIST: Yes, I agree with that. But what if three voters, one with profile $x < y < z$, one with profile $y < z < x$, and one with profile $z < x < y$, all stay home?

PHILOSOPHER: Then I suppose that should make no difference to the outcome, for the three profiles together create a cycle, and no preferential information can possibly be extracted from that. Yes, we should be able to combine these three profiles to form a tie.

ECONOMIST: That's exactly right. What this means is that we can proceed by counting ties first, and then see what remains. So the above picture can be simplified. For there are two of those preferential cycles. First there is the one you just mentioned. Let's mark it with •. Then there is the one that runs in the opposite direction: $z < y < x$, $y < x < z$, and $x < z < y$. Let's mark this with ⋆:

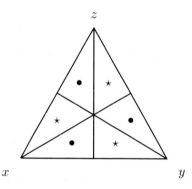

PHILOSOPHER: And now you are going to simplify the picture by subtracting the largest possible fixed numbers from regions with the same mark?

ECONOMIST: That's right. Here is the result of counting all triples of voters whose profiles cancel out as ties: *(Draws a new picture:)*

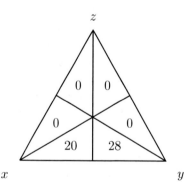

PHILOSOPHER: Wow, a clear win for candidate y.

LOGICIAN: All this theorem proving and analyzing voting profiles makes one crave a refreshment. The NIAS restaurant boasts an excellent espresso machine. Shall we go inside for some coffee or cappuccino?

ECONOMIST: Good idea.

Chapter 7
Ends and Means, Values and Virtues

Jan van Eijck and Martin van Hees

Our philosopher, economist, political scientist, computer scientist and logician convene yet again after enjoying one of Paul's lunches. Outside it is showering with heavy rain. Autumn finally seems to have arrived.

PHILOSOPHER: It has taken me a while but I think I now see what social software is trying to get at. Its ultimate driving force seems to be a desire to help solve social problems. For this, one should of course understand these problems and get a good grasp of their structure. So, and that's the second element, we focus on the analysis of such social problems. Finally, the way of going about in both the analysis and the formulation of the possible solutions is to make use of formal techniques that originate from a variety of disciplines—economics, logic, computer science. And this is what gives the enterprise its cross-disciplinary flavor.

LOGICIAN: That sounds about right. We agreed in an earlier discussion that it may not be expedient to try and give a precise definition of social software (see p. 38).

POLITICAL SCIENTIST: *(To the philosopher:)* But I get the impression that you have reservations about the whole enterprise. In fact, you have been somewhat grumpy all along.

PHILOSOPHER: I'm sorry to hear that I came across as grumpy. I must confess I have a worry about the almost exclusive focus on the three elements of solution, analysis, and methodology. We do indeed talk at length about specific problems, solutions to those problems and all sorts of techniques that could be used. But we have not really addressed the question what it is that constitutes a problem nor about when a specific proposal can count as a solution and when it cannot.

LOGICIAN: We can't have it all at once, can we? In fact, isn't it better to go about in a kind of piecemeal way rather than posing all those big questions at once?

ECONOMIST: I am not even sure that I understand what it is that we are supposed to have neglected.

PHILOSOPHER: Ok, I'll try to explain but let me say at the outset that I do not try to argue for the return to a "grand" analysis of big philosophical questions. I am very much convinced of the necessity of breaking up big problems, and I agree that formal methods are an excellent tool for that. What I want to point out is that we should be more sensitive to the normative assumptions underlying our detailed analysis *in order to* improve upon that analysis. To illustrate, consider the various alternative solutions to the Solomon verdict that we discussed earlier. Those solutions were based upon the idea that the professed mothers make a bid for the child. Game-theoretical analysis shows that under such schemes we can make sure that the only equilibrium outcome is the one in which the real mother gets the child, at no cost at all.

ECONOMIST: Yes, what could possibly be wrong with that?

PHILOSOPHER: I wish to maintain that cheerfully proposing algorithms to solve social problems without worrying about moral side constraints is a questionable way to proceed. Has anyone considered the possibility that it may be immoral to ask a mother to assign a value to her child's life?

LOGICIAN: Why is that? Note that the auction solution simply exploits the fact that the true mother will hold the child dearer than her own life. The solution works precisely because a child is priceless to the real mother and not to the fake mother.

COMPUTER SCIENTIST: I see the point about moral side constraints if we consider algorithms like "Apply physical or psychological coercion until the suspected terrorist has named all his contacts". I agree there might be something wrong with that one.

LOGICIAN: Yes, and the rule of law in civilized countries is meant to prevent such criminal methods.

ECONOMIST: According to an article in the *New Yorker* that I have read [148], a CIA program to outsource torture by means of "extraordinary rendition" of suspected terrorists to countries like Syria or Egypt existed already in the 1990s. Mind you, these are countries where they would almost certainly be tortured. And it got completely out of hand after 9/11.

PHILOSOPHER: To get back at something closer to the Solomon verdict, consider the gruesome scenario of *Sophie's Choice*, William Styron's famous novel [226] about a choice a mother is forced to make by a sadistic Nazi officer. She is made to choose which of her two children stays alive, and which gets killed. If she refuses to choose, the Nazis will kill both children. It has been argued that part of the gruesomeness of this choice has to do with Sophie's identity as a mother. According to the philosopher Joseph Raz [192], the mother is asked by the Nazis to do something that violates the essence of what it means to be a parent: not to choose between one's children. The parallel with the Solomon verdict is that we there ask a mother to state how much she values her own child. But, if Raz is right, that is something that she cannot do without violating her own identity as a parent. Hence, what looks like a neat solution turns out to be based on a gross violation of one of our central values.

COMPUTER SCIENTIST: I don't see what you are getting at with this example. Surely, imposing such a choice on a mother is immoral. We all agree.

ECONOMIST: Imagine yourself in the position of Sophie. Being put in such a situation is gruesome and immoral. But it does not make things better if she refuses to make a choice, or does it? That way, she condemns both of her children. Suppose she would ask her children: what should I do, nothing, in which case both of you will be killed, or flip a coin? What do you think they would say?

LOGICIAN: Let's not get carried away. This may all be beside the point. To make a choice between one's two children, and to express how much one values one's only child seem very different things to me.

ECONOMIST: Yes, and the artillery is a bit heavy, too. Maybe there is a way to make your point without bringing in Nazi practices?

PHILOSOPHER: The point of the story was not that it is impossible to assign a value to a human life. In fact, I not only believe that to be possible but am convinced that we do so on a regular basis, for example when we decide what kind of safety devices to buy for one's car. What I said is that forcing parents to assign a value to the lives of their children violates their identity as parents and may therefore be immoral.

LOGICIAN: Put yourself in the place of Solomon, then. You are holding court, and two raging women are brought into your courtroom. A soldier carries in a crying baby. The women both claim that they are the mother of the child. You have the legal authority to enforce a decision. You also have a reputation of wisdom to lose. What do you do?

PHILOSOPHER: I must confess I don't know. I would have to reflect on this.

COMPUTER SCIENTIST: I would not object to be in the place of Solomon. All those beautiful concubines . . .

LOGICIAN: Listen, everyone agrees that Solomon's method is harsh. But if you object to that, you have to come up with something better. Flipping a coin would have avoided putting pressure on the women in a way that you deem morally dubious. Trouble is that now there is a fifty percent chance that the child gets handed over to the impostor.

PHILOSOPHER: Fair enough. Well, let me think. I guess I would try to find a way that ensures the child goes to the real mother but which does not suffer from unwanted and avoidable side-effects. So can we design a procedure that also has the desired outcome but in which we need not ask the mother to assign a value to her child's life? Suppose that Solomon asks each of the women to write down whether they still want to claim the child. He tells them beforehand that if exactly one of the two makes such a claim, the child will go to her. If however they both claim the child (or if neither of them does) the child will be raised in the palace and each woman should pay a fine that is equivalent to say her annual income. Given her love for the child, the real mother will claim the child: she prefers any situation in which she has tried to get her child back. Realizing this, the other pulls out. After all, given the real mother's claim, there is no chance that she will get the child and she will therefore want to make sure that she does not have to pay the fine. So we have the desired outcome without having asked the mother to assign a value to her child.

ECONOMIST: That's neat. But aren't you making an implicit extra assumption about the motives of the fake mother? That is, if her wish to have the child is primarily based on a desire to frustrate the real mother then she may prefer paying the fine after all.

PHILOSOPHER: Yes, you are right. But note that such an assumption is also made in the solution that I protested against.

LOGICIAN: And can we be sure that the real mother prefers the situation in which the child is at the palace to the one in which the child is with the fake mother but in which she is not fined?

PHILOSOPHER: Yes, I do make that assumption. For which parent would not prefer a situation in which she has done everything she can to keep her own child? Wouldn't you prefer to pay a fine to having to live with the thought that you did not claim your own child, a child who now is raised by an impostor mother? The only reason why one could prefer the latter is, I think, if one fears that the child will have a very nasty life at the palace, say because he will become a slave there. But Solomon can preclude such a complication by ensuring the women that the child will have a decent upbringing in the palace.

ECONOMIST: Your proposal brings to mind the famous disagreement between deontology and consequentialism in ethics. Deontologists stress duty or deon, consequentialists look at whether the outcome is fair or desirable. Maybe designers of social mechanisms are more often consequentialists than deontologists ...

PHILOSOPHER: In this case the solution is based on the woman having what is called a procedural preference: she prefers to have done everything she could to obtain the child irrespective of the consequences [112].

ECONOMIST: The solution hinges on the assumption that the women try to realize their preferences—procedural or not—as well as possible. But I don't see why it discredits the view that consequentialists do a better job in finding solutions to practical social problems.

PHILOSOPHER: Deontologists and consequentialists often disagree about what the problems are so you can't say in general that one approach works better than the other. In the Solomon case my worry was about an aspect of the solution that was proposed, not about the nature of the problem itself. And in some cases in which there is agreement about what the problem is I would rather not leave the solution of those problems in the hands of people who think that the ends justify the means.

LOGICIAN: Some time ago I came across an interesting book by James Wood Bailey, where the view is defended that utilitarianism, which I suppose is a form of consequentialism, is a useful basis for political theory [10]. Bailey does not deny that individuals within institutions have moral responsibilities that cannot be defined in terms of utility alone. But utility can be used as a yardstick for valuing institutions. It allows us to identify morally valuable institutions. The argument is based on a definition of institutions as equilibria in complex or iterative games.

COMPUTER SCIENTIST: Wait, let me guess. I see how his argument would go. I bet he just redefines my duty to abstain from stealing, say, in terms of maximizing my long-term interest. Why is stealing a bicycle morally wrong? Because it is not in my long term interest. I will get caught, or if not, my own bike will get stolen tomorrow, or I will have to invest in an expensive lock to prevent my bike from getting stolen, and so on. This is just an iterative version of the prisoner's dilemma game, where 'cooperate unless challenged' is the most successful strategy. So it turns out that what is morally right is what is good for me in the long run. See Axelrod's book on the evolution of collaboration [9], or Maynard Smith on evolution and the theory of games [149] that we discussed before (p. 64).

LOGICIAN: In Amsterdam the only reasonable thing to do is to ride on a cheap bicycle and invest in two expensive bike locks. Any bike thief will prefer to steal a more expensive bicycle locked with a single lock. But this is prudence, not morality. You are right, by the way, about Bailey's argument.

PHILOSOPHER: I am not sure a reduction of norms and values to our long-term interests is needed for the design of social algorithms. Consider the problem of fair division. There may be all sorts of different considerations that affect whether a division of a legacy is fair or not. In some cases it may be fair to give each of the children an equal share. In other cases we may want to give one of the children a bigger share, say because the others have squandered a large part of the family fortune. If we take the long term perspective, we should describe the problem as forming a small part of a much larger 'game of life' [32] which explains—in terms of our interests—the relevant moral side constraints in the division problem at hand. It would of course be great if this were possible, but I don't see why we should embark on it for a particular division problem. It seems to me that it suffices to be aware of the fact that different moral considerations may affect what is a problem and what is not, and what is an appropriate solution to a problem. We should thus be sensitive to those considerations both in the formulation of our problems and in the analysis of our solutions to them.

POLITICAL SCIENTIST: Ah, that's what you are getting at! Of course, the solutions that we have discussed are based on the assumption that they all have a right to an equal share.

PHILOSOPHER: So you're saying that the solution only works for certain problems of fair division?

LOGICIAN: Of course, if there is debate about whether fair division is the correct procedure to be applied to a certain case, then that debate should be settled first.

COMPUTER SCIENTIST: This seems like an orthogonal issue to me. Scientists have learnt to disentangle such issues. But you philosophers seem to enjoy an occasional bit of conceptual confusion.

ECONOMIST: We should bear in mind that a model by definition leaves things out. Models are meant to get us started with thinking about solutions to well-defined versions of problems, without immediately taking aboard messy notions like moral rights and obligations. This still seems to me the most expedient route. And now I need a cigarette, if you'll excuse me.

(The economist goes outside to have a smoke. The others get a cup of

coffee. After a few minutes, the economist returns, a bit wet. It is still raining outside.)

PHILOSOPHER: I really don't understand why you don't get it. What is so controversial about my point? Clearly, if we are interested in providing solutions to social problems then we cannot ignore normative considerations. To say that something is a problem is to take a normative stance. The same applies to the formulation of a solution to a problem. Whether something is a solution or not is not a purely value-neutral issue.

LOGICIAN: Yes, you sort of said this before. Maybe it helps if you give a concrete example of what you have in mind.

PHILOSOPHER: Take an example from economics, then. The economist and philosopher Amartya Sen [211, 168] argued that notions like rights, freedom and equality are of utmost importance for our understanding of human well-being. For him, the importance of these considerations was not a reason to abandon the economic framework, but rather to broaden the framework so as to make room for these new concepts.

ECONOMIST: This has had profound consequences for our thinking about poverty. For a long time, economists were accustomed to define poverty in terms of Gross Domestic Product (GDP)—the lower the GDP per capita, the poorer the country was said to be. As a result, policies aimed at reducing poverty primarily were primarily aimed at increasing GDP per capita.

PHILOSOPHER: I suppose you need some indicator to measure success of an economic policy.

ECONOMIST: That's right, but Sen argued that GDP was a poor indicator for poverty. First of all, the focus on aggregate country data means that we lose sight of certain very relevant differences in well-being. Afro-American men in the U.S., for instance, have a lower life expectancy than males in China, yet the GDP of the U.S. is much higher. Moreover, the focus on GDP entails that we overlook certain crucial differences between countries. Take the example of large scale famines, which, as Sen points out, have never happened in democracies. Sen argues that this is not a coincidence: famines can only happen in authoritarian systems lacking openness of information and transparency of procedures. Sen's advocacy of capabilities or entitlements led to a change of policy of the UN: instead of reporting on economic development only, they now report on a wide range of issues under 'economic and social development'.

POLITICAL SCIENTIST: Sen was right: the formulation of the problem of the existence of poverty is of utmost importance. Sen's own proposals for how to view the problem of poverty can of course also be questioned. Some of those who shared Sen's criticism of GDP as an indicator for poverty have disagreed with his alternative to it. But how does this translate to the social software enterprise? We are not yet focusing on world-scale problems like poverty. Can we be sure we need reflection on our normative assumptions?

LOGICIAN: Consider the issue of strategic behavior, the topic of the Gibbard-Satterthwaite theorem. The theorem states that almost every social choice function is vulnerable to manipulation, that is, that it may be advantageous for one or more of the individuals not to submit their real preferences. Or, as it also has been formulated, individuals may have an incentive to lie about their preferences.

ECONOMIST: Within economic theory, that theorem gave rise to a specialized subfield: implementation theory. The idea there is to find mechanisms that 'implement' manipulable social choice functions. A mechanism is said to implement a social choice function if, when the mechanism is used rather than the social choice function, the strategic behavior of the individuals will result in the same outcome as what would have resulted if they had all expressed their real preferences under the social choice function.

POLITICAL SCIENTIST: This sounds like a nice example of social software. A problem is formulated—the manipulability of social choice functions—and an algorithm is formulated—the implementation mechanism—to solve the problem.

PHILOSOPHER: Yes, indeed. But still I think we should examine the normative assumptions underlying the approach. Why is strategic behavior considered to be a problem? In a recent paper [119] Dowding and van Hees argue that in a context of political decision making strategic behavior may be a virtue rather than a vice. They argue that if a procedure is manipulable, that is, if strategic behavior may pay off, then rational individuals have to make a calculation about what is best for them to do. This means that they will try to collect information about the beliefs and preferences of the other individuals, about the way in which the social choice function operates, about the possible ways the others may act, and so on. In sum, the greater the incentives to manipulate, the greater the incentive to obtain information about the decision problem. If having more information about the process is considered to be a valuable thing, and many theorists of democracy have indeed argued so, then it is a good thing that the social choice function is manipulable. There need not be a problem for an implementation theorist or a social software designer to solve. In fact, the use of a mechanism that makes manipulation impossible may in fact be creating a problem rather than that it solves one: it impoverishes the political process.

POLITICAL SCIENTIST: When it was pointed out to Jean-Charles de Borda that his election scheme—where voters distribute points over candidates to indicate an order of preference—is highly susceptible to strategic manipulation, he is said to have exclaimed: 'My scheme is intended only for honest men' [33, p. 182].

LOGICIAN: Well, that severely limits its usefulness.

ECONOMIST: Surely manipulation may pose problems, even in a political context. Think of the cost of getting all this extra information. Also, it makes the decision process more unpredictable.

POLITICAL SCIENTIST: And will it not be unfair for those individuals who do not have the same strategic skills as others?

ECONOMIST: That disadvantage would also apply to the implementation mechanisms.

PHILOSOPHER: The argument does not yield that manipulability is *always* a good thing; it merely challenges the view that it is *never* a good thing. Again, my point is that we should be careful about what we believe to be a problem that needs solving. Take the decision making process at university department meetings. Say we want to "solve" the problem of inefficiency or non-transparency of such meetings, a problem that we are probably all familiar with. It may well be the case that getting rid of inefficiency or non-transparency creates new problems that are more serious than the ones we intended to solve.

LOGICIAN: Abolishing departmental meetings altogether also has its drawbacks, you mean?

COMPUTER SCIENTIST: I agree that we should always think carefully about the severity of a disease before administering potent cures. Good doctors try to avoid iatrogenic illness, problems arising from the treatment itself. But how does one do that? Does philosophy have a patent cure-all? Should we assume that meetings at philosophy departments are conducted in more constructive and efficient ways than elsewhere?

PHILOSOPHER: Well, at least we have learnt from long experience that we agree more easily on pragmatic solutions than on fundamental principles.

LOGICIAN: Ahem—hardly what I would call a systematic method.

PHILOSOPHER: The interesting thing is that when there are strong disagreements about fundamental principles, a solution can only be pragmatic if it does not go against any of those principles. In order to be pragmatic, one should know what it means not to be pragmatic. And here insights from ethics are often of use. There are all sorts of ways of going about. For instance, one can distinguish between consequentialist and non-consequentialist accounts of what a problem is.

COMPUTER SCIENTIST: I attended the occasional lecture on ethics, but what vexes me is the exclusive focus on moral problems, or should I say, moral puzzles. The whole enterprise seems to miss a fundamental point about how people behave. Ethicists, at least those I have listened to, seem to assume that people when reflecting on a course of action analyze the morality of it, reach a conclusion, and then act accordingly. But what we see is that humans have great trouble to do what is in their best interest, and even greater trouble to do what their conscience tells them to do.

PHILOSOPHER: "Following one's conscience" is just a metaphor, although one that Church philosophers like Augustine and Thomas Aquinas took quite seriously.

COMPUTER SCIENTIST: What I meant is making resolves, and then failing to stick to them. Oblomov behavior. See, people are not like computers at all. A mouse-click on the "do A" button, but nothing happens.

PHILOSOPHER: That is what philosophers call 'akrasia', or inability to act in accordance with one's best judgment [183].

LOGICIAN: "O Lord, give me chastity, but not yet." The only quote from St. Augustine that I know by heart [7]. Very human, indeed.

COMPUTER SCIENTIST: When I teach programming skills, I have found out that it is no use to explain to my students that master programmers write clear code with documentation, insert tests that can serve as specifications, and restructure their programs whenever needed. Instead, I just drill them and give them feedback—letting them rewrite their unstructured rubbish until it satisfies my standards—until writing clear code is second nature to them. Not very different from instilling moral behavior in my young children. I mean skills like not hurting other children, not being rude, being honest, being polite. I have never heard ethicists address the issue of moral education, and that is precisely why I find ethics as an academic discipline so utterly boring and irrelevant.

LOGICIAN: Aristotle's *syllogistics* may be just a footnote to modern logic, but Aristotle's *Ethics* [5] is more inspiring than many of today's sterile discussions.

PHILOSOPHER: Thank you very much. I don't accept this dismissal of armchair philosophy though. If for instance thinking about the distinction between facts and values is a form of armchair philosophy, then I am happy to be an armchair philosopher. Moreover, you may want to catch up on the developments. The kind of armchair philosophy that you are criticizing hardly serves as an accurate picture of contemporary ethics. Whether it concerns a new field like neuro-ethics [125], developments in moral psychology [107], the study of the evolution of norms [239], or the revival of virtue ethics, we can witness an empirical turn in our thinking about moral issues. As to the revival of virtue ethics, the plea that ethics should take psychological insights into account can already be found in a landmark paper by Elizabeth Anscombe that was published in 1958 [3].

COMPUTER SCIENTIST: Ahem, 1958 is a long time ago. Was this a plea for a return to the Aristotelian view of ethics, with much greater emphasis on psychology? And did academic philosophers pay any attention?

PHILOSOPHER: As a matter of fact, many of them did, and there are quite a lot of places where you could start. A book I very much recommend is *Moral Goodness* by Philippa Foot [93]. It revives the ancient idea of a link between human happiness and virtue. It marks a fresh start in thinking about moral issues, and is already a classic. Foot was one of the founders of Oxfam, by the way. And it may interest you that Foot introduced the trolley problem that Rohit Parikh mentioned in his lecture here at NIAS (see p. 55). Another gem is *Ethics and the Limits of Philosophy*, by Bernard Williams [240]. I am almost sure you will like it, for Williams is about as skeptical as you are about what philosophy can have to say about moral issues. Only more knowledgeable, of course.

COMPUTER SCIENTIST: *(With a smile:)* Of course.

LOGICIAN: I don't know about Foot or Williams, but Aristotle is a good practical psychologist, and that is why much of what he has to say about reaching one's full potential by training oneself to be an excellent man— or woman, one has to add—is still relevant today. We may want to study ethics in order to improve our lives, and the principal concern of the subject, according to Aristotle, is the nature of human well-being.

COMPUTER SCIENTIST: I like the view that people must be trained to be moral. It reminds me of the well known Zen simile of the training of the mind as "taming the wild ox" [194]. And a friend in cognitive science told me that the image of a wild animal and a rider with limited control squares quite well with modern findings of how emotion and reason interact in determining action [55].

LOGICIAN: *(At the economist:)* It explains why you have difficulty giving up smoking. Your habit is endangering your health, and you know it. The warning message printed on your fags reminds you. Your insurance company makes you pay a premium for the extra risk. You can work out the statistics.

Still, you can't give up, because the ox is stronger than the rider.

COMPUTER SCIENTIST: To smoke or not to smoke: that question may have something to do with ethics after all. I am sure Aristotle would have agreed that an addicted smoker is lacking in the quality of temperance.

PHILOSOPHER: If ethicists are censored for their bad habits, there is always an easy rejoinder: "Who has ever seen a signpost walk in the direction that it points to?"

POLITICAL SCIENTIST: Let's leave a discussion of the virtues for another occasion. I think we have talked enough for one lunch.

Chapter 8
Common Knowledge and Common Belief

Hans van Ditmarsch, Jan van Eijck, Rineke Verbrugge

PHILOSOPHER: Today, I suggest we discuss the important concepts of common knowledge and common belief. As far as I know, the first one to give a formal analysis of these concepts was the philosopher David Lewis, in his book *Convention* [140]. One of his examples is traffic conventions, about the role of common knowledge in how one behaves in road traffic. To explain this properly, I wonder if you would care to play a little game with me.

COGNITIVE SCIENTIST: Sure.

PHILOSOPHER: Imagine yourself driving on a one-lane road. You have just come out of the Channel Tunnel on the British side and it is well-known that drivers who just went from France to England, or vice versa, tend to forget on which side of the road they have to drive, particularly if they find themselves on a quiet one-lane road where they are suddenly confronted with oncoming traffic. In case traffic comes towards you from the other direction, you will have to swerve a bit to the side to let it pass. In fact, you each have to swerve a bit.

ECONOMIST: Ah, this is beginning to sound familiar! If you swerve, you're a chicken. If not, and if you force the other to swerve, you're a tough guy. Unfortunately, when two tough guys come together, they will crash. There is interesting equilibrium behavior in examples like this. It's a standard setting for a two-person game in game theory [31].

PHILOSOPHER: Yes, you are right, but that is not what I wanted to explain. *(To the cognitive scientist again:)* Will you swerve left or right?

COGNITIVE SCIENTIST: Well, if I remember that I am in England, where people have to drive on the left, I will swerve left. Otherwise, I will swerve right.

PHILOSOPHER: Yes, and how about the guy coming towards you? He and you may both be cautious drivers, but if he will swerve right and you left, you will *still* crash. The point is that it is not enough for you and the on-comer both to know that you have to drive left. You would also like to know *that the other knows*. And this will affect your behavior. Wouldn't you agree that you will drive *more* cautiously—and swerve slightly more to the left—if you are uncertain whether the oncoming driver *also* knows that he has to drive on the left, than when you know that he knows to drive on the left?

COGNITIVE SCIENTIST: Surely.

PHILOSOPHER: Then we are approaching common knowledge. Because surely you then also agree that this holds for the other driver as well. Now if you knew that the other driver did not know whether you knew to drive on the left, would that still affect your driving behavior?

COGNITIVE SCIENTIST: It seems reasonable to be slightly *more* cautious when I do not know if he knows that I know, than when I know that he knows that I know, as his driving behavior will be slightly less predictable given his doubt about my knowledge—he might be tempted to avoid collision by a last-minute unexpected strong swerve to the right instead of to the left, if he were to think—incorrectly—that I am initiating that too.

PHILOSOPHER: Exactly. You are *very cautious* if you do not know, *slightly less cautious* if you know but not if the other knows, *even less cautious* if you know and also know that the other knows but not if he knows that, *and so on*: by repeating the above argument, you will all the time become slightly more confident about the other's road behavior but never entirely so. Driving on the left-hand side is what Lewis calls a *convention*, and this means that you know that I know that you know ... up to any finite stack of knowledge operators.

ECONOMIST: As another instance of how relevant the concept of common knowledge is, you may care to mention that analyzing the properties of common belief is what earned the economist Robert Aumann the 2006 Nobel Prize for economics. In fact, independently from the logicians and philosophers, Aumann developed the concepts of common knowledge and common belief as ways to describe perfect rationality. Strategic choice assumes such common knowledge of each other's possible actions.

COMPUTER SCIENTIST: Ah, Aumann on agreeing to disagree. I have a surprise for you here. Recently at a very interesting workshop on new directions in game theory in Amsterdam, the famous game theorist Dov Samet gave me a copy of an article by sociologist Morris Friedell, "On the structure of shared awareness", that already appeared in January 1969 in *Behavioral Science* [97]. This is based on a technical report from 1967, so it is even earlier than Lewis' much less technical book. Friedell's paper contains a proper definition of common knowledge, and it also has a wealth of fascinating examples of common knowledge in social situations. In fact, without knowing it, many later authors on common knowledge are just expanding on examples introduced by Friedell. So if anyone is the father of common knowledge, it is Friedell.

ECONOMIST: It is commonly believed among economists that Aumann was the first to give a formal analysis of common knowledge.

PHILOSOPHER: And it is commonly believed among philosophers that Lewis was the first.

LOGICIAN: But what Dov Samet was telling my colleague here shows that those common beliefs were wrong. A nice illustration of the fact that common beliefs may happen to be false.

PHILOSOPHER: Unlike cases of common knowledge. Maybe even something stronger was true: maybe it was commonly believed among economists that it was common knowledge that Aumann was the first to give this formal analysis. And *that* common belief was also false.

COMPUTER SCIENTIST: Friedell also has interesting things to say about ways of achieving common knowledge. Our dear Philosopher makes it sound like common knowledge is very hard to achieve. But that would be a mistake. Common knowledge is often easily achieved, by means of public announcement.

COGNITIVE SCIENTIST: And what do you mean by public announcement, exactly?

COMPUTER SCIENTIST: Well, I suppose a public announcement is an event where something is being said aloud, while everybody is aware of who is present, and it is already common knowledge that all present are awake and aware, and that everybody hears the announcement, and that everybody is aware of the fact that everybody hears it, and ...

COGNITIVE SCIENTIST: Ahem, an example may be clearer.

COMPUTER SCIENTIST: OK, at your service. It is already common knowledge among us that no one here has hearing difficulties and that everyone is wide awake, right? *(In a loud, solemn voice:)* I herewith announce to you all that the concert by Heleen Verleur and Renée Harp will take place on January 25. *(In a lower voice again:)* There you are. The date of the concert is now commonly known among the five of us.

ECONOMIST: Actually, this concert has already been announced by internal NIAS email. But the thing is, several fellows don't read their email, or only very irregularly. Should we still consider these email notifications as proper public announcements?

PHILOSOPHER: I have a hard time remembering all those emails that I receive here.

LOGICIAN: There are various scenarios for which one can prove that it is impossible to achieve or increase a group's common knowledge [136, 153, 90].

COMPUTER SCIENTIST: I suppose the fact that fellows don't read their emails means that that channel is unreliable. Analysis of message passing through unreliable channels is old hat in computer science. We call it the *problem of the two generals*, or the *coordinated attack problem*. Would anyone like me to elaborate?

COGNITIVE SCIENTIST: Yes, please.

COMPUTER SCIENTIST: To immediately make the link with the topic at hand: it was proved by Halpern and Moses [109, 110] that message exchange in a distributed environment, where there is no guarantee that messages get delivered, cannot create common knowledge. They use the example of two generals who are planning a coordinated attack on a city. The generals are on two hills on opposite sides of the city, each with their own army, and they know they can only succeed in capturing the city if their two armies attack at the same time. But the valley that separates the two hills is in enemy hands, and any messengers that are sent from one army base to the other run a severe risk to get captured. The generals have agreed on a joint attack, but they still have to settle the time.

PHILOSOPHER: So the generals start sending messengers. But they cannot be sure that the messengers succeed in delivering their message. And if they get through, there is no guarantee that the message of acknowledgment will get delivered. And so on.

COMPUTER SCIENTIST: You got the picture.

PHILOSOPHER: Suppose the general who sends the first messenger keeps sending messengers, all with the same story, until he gets an acknowledgment back, and then he keeps sending messengers to confirm the acknowledgment?

COMPUTER SCIENTIST: That procedure is known in computer science as the "alternating bit protocol" for sending bits over an unreliable channel. The sender repeats the transmission of a bit until an acknowledgment is received, then the sender acknowledges the receiver's acknowledgment until that is in turn acknowledged by the receiver, and only then the next bit is sent until that bit gets acknowledged, and so on.

LOGICIAN: The alternating bit protocol is also covered by Halpern and Moses' impossibility result. After the bit gets through, the receiver knows the value of the bit. After the acknowledgment gets back, the sender knows that the receiver knows the value of the bit. After the acknowledgment of the acknowledgment gets back, the receiver knows that the sender knows that the receiver knows the value of the bit, and if this gets confirmed, the sender knows that the receiver knows that the sender knows that the receiver knows the value of the bit. Still, this will not achieve common knowledge.

PHILOSOPHER: OK, you have made it quite plausible that message passing through unreliable channels cannot create common knowledge. And NIAS email is perhaps not the proper medium for NIAS public announcements. But maybe we should turn it around: what are the properties of events that succeed in creating common knowledge? It seems to me that they all involve a shared awareness that a common experience takes place. It can involve various senses: hearing, seeing, maybe even touching or smelling.

COMPUTER SCIENTIST: This is getting sensual. Maybe intimate experiences such as eye-contact and touching are privileged in creating common knowledge? Friedell formulates the following obvious but important principle:

> If B sees A look at B, then A sees B look at A. From this and a few simpler properties one can demonstrate that eye contact leads to common knowledge of the presence of the interactants. It is no coincidence that eye contact is of considerable emotional and normative significance [97, p. 34].

COGNITIVE SCIENTIST: Would you stop looking me in the eye so intently, dear Computer Scientist? We already *have* common knowledge that we're both here ... *(blushes)*

COMPUTER SCIENTIST: Indeed, here are those touchy situations that Friedell also analyzes, where some proposition is common knowledge, but the participants mutually pretend that the contrary proposition is the case [97]. If I'm not mistaken, such "open secret" situations will be extensively discussed during the NIAS lecture closing off our project (see p. 183).

PHILOSOPHER: There is a nice philosophy paper by Clark and Marshall about common knowledge as a background for mutual reference in discourse. They remark that common knowledge is often established by what they call "co-presence" [48].

COGNITIVE SCIENTIST: Yes, but how does one know that an announcement has become common knowledge? I might have let my attention wander for a moment, or I might have misheard you. Actually, for smelling one would prefer some things *not* to be commonly observed. It is common practice in polite society to pretend one does not notice certain smells. This prevents what is generally known from becoming common knowledge.

PHILOSOPHER: I would put that differently. I would say it makes it possible to pretend of things that are in fact already common knowledge that they are not.

COMPUTER SCIENTIST: Seriously, whether you paid attention or not may not be the point. If an announcement is made, you were *supposed* to pay attention, and therefore the information can now be assumed common knowledge.

PHILOSOPHER: That is what happens in the public arena all the time. At the basis of legal relations between individuals and the state, or of the mutual legal relations between individuals, is the assumption that the law is common knowledge.

COGNITIVE SCIENTIST: But this is a fiction. Professional lawyers have a full-time job to keep up with the law. Ordinary citizens can simply not be expected to cope.

PHILOSOPHER: You may call it a fiction. I prefer to say that it is a necessary presumption. Roman lawgivers found out long ago that if citizens within their jurisdiction could plead innocence because of being unaware of the law, no offender could ever get convicted. So they were quick to invent principles like *Ignorantia legis neminem excusat,* "ignorance of the law excuses no one".

COMPUTER SCIENTIST: And the counterpart of that is that the laws have to be properly published and distributed. By being printed in a government gazette that every citizen has access to, for instance. Of course, the citizens are not supposed to read all that boring stuff. What matters is that they should be able to find out about it whenever they want. In this way, the publications in the government gazette amount to public announcements.

COGNITIVE SCIENTIST: This connects to the conventions of driving that we started our discussion with. The traffic regulations are assumed to be common knowledge, although few people will be able to accurately reproduce all traffic rules. But if you are ignorant of the rules and cause a traffic accident, you are obviously still liable.

PHILOSOPHER: To prepare for this discussion I reread a classic publication from 1978 analyzing the concept of common knowledge, by Jane Heal [116]. Still a nice piece of philosophical exposition. The introduction is fabulous. Her work anticipates combining reasoning about knowledge and plausibility. If we're having dinner together and I drop a hot potato, it may be that

> I know that I have dropped that potato and so do you; but I hope and I believe that you do not know, and you hope that I do not know that you know [116, p.116]

It also anticipates ways of linking knowledge to action for which, as far as I know, even now no good explanations can be given. Consider two agents, separated by a screen, who both repeatedly select one option from a set of many, simultaneously. When their selection is the same, a reward is given, and it is assumed to be common knowledge that they both get notified when that happens. But the notifications are private.

COMPUTER SCIENTIST: I don't think that is miraculous at all. This is a case where the private announcement "you get a reward for this choice" can achieve the effect of a public announcement, just *because* it is already commonly known that whenever one player gets the private announcement, the other player gets it as well. So what will happen is that after the first random common choice of C, the two players will keep choosing C to get rewarded again.

PHILOSOPHER: Ahem—exactly.

COMPUTER SCIENTIST: Michael Suk-Young Chwe's book *Rational Ritual* [47] also discusses such matters. Interestingly, Chwe pays attention to the *size* of groups for which common knowledge gets established. A brand name that is common knowledge in a large group is worth a lot of money. Chwe analyzes the example of advertisements broadcasted during the American football Super Bowl. He compares the enormous cost of making something common knowledge by means of such advertisements to the obvious benefits. Part of the benefit is in the fact that the advertisements create common knowledge. An important consideration when deciding to buy a Blu-ray media player, for example, is the knowledge that others are going to buy it too. The common knowledge created by an advertisement in the break of a nationwide TV-event gives the reassurance that lots of titles will soon become available in the new format.

COGNITIVE SCIENTIST: I know that book. Actually, Chwe uses the example of the announcement of the new Apple Macintosh computer during a football Super Bowl, in 1984 I think. What I particularly like about the book is that it treats formal issues in a lucid not-technical way. But it assumes a firm grasp of technicalities, such as the distinction between general knowledge and common knowledge.

LOGICIAN: General knowledge among the members of a group of agents means that all individuals in the group know a certain fact, and *common* knowledge means: everybody knows that everybody knows, and so on [153, 90].

COMPUTER SCIENTIST: Let me propose a definition of common knowledge. A proposition φ is common knowledge if everybody knows that φ and everybody knows that φ is common knowledge.

PHILOSOPHER: That can hardly qualify as a definition. What you are saying is obviously circular. Besides, if I know that φ is common knowledge, then it logically follows that φ is common knowledge, for knowledge implies truth.

COMPUTER SCIENTIST: Yes, of course, but the definition states an equivalence. Truth does not in general imply knowledge, but in the case of common knowledge it does. If φ is common knowledge, then I know (and you know) that φ is common knowledge. And the circularity is not vicious.

PHILOSOPHER: I am of course familiar with recursive definitions, with a base case and a recursive case.

COMPUTER SCIENTIST: But this is an instance of what in computer science is known as a definition by co-recursion. Co-recursive definitions are like recursive definitions, but with the crucial difference that there is no base case. And they define infinite objects. Let me give you a simple example. An infinite stream of zeros, call it *zeros*, can be defined as: *zeros* equals a zero followed by *zeros*. In lazy functional programming this is written as

```
zeros = 0 :  zeros
```

If you execute this program in Haskell you will get an infinite stream of zeros flashing over your screen.

PHILOSOPHER: I suppose you mean an initial segment of an infinite list?

COMPUTER SCIENTIST: Yes, that is what I mean, of course. Even you are bound to get bored at some point, and break it off.

PHILOSOPHER: Ahem, nice example. Haskell is a programming language, I suppose?

COMPUTER SCIENTIST: Haskell is a language for functional programming, well suited for defining programs by co-recursion. As you can see from the example, Haskell uses colon for putting an element in front of a list. If you are interested, I can give you a reference to a textbook on Haskell programming with a whole chapter devoted to co-recursive definitions [67].

And I hope to have convinced you that my definition of common knowledge was as acceptable as my definition of the stream of zeros.

PHILOSOPHER: Yes, your recursive definition does make intuitive sense.

COMPUTER SCIENTIST: It is a co-recursive definition, not a recursive definition.

PHILOSOPHER: Thank you. I will try to keep the distinction in mind, at least while you are present. But let us move to the distinction between distributed knowledge and common knowledge. Am I right in saying that distributed knowledge is what a group would know if it had pooled their knowledge? If I know that p implies q, and you know p, then we have distributed knowledge of q.

COMPUTER SCIENTIST: Yes, that's right. Suppose Alice knows that p, Bob knows that p implies q, and Carol knows that q implies r. Then if they combine their resources they can figure out together that r is the case, so they have distributed knowledge that r. One obvious way to make r common knowledge is for Alice to shout p, for Bob to reply with announcing that p implies q, and therefore q, and for Carol to conclude by stating loudly that q implies r, and therefore r. In short, they each make a public announcement of what they know, and their distributed knowledge turns into common knowledge.

LOGICIAN: Your example illustrates the difference quite nicely. Let us use Cp to express that p is common knowledge. If I know that p and you know that p implies q, these together do not imply Cq. But if Cp and $C(p \to q)$ then Cq. If p and $p \to q$ are common knowledge then the conclusion q is also common knowledge.

COMPUTER SCIENTIST: Indeed, that is all in accordance with the definition that I gave you.

ECONOMIST: *(Smiling:)* Well, it is common knowledge among economists that the analysis of common belief is crucial for understanding the way the stock-market functions. There may be rules of thumb for computing the value of stock like 'a share in company X should not cost more than twenty times the profit per share of company X', but these are not practical.

PHILOSOPHER: I suppose these days it is quite uncommon for companies to have an uninterrupted existence of twenty years. Without mergers or split-ups, I mean. Besides, nobody is willing to look that far ahead.

ECONOMIST: John Maynard Keynes, in his *General Theory of Employment, Interest and Money* [132] has something amusing to say about this:

[...] professional investment may be likened to those newspaper competitions in which the competitors have to pick out the six prettiest faces from a hundred photographs, the prize being awarded to the competitor whose choice most nearly corresponds to the average preferences of the competitors as a whole; so that each competitor has to pick, not those faces which he himself finds prettiest, but those which he thinks likeliest to catch the fancy of the other competitors, all of whom are looking at the problem from the same point of view. It is not a case of choosing those which, to the best of one's judgment, are really the prettiest, nor even those which average opinion genuinely thinks the prettiest. We have reached the third degree where we devote our intelligences to anticipating what average opinion expects the average opinion to be. And there are some, I believe, who practise the fourth, fifth and higher degrees.

That is from Chapter Twelve, called "The State of Long-term Expectation".

PHILOSOPHER: You impress me. So you do really know your classics by heart?

ECONOMIST: Well, to be completely honest with you, I admit that I looked this one up for the occasion.

PHILOSOPHER: Your quote is interesting, for it talks about levels of mutual belief, and in the limit about common belief. The prize in the beauty contest goes not to the person who picks the prettiest girl, but to the person who picks the girl that is commonly believed to be the prettiest girl. If Keynes is right that the stock-market is about common belief, then the value of a share is what people believe it is. As long as a stock is commonly believed to be worth a lot, it does not matter if it is overvalued.

ECONOMIST: Until a stock-market crash occurs. Keynes himself was an avid speculator, and his friends had to bail him out during the crash that preceded the Great Depression.

LOGICIAN: That reminds me of the current credit crunch. I'm afraid that epistemic logic and the concept of common belief do not suffice to explain what's going on there. For example, imagine a rumor that a bank is going to go bankrupt. The rumor may be false, but it can start a chain reaction which results in the bank actually going bankrupt. If we want to be serious about social software, we need to be able to explain such a phenomenon, and possibly even to devise mechanisms to prevent them.

ECONOMIST: In fact, it does seem to me that epistemic game theory and behavioral game theory can already account for both epistemic and psychological aspects of the agents. In a recent paper by Bicchieri and Xiao [30], for example, the authors take on the challenge to investigate how social norms influence individual decision making. It turns out that what we expect others to *do* significantly predicts our own choices, much more than what we expect others to *think we ought to do*. Such findings are important if you want to design policies aimed at discouraging undesirable behavior [2].

COMPUTER SCIENTIST: So all this talk by the Dutch prime minister about norms and values will not influence the Dutch citizens' behavior one iota if we do not see the desired behavior around us.

LOGICIAN: That's what I always tell my spouse: It doesn't help to *tell* our children not to smoke or drink or lie: We should consistently set the right example. It's sure tiring to be a parent ...

COGNITIVE SCIENTIST: Speaking about psychological aspects and children, common knowledge must also be relevant for what in cognitive science and psychology is known as 'theory of mind'. Around the age of four, children appear to develop a notion of another person's mind. They discover that what others think can be different from their own thoughts and that you can explain and predict other people's behavior in terms of their mental states. A well-known setting is Wimmer and Perner's 'Sally-Anne' experiment [243], where a doll, Sally, puts a marble into her basket and then leaves the scene. While Sally is away and cannot see what happens, Anne takes the marble out of Sally's basket, and places it into her own box. Sally then returns and children have to answer the question where Sally will first look for her marble. Only from the age of four, children seeing the marble being moved will anticipate that Sally, who has *not* observed this move, will therefore later not know the new location of the marble.

PHILOSOPHER: Ah, that would explain why under-four-year-olds do not see the fun of performing magic tricks, for instance. The child knows that the coin is hidden beneath the sheet of paper, and the audience pretends to believe it has disappeared, and starts uttering sighs of amazement.

LOGICIAN: Yes, my five-year-old daughter loves that. Of course, the grown-ups have to play along by displaying their complete bafflement.

LOGICIAN: There may well be a relation between how conventions are formed in general and how a theory of mind develops in children. It seems only one step from whether you know that the other knows the location of a ball, to whether you know that the other knows on which side of the road to drive. But in such psychological experiments the higher-order setting never plays a role, as far as I know.

---

[2] These remarks about the 2008 credit crunch were inspired by contributions to an email discussion by Rohit Parikh, Adam Brandenburger and Cristina Bicchieri.

COGNITIVE SCIENTIST: The standard setting of the Sally-Anne experiment does not test for higher-order aspects of knowledge: the child only needs to make a first-order false-belief attribution, that Sally believes that the marble is still in her own basket.

LOGICIAN: But recent investigations [155, 238, 92] pay special attention to just that higher-order aspect, and discuss experimental settings that corroborate the emergence of higher-order theory of mind, but only after the age of about six. It appears that even adults have some difficulty in applying third-order attributions such as "John doesn't know that Alice believes that he wrote a novel under pseudonym". That is, of course, if they are not logicians.

COGNITIVE SCIENTIST: Wow, if reasoning on three orders is already so hard for most of us, how can people ever draw correct conclusions about common knowledge, with all that complicated co-recursion it involves?

ECONOMIST: Indeed, it seems that in game settings people often just approximate common knowledge by a low stack of "we know that we know . . .", maybe only three or four levels [220].

PHILOSOPHER: Ah, now we are back on the English road where we started our discussion! As long as we know that we know that we know to drive on the left, we feel safe enough to proceed without swerving. At least I do.

ECONOMIST: I hope you don't mind if I get serious again. In "Agreeing to disagree" [8] Aumann introduces common knowledge as "everybody knows that everybody knows that . . .". In the economics setting, instead of different *possible* situations—such as driving on the left, or on the right—the preferred model is that of different *probable* situations, and how events relate prior to posterior probabilities. Aumann shows that if agents have common knowledge of their posterior probabilities of an event, that these must then be the same. In other words, they can only agree to agree and they cannot agree to disagree. His presentation is elementary but it would still carry a bit too far to explain the details here.

LOGICIAN: What do you mean, carry us too far? Let *me* explain, then. The easiest way to explain what is behind Aumann's proof is this. It is not rational to agree to disagree, in an economic context at least, because this agreement would entail awareness of the fact that the disagreement can be exploited. What does it mean that you believe that the probability of an event is one half? Simply that if you are taking bets on this, then you will consider a bet with a return of two to one a fair bet. And if you believe that the probability is one in four and you are in a betting mood, then you will consider a bet with a return of four to one (including the stake) a fair bet.

COMPUTER SCIENTIST: Isn't that what bookies call an odds of three to one against? If the event happens you win three times your stake, otherwise you lose your stake.

LOGICIAN: That's right. Now consider what happens if I know that you believe that the probability of Barack Obama winning the presidential election is one fourth, and you know that I believe that this probability is one half. Then I know that you are willing to take odds of three to one against, and you know that I am willing to take only equal bets. Then we should both be aware of the fact that someone can make money out of us, irrespective of how the election turns out.

COMPUTER SCIENTIST: Ah, I see. Assume Hillary Clinton places her bet of a thousand bucks with the guy who offers odds of three to one against Barack winning, and bets for two thousand bucks that Barack will lose with the guy who offers equal odds. If Barack wins, Hillary collects three thousand bucks from the first guy and loses her stake with the other, so she gains a thousand bucks. If Barack loses, Hillary loses her stake with the first guy but collects two thousands bucks from the other bloke, so again she pockets a profit of a thousand bucks.

PHILOSOPHER: Isn't that what gamblers call a Dutch book?

LOGICIAN: That's right. A Dutch book, a set of odds and bets which guarantees a profit, regardless of the outcome of the gamble, is what we have here. That's why agreeing to disagree is not rational for people who are willing to put their beliefs to the test by taking bets.

PHILOSOPHER: The explanation of degree of belief in terms of willingness to act, or to take bets, reminds me of Frank Ramsey's famous foundation of probability theory in terms of degrees of belief [189]. Ramsey remarks that the frequency account of probability does not explain what we mean by probability in cases of non-repeatable events. The election or non-election of Barack Obama is an example.

LOGICIAN: Actually the proof that Aumann gives does not involve betting or Dutch books. It is simply the observation that if φ is common knowledge between Alice and Bob, then φ has to hold in a set of members of the knowledge partition for Alice, and similarly for Bob.

ECONOMIST: There is also more recent stuff: in game theory, a lot of work is made of the analysis of strategic choice under assumptions of limited rationality. A case of opponent modeling where common knowledge is absent would be an example [69].

PHILOSOPHER: I am still wondering about this funny kind of definition that you call co-recursion. It seems like some kind of infinitary process is going on. How can we make sure it ever stops? I mean, imagine sending a romantic email, with 'I adore you' or that sort of thing. You get a reply "I am so glad to know that you adore me", you send a reply back "Now I am delighted, for I know that you know that I adore you", only to get an exciting response: "How sweet for me to know that you know that I know that you adore me." Obviously, this nonsense could go on forever, and never achieve common knowledge of the basic romantic fact.

LOGICIAN: That's brilliant. For it *does* never stop if you do it like this. But if the two lovebirds get together, they may still go through the whole exchange that you mentioned, but only for the fun of it. For the first "I adore you" creates common knowledge.

ECONOMIST: Of course. And there are lots of everyday examples where the creation of common knowledge is crucial. Indeed, certain rituals are designed for it, and it is unwise not to observe them. Take the old-fashioned ritual that takes place when you withdraw a large amount of money from your bank account and have it paid out to you in cash by the cashier. The cashier will look at you earnestly to make sure she has your full attention, and then she will slowly count out the banknotes for you: one thousand (counting ten notes), two thousand (counting another ten notes), three thousand (ten notes again), and four thousand (another ten notes). This ritual creates common knowledge that forty banknotes of a hundred dollars were paid out to you.

PHILOSOPHER: Such rituals are important, indeed. Suppose you have four thousand bucks in an envelope, and you hand it over to a friend who is going to do a carpentry job at your home, say. Then what if this friend calls you later with dismay in his voice, and the message that there were just thirty-five banknotes in the envelope?

ECONOMIST: Then you are in trouble indeed, for you have failed to create common knowledge that the forty notes were there when you handed over the envelope. You failed to observe an important ritual, and this failure may result in the end of a friendship.

LOGICIAN: Maybe you only got what you deserved. Why pay for a carpentry job in cash unless one of you wants to fool the tax office?

PHILOSOPHER: Let us move on to the logic of common knowledge. How do we know that the concept of common knowledge is well-defined? And how do we know that common knowledge can be achieved in a finite number of steps?

LOGICIAN: The answer to the first question lies in a famous theorem by

Tarski and Knaster. Let F be the operation of mapping a set of situations X to the set of situations where X is general knowledge and where $F(X)$ is also general knowledge. Then this operation is monotonic. This means that it preserves the ordering on situations. If X is less informative than Y then $F(X)$ will also be less informative then $F(Y)$. Then F is guaranteed to have a fixpoint.

PHILOSOPHER: What do you mean by "less informative"?

ECONOMIST: And what is a fixpoint?

LOGICIAN: What 'less informative' means depends on the context. For sets of situations this will be reverse inclusion. If you can exclude more situations, you know more. Anyhow, Tarski and Knaster [133] prove that all monotonic functions have fixpoints. A fixpoint or fixed-point of a function F is a value X for which $F(X) = X$.[3]

COMPUTER SCIENTIST: Here is an easy example. The Dutch mathematician and philosopher of mathematics Brouwer proved a famous theorem stating that every continuous function from a compact convex set into itself has a fixpoint. Each map of the town of Wassenaar, where we are located here at NIAS, can be seen as the image of a continuous function that maps the real town onto its representation on the map. It follows from Brouwer's theorem that the map of Wassenaar that I have in front of me has the property that one point on the map coincides precisely with its pre-image.

LOGICIAN: Yes, of course, but you have to look really closely to see it. The fixpoint is the location of NIAS on the map. There is also a more procedural analogy for fixpoints. This is perhaps more illuminating in the context of common knowledge. Suppose you are painting your walls and you would like to mix exactly the same kind of beige as the small amount you have still left in your tin, which you now dub your "reference tin". Then you take a large new tin of white paint, and you keep adding small drops of brown and mixing, until you think you've almost attained the intended beige. At that moment you add a drop from the reference tin to the new mixture, without mixing, and look closely whether the reference drop is still darker than the new mixture. If it is, you go on adding drops of brown to the new tin and mixing, taking care to check at regular intervals. If you're careful, this procedure is bound to lead to the fixpoint. This works much better than trying out your new paint on the wall next to the old beige!

PHILOSOPHER: I like this. Let us move on.

LOGICIAN: As you all know, an agent a is said to know φ in a state s if the

---

[3] A lucid account of this material is in Davey and Priestley's textbook [58].

proposition φ holds in all states that a cannot distinguish from s. These are called the "accessible" situations. Intuitively, "accessible from s" means "consistent with a's information in state s". You can picture this as a link with a label for the agent. If a state s where p is true is linked for agent a to a state s' where p is not true, this represents the fact that a does not know whether p is the case.

PHILOSOPHER: So when you talk about what agents know about what other agents know, this corresponds to more than one such step.

LOGICIAN: That's right. Let's take the case of two agents, Alice and Bob, who want to achieve common knowledge on who is going to collect the kids from daycare. Common knowledge is important here, for it is not enough that Alice knows that Bob knows that it is his turn today. Bob should also know that she knows. And so it goes on. *(Writes on the whiteboard:)*

$$1 \text{ --- Alice --- } 2 \text{ --- Bob --- } 3 \text{ --- Alice } 4 \text{ --- Bob --- } 5 \text{ --- } \cdots$$

So there is a path, with a link from state 1 to state 2 for Alice because Alice cannot distinguish these states, followed by a link from 2 to 3 for Bob, for Bob cannot tell 2 and 3 apart, and so on. Something is common knowledge for Alice and Bob if it is true in all situations that are on such a path.

PHILOSOPHER: Ah, now I see how fixpoints come in. For common knowledge you have to compute the transitive closure of the union of the accessibility relations for Alice and Bob.

LOGICIAN: Exactly.

COMPUTER SCIENTIST: Let me elaborate. The fixpoint procedure for making a relation transitive goes like this:

1. Check if all two-step transitions can be done in a single step. If so, the relation is transitive, and done.

2. If not, add all two-step transitions as new links, and go back to 1.

Wait, let me draw a picture.

PHILOSOPHER: I suppose we can think of the link from 1 to 2 as a link for Alice, and the link from 2 to 3 as a link for Bob, and so on?

COMPUTER SCIENTIST: That's right, but I have blurred the distinction by taking the union of Alice's and Bob's links. Anyway, our check reveals that not all two step transitions can be done in single leaps, so the relation is not transitive. In the first step, we add all two-step links as new links:

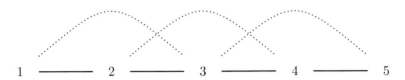

Now we check again. No, this is not yet transitive. So we add all two-step links in this new picture as extra links:

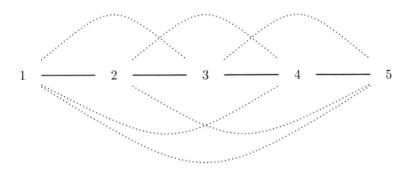

PHILOSOPHER: I can see that this is an example of a fixpoint procedure. You are changing the relation step by step, until it has the required property. After your final step the relation has indeed become transitive: all states are now connected by direct links. So a proposition is common knowledge between Alice and Bob if it is true in all those states.

COMPUTER SCIENTIST: I have another nice example for this, a simple card game situation [66]. Consider the situation where Alice, Bob and Carol each receive a card from the set *red, white* and *blue*. They can all see their own card, but not those of the others. I will draw a possible worlds model of this situation. *(Draws on the whiteboard:)*

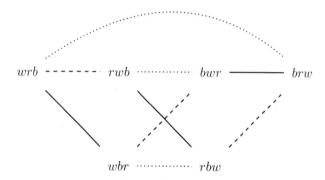

Each world represents a card distribution in alphabetical order of the agents, with obvious color abbreviations. For example, wbr represents the state in which Alice has white, Bob has blue and Carol has red. The solid lines are for Alice. If she has white, she can see that she has white, but she cannot distinguish wbr from wrb. And similarly for the cases where she holds blue, and for the cases where she holds red.

PHILOSOPHER: Let me see. Then the dotted arrows must represent Bob's knowledge relation, and the dashed arrows Carol's. So now one can say things like "Alice holds white" by means of propositional atoms such as w_{Alice}.

COMPUTER SCIENTIST: That's right. "Alice holds white" is true in wbr and wrb but not in the other four worlds. Also, in both of these worlds "Alice knows that she holds white" is true, for the knowledge relation for Alice links wbr and wrb, and links no other worlds to these two, and in both of these w_{Alice} is true.

PHILOSOPHER: So in situation wbr it is common knowledge among Alice, Bob and Carol that Alice doesn't know that Bob has blue? *(Writes on the whiteboard:)*

$$wbr \models C_{\{Alice,Bob,Carol\}} \neg K_{Alice} b_{Bob}$$

COMPUTER SCIENTIST: That's right. This is because all six worlds can be reached from wbr in one or more steps by accessibility relations for agents in the group, and it is clear that $\neg K_{Alice} b_{Bob}$ in all worlds, for it holds everywhere that Alice can access at least one world in which Bob doesn't have blue.

LOGICIAN: There is a slight further subtlety. In the literature one finds both the transitive closure, and the reflexive transitive closure as definitions of the accessibility relation for common knowledge. The first is common among philosophers, and the second among computer scientists. Even standard textbooks take different stances on this issue.[4] When modeling knowledge and not belief, both definitions amount to the same, because of the assumed property that *known* propositions are true. Nobody is so presumptuous as to claim the opposite implication that truths are always known. Computer scientists are more interested in knowledge. But for beliefs there is a real difference, and the most natural interpretation of common belief uses transitive closure only.

PHILOSOPHER: If you do not require that individual beliefs are true but then all of a sudden require that common beliefs are true, you get a rather confusing mix. So I suppose the philosophers were right in proposing transitive closure for both common knowledge and common belief.

COMPUTER SCIENTIST: When reading about societal problems like climate change, the confusing thing is the disagreement about what is common knowledge and what is common belief, which sometimes amounts to a common illusion.

LOGICIAN: Yes, and what makes it worse is that there are certain think-tanks involved in the Republican War on Science [157] who are trying to create a common illusion *that* the greenhouse effect is a common illusion. But maybe we should save these matters for another discussion and stay with our present topic now. (See p. 219.)

COGNITIVE SCIENTIST: I am still puzzled about some aspects of this common knowledge. In developmental psychology, even though we at some stage think to discover the *presence* of a theory of mind, we find it very hard to explain how such knowledge of others' knowledge is *formed*. Are we to think of this as some kind of category shift? Something that is not there initially, and then appears all of a sudden? If I understand this fixpoint process right, it must be very hard to achieve common knowledge in real-life situations. Can anyone say more about how this is possible?

LOGICIAN: I see this picture of computing transitive closure by means of a gradual process of adding links to a relation has confused you, and I am sorry. You should not think about common knowledge as a new relation that gets computed in stages, but as something that can be achieved in one go. Common knowledge of φ can be seen as the result of removing all non-φ situations from the picture. This can be done very easily, by means of a public announcement. Think of the card situation again. Suppose Alice

---

[4] Meyer and van der Hoek [153] take the reflexive transitive closure; Fagin et al. [90] the transitive closure.

suddenly says aloud: "I am holding white". Then the picture simplifies to this:

$$wrb \quad\text{————}\quad wbr$$

Now it has become common knowledge that Alice holds white. And it is common knowledge that the only uncertainty that remains is Alice's uncertainty about the cards of Bob and Carol.

COGNITIVE SCIENTIST: So the result of publicly announcing φ is that φ will become common knowledge.

LOGICIAN: Well, not quite. Suppose instead of "I am holding white", Alice would have announced "I am holding white, but you guys don't know it yet." Then the second part of this becomes false as an effect of the announcement.

PHILOSOPHER: Alice is using a variation on the famous Moore sentence [158, p.543]: "I went to the pictures last Tuesday, but I don't believe that I did."

LOGICIAN: Yes, the effect can be truly destructive. "Your wife is cheating you, but you don't know it yet." After that announcement the addressee *does* know, so the statement has made itself false.

COGNITIVE SCIENTIST: Moore sentences have the property that you cannot truthfully repeat them. So indeed, not all φ can be made common knowledge by publicly announcing them. I see that now.

COMPUTER SCIENTIST: By the way, the application of fixpoints to the logic of knowledge may originate with John McCarthy. In a small note in the early 1970s that at the stage he did not even consider important enough to publish[5] McCarthy formalizes two logical puzzles, one called the "Wise Men" puzzle (this is also known as "Muddy Children"), and the other a puzzle about numbers, called the "Sum and Product"-riddle. In the course of solving those riddles he almost off-handedly introduces the reflexive transitive closure of accessibility relations, and he uses this to account for what agents learn from the announcements made in those riddles. He also promises a further analysis in terms of a knowledge function, and handling time and learning, but I don't think that follow-up paper ever appeared.

COGNITIVE SCIENTIST: So it seems we have another pioneer of the logic of common knowledge.

---

[5] It was only later included in an overview of previously unpublished notes [151].

LOGICIAN: A lucid account of the interaction of public announcement and common knowledge can be found in a short note by Johan van Benthem from 2000, available on the Internet [17]. The crucial logical operation here is relativization. Imagine an information state involving several agents, with several worlds connected by agent accessibilities. Then the effect of a public announcement A is that all non-A worlds get eliminated from the picture. Van Benthem's key observation is that this *semantic* process of elimination of non-A worlds has as its *syntactic* counterpart the well-known logical operation of relativization of a formula to A. In the model that results from updating with the public announcement A a formula φ is true if and only if the relativization of φ to A is true in the original model. In the note Van Benthem then introduces the concept of relativized common knowledge, and conjectures that relativized common knowledge cannot be expressed in terms of plain common knowledge.

COMPUTER SCIENTIST: That squares well with an observation made by Baltag, Moss and Solecki in [11]. There it is shown that there is no sentence of the language of epistemic logic extended with a common knowledge operator that expresses "after public announcement of φ it is common knowledge that ψ".

PHILOSOPHER: I suppose relativized common knowledge is common knowledge relativized to an announcement? So it expresses what has to be true in model *before the public announcement* in order to create common knowledge *after the announcement*?

LOGICIAN: More precisely, after a φ announcement it is plain common knowledge that ψ if and only if it is φ-relativized common knowledge that after a φ announcement ψ holds. Later on, Van Benthem showed together with Van Eijck and Kooi [24] that if you take propositional dynamic logic as your epistemic language then the effect of *any* update that can be represented as a so-called finite action model is expressible in the epistemic language.

PHILOSOPHER: I thought propositional dynamic logic was designed for reasoning about the correctness of computer programs.

COMPUTER SCIENTIST: That's right. Propositional dynamic logic, or PDL for short, is an extension of Hoare logic.

LOGICIAN: But the beauty of formal systems is that they can be reinterpreted and reused. For instance, PDL has a construct for program composition: first execute program P, next execute program Q. We can reinterpret this to express the epistemic relation of what Alice knows about Bob's knowledge. Similarly, PDL has a construction for non-deterministic choice between two programs P and Q. We can reinterpret this as the relation of what Alice and Bob both know. Finally, PDL can express reflexive transitive closure, for executing a program P an arbitrary finite number of times. We reinterpret that as the reflexive transitive closure of a knowledge relation.

PHILOSOPHER: And taken together these PDL constructs can express common knowledge?

LOGICIAN: Yes, common knowledge between Alice and Bob that φ is expressed as follows. *(Writes on the white-board:)*

$$[(a \cup b)^*]\varphi$$

This is true if in every world that is reachable via the reflexive transitive closure of the union of the accessibility relations of Alice and Bob it holds that φ.

PHILOSOPHER: That is indeed what common knowledge amounts to. Now I suppose that PDL also has a construct that can be used to express relativized common knowledge?

LOGICIAN: Right again. For that you need PDL-tests, formulas that check that a condition holds somewhere in a program. The familiar programming construct of 'if φ then P else Q' is expressed in PDL by: *(Writes on the white-board again:)*

$$(?\varphi; P) \cup (?\neg\varphi; Q).$$

What you need for relativized common knowledge is test for a property along a path, to express that in every world that is reachable via a sequence of φ worlds along the reflexive transitive closure of the union of the accessibility relations of Alice and Bob, it holds that ψ. Here is the formula: *(Writes on the white-board:)*

$$[(?\varphi; (a \cup b))^*]\psi.$$

PHILOSOPHER: Beautiful. Let me guess now. The principle that expresses the effect of public announcements on common knowledge will state that after public announcement of φ it has become common knowledge for Alice and Bob that ψ if and only if it is already φ-relativized common knowledge for Alice and Bob that ψ. Is that right?

LOGICIAN: Almost right. Let me use $!\varphi$ for a public announcement. Then this is what we get: *(Writes on the white-board:)*

$$[!\varphi][(a \cup b)^*]\psi \leftrightarrow [(?\varphi; (a \cup b))^*][!\varphi]\psi.$$

This has the shape of a reduction axiom: note that the public announcement $[!\varphi]$ occurs on both sides in the equivalence, but on the right-hand side the formula it has scope over has lower complexity. This means that the axiom can be used to define a translation from the language of PDL plus public announcement operators to the language of PDL without public announcement operators. And in [24] it is shown that this trick not only works for public announcements, but that something similar can be done for *any* update action.

COGNITIVE SCIENTIST: This bit on relativized common knowledge went over my head, I am afraid. But I can appreciate the logical puzzles that have to do with common knowledge, such as the Wise Men puzzle and this Sum and Product riddle.

COMPUTER SCIENTIST: Then it may interest you that both of these riddles have old roots. The wise men riddle occurs in a puzzle book by Gamow and Stern from 1958 [100], but a friend of mine claims having seen this in Russian puzzle books from the first half of the twentieth century. The 'Sum and Product' riddle almost certainly originates with the Dutch topologist Hans Freudenthal. He stated it in the Dutch-language mathematics journal *Nieuw Archief voor Wiskunde* (New Archive for Mathematics) in 1969 [95] and presented its solution in the next issue [96]. McCarthy only later became aware of that source of the riddle.[6]

LOGICIAN: In any case, it is clear that McCarthy's promise of follow-up was eventually fulfilled by the development of dynamic epistemic logic over the past 25 years or so![7]

---

[6] Details on the dissemination are in [65].

[7] Overviews of that development can be found in [90, 13, 66].

Chapter 9
Game Theory, Logic and Rational Choice

Johan van Benthem and Jan van Eijck

A game theorist has joined the group. Our usual protagonists use the occasion to clarify what game theory and logic might have to say about rationality of actions.

PHILOSOPHER: What I would like to understand better is how game theory can help us to understand rational choice, and how this is related to logic. Philosophy has a long-standing interest in rational behavior. The hallmark of rationality is always taken to be the "good reasons for acting" that rational people can give. But game theory seems more concerned with what people actually do than in the reasons they might care to give for their actions.

GAME THEORIST: In game theory, it is common practice to analyze problems of rational choice as problems of finding the best move in a game. A player is rational if she plays according to an optimal strategy. Game theory has various ways of determining whether a given strategy is rational. For finite games of complete information the preferred method is backward induction. I take it that you all know how that works.

PHILOSOPHER: Yes, yes. But I suppose it will do us no harm if you briefly remind us.

GAME THEORIST: Backward induction is a technique to solve a finite game of perfect information. First, one determines the optimal strategy of the player who makes the last move in the game. Then, taking these moves as given future actions, one determines the optimal strategy for the next-to-last player in the game. And so on, backwards in time, until the beginning of the game is reached. As it turns out this determines the Nash equilibrium of each subgame of the game.

PHILOSOPHER: Splendid. And what, again, if I may ask, are Nash equilibria

and subgames?   I have heard of John Nash, of course. I enjoyed watching
A Beautiful Mind.

GAME THEORIST: The movie is certainly entertaining, but the book [161]
on which it is based gives a more accurate picture of the life of John Nash.
But I see you want further memory refreshment. A Nash equilibrium, also
called strategic equilibrium, is a list of strategies, one for each player, which
has the property that no player can achieve a better payoff by unilaterally
changing her strategy. A subgame is a piece of a sequential game beginning
at some node such that each player knows every action of the players that
moved before him at every point.   There are excellent textbooks where
further details can be found.   I particularly recommend [225] and [171].
And [134] collects all contributions to game theory by John Nash, with an
enlightening introduction.

LOGICIAN: Of course it is also possible to take games as objects in their
own right, and study transformations on them.   Instead of condemning a
particular move as irrational, one might wish to take the move as a revelation
of an agents preference. This transforms a given game into a new one, with
different preferences. Also, maybe a move reveals an agent's belief about
the beliefs of the other game participants. This would correspond with a
game transformation where beliefs change. Still a different way of changing
a game is by making a promise: This changes other agents' expectations,
so it also corresponds to a game transformation.

COMPUTER SCIENTIST: This smells of the update operations of dynamic
logic.

LOGICIAN: You are quite right. A more general study of game transformations would involve dynamic and epistemic game logics. But I propose not
to dive into that, but instead to look at the structure of very simple choices.
Suppose you have a choice between two available actions Left and Right.
(Writes on the whiteboard:)

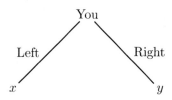

The choice is yours. What will you do?

GAME THEORIST: Well, I suppose that without further information no prediction can be made. A game theorist would say that we need to know the values you attach to the outcomes x and y. Or stated in another way, your preferences between these.

COMPUTER SCIENTIST: It looks to me that the logical form of the prediction is this:

> You must (and can) do Left or Right.
> You prefer outcome x.
> Therefore: You will perform action Left.

LOGICIAN: Surely, there is no compelling logical reason why you must do what is best for you. Much of the greatest world literature is about people who do not. But one might say that rational people behave according to this inference pattern, and hence we could take it as a definition of behavior for a certain kind of agent.

COMPUTER SCIENTIST: I suppose the pattern of inference could also be invoked post hoc. When I want to explain the way you behave when you choose Left, I conclude that you must have liked outcome x better than outcome y.

PHILOSOPHER: We do this all the time when "rationalizing" our own actions to ourselves or others. You chose action Left without thinking about the consequences in the cozy half-dark of a late night bar—but in the harsh light of the next morning, waking up with a headache in some unknown place, you have no shortage of good reasons for your behavior.

COMPUTER SCIENTIST: Yes, we humans may not be very good in taking rational decisions with a strict logical discipline beforehand, but we are wizards in rationalizing our actions afterwards.

LOGICIAN: Moaning over human nature gives great satisfaction, doesn't it? Snap out of it, guys. I have something more interesting for you to look at, a case where two agents interact. Let's assume payoffs are also given, to represent the agents' preferences. You first choose Left or Right. If you choose Left the game is over; while if you choose Right, it is then my turn to choose between Left and Right. The payoffs are indicated in the following game tree, with your value written first, then mine. *(Writes on the whiteboard:)*

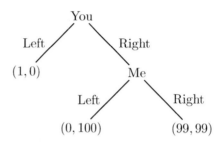

GAME THEORIST: OK. The standard procedure in game theory for this scenario is BI (Backward Induction). We start at the bottom: as a "rational" player, I will choose to go Left, since 100 is better than 99. You can see this coming: so going Right gives you only 0, whereas going Left gives you 1. Therefore, you will choose Left at the start, and we both end up getting very little, while I lose most of all.

COMPUTER SCIENTIST: Ahem, rationality seems to come at a rather high price in this example.

GAME THEORIST: Much more sophisticated scenarios exist where standard game solution procedures have strange effects.

LOGICIAN: Let's not quibble about whether this is right or wrong. Let us look instead at what the example can teach us about the logical underpinnings of BI. What we see is interaction between agents, where your expectations about my behavior determine the outcome. In particular, you assume that I am rational in the game theoretical sense, choosing Left, predicting that Right will end in $(0, 100)$. And so on, in more complex games. BI is often considered the "standard solution procedure" for games. But what is the status of this mixture of available actions, preferences, and expectations?

GAME THEORIST: BI-style rationality has a remarkable staying power. It may not be a great predictor of human behavior, but it has its use for rationally reconstructing it. And, as was remarked earlier, there seems to be a universal need for such rationalizations.

PHILOSOPHER: But if I assume that your preferences only reveal themselves in how you play, then your rationality becomes a truism. Suppose that your preferences between the outcomes of some given game are not known. Then I can always ascribe preferences to you which make your actions rational in the BI sense. In the simplest scenario, if you choose action Left over Right, I can always make your given choice appear rational *a posteriori*, by assuming that you prefer the former outcome over the latter.

GAME THEORIST: Yes, but let us pursue this. This style of rationalization carries over to more complex interactive settings. For now one must also think about me, i.e., the other player that you are interacting with. Let a finite two-player extensive game **G** specify my preferences, but not yours. Moreover, let both our strategies $\sigma_{\mathrm{me}}, \sigma_{\mathrm{you}}$ for playing **G** be fixed in advance, yielding an expanded structure that is sometimes called a "game model" **M**. Now, here is a technical question. When can we rationalize your given behavior σ_{you} to make our two strategies the BI solution of the game?

LOGICIAN: In principle, to achieve this, we have complete freedom to just set your preferences, or equivalently, set the values which you attach to outcomes of the game. And this can be done independently from my already given evaluation of these outcomes.

GAME THEORIST: Even so, not all game models **M** support BI. In particular, my given actions encoded in σ_{me} must have a certain quality to begin with, related to my given preferences. Note that, at any node where I must move, playing on according to our two given strategies already fixes a unique outcome of the game. What is clearly necessary for any successful BI-style analysis, then, is this. My strategy chooses a move leading to an outcome which is at least as good for me as any other outcome that might arise by choosing an action, and then continuing with $\sigma_{\mathrm{me}}, \sigma_{\mathrm{you}}$.

LOGICIAN: There is a folklore result about such games that are "best-responsive" for me.

> In any game that is best-responsive for me, there exists a preference relation for you among outcomes making the unique path that plays our given strategies against each other the BI solution.

To see why this is true, start with final choices for players near the bottom of the game tree, assigning values reflecting preferences for you as described before. Now proceed inductively. At my turns higher up in the game tree, their being best-responsive for me ensures automatically that I am doing the right thing, provided our strategies in the subgames following my available moves are already in accordance with BI. Next, suppose it is your turn, while the same inductive assumption holds about the immediate subgames. In particular, then, these subgames already have BI-values for both you and me. Now suppose your given move a in σ_{you} leads to a subgame which has a lower value for you than some subgame produced by another move of yours. In that case, a simple trick makes a the best for you. Take some fixed number N large enough so that adding it to all outcomes in the subtree headed by a makes them better than all outcomes reachable by your other moves than a. Now, it is easy to see the following feature:

> Raising all your values of outcomes in a game tree by a fixed amount
> N does not change the BI-solution, though it raises your total value
> by N.

So doing this to a's subtree, your given move at this turn has become best.

PHILOSOPHER: An example would do me no harm at this stage.

LOGICIAN: At your service. Here is a picture of an example game between you and me, with solid arrows for your given moves and dotted arrows for mine. No payoffs are indicated, for it is assumed that your payoffs are not known.

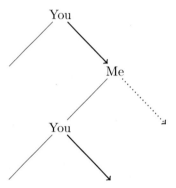

Let us fill in payoffs for you that make it appear that your behavior in the game was irrational.

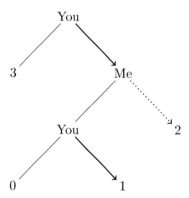

Assume that the value 3 on the left has been assigned in some subgame already. Now adjust the values in the subgame that results from your first move. An adjustment that works is adding 2 to all of them. Of course, the adjustment can be made in many ways to get BI right.

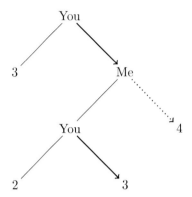

GAME THEORIST: So the conclusion must be that one can always pretend that you did the rational thing by tinkering *post facto* with your preferences. This is the basis for re-analysis of games in practice, replacing initial assignments of values for players by others so as to match observed behavior.

LOGICIAN: But there are alternative ways of rationalizing observed behavior. What we have seen so far takes the strategies, with their accompanying beliefs, as given, and uses these to work out the preferences for one of the players. But one could also start from given preferences for both players, and use these to modify the beliefs of the players to rationalize the given behavior.

PHILOSOPHER: A simple example again, if you please.

LOGICIAN: Look again at our very first example. *(Points at the whiteboard:)*

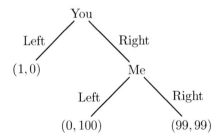

Suppose you choose Right in this game. One can interpret this rationally if we assume that you believe that I will go Right as well in the next move.

This rationalization is not in terms of your preferences, but of your beliefs about me.

GAME THEORIST: This style of rationalizing need not produce the BI solution.

LOGICIAN: No, but it still presupposes a certain pattern in a game **G**, or better, game model **M**. This time, consider a finite extensive game as before, with your strategy σ_{you} and your preference relation given. My preference relation does not matter in this scenario.

GAME THEORIST: Not all behavior of yours can be rationalized in this way. For suppose that you have a choice between two moves Left and Right, but all outcomes of Left are better than all those arising after Right. Then no beliefs of yours about my subsequent moves can make a choice for Right come out "best".

LOGICIAN: To put it differently, a game model which can be expanded so as to make your moves best in terms of your beliefs about my strategy must satisfy the following condition:

> Your strategy σ_{you} never prescribes a move for which each outcome reachable via further play according to σ_{you} and any moves of mine is worse than all outcomes reachable via some other move for me.

GAME THEORIST: That's right. In case you are the last to move, this coincides with the usual decision-theoretic requirement that you must choose a move that guarantees a best possible outcome for you.

LOGICIAN: Let us call a game model satisfying this condition "not-too-bad" for you. [21] has the following theorem: In any game that is not-too-bad for you, there exists a strategy τ for me against which, if you believe that I will play τ against your σ_{you}, is optimal. Why is this true? This time, the adjustment procedure for finding the rationalizing strategy is a bit different. The idea works *top-down* along the given game tree. Suppose that you make a move a right now according to your strategy. Since your given strategy σ_{you} is not-too-bad for you, each alternative move b of yours must have at least one reachable outcome y (via σ_{you} plus some suitable sequence of moves for me) which is majorized by some reachable outcome x via a. In particular, the *maximum outcome value* for you reachable by playing a will always be better than some value in the subgame for the other moves.

GAME THEORIST: You still have to explain why your given move a is optimal.

LOGICIAN: Right. Here is the expected strategy for *me* which makes it optimal. Choose later moves for me in the subgame for a which lead to the outcome x, and choose moves for me leading to outcomes $y \leq x$ in the subgames for my other moves b. Doing this makes sure a is a best response against any strategy of mine that includes those moves. This does not yet fully determine the strategy that you believe I will play, but one can proceed downward along the given game tree. *(To the philosopher:)* And now I suppose you want to see an example again?

PHILOSOPHER: Yes, if you don't mind.

LOGICIAN: Not at all. Here is a game with your moves marked as solid arrows, and with the necessary rationalized beliefs about me indicated by the dotted arrows. Note that in contrast with the folklore result I mentioned before, the outcome values for you are now given beforehand. *(Writes on the whiteboard:)*

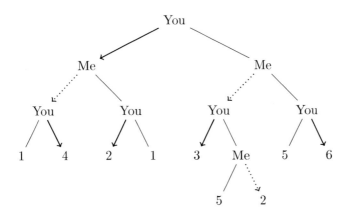

Your initial choice for going Left has been rationalized by forcing the outcome 4—assuming that I will go Left—which is better than the forced outcome 3 on the right—assuming that I would go Left there, too. Likewise, one step further down, in the subtree with outcomes 3, 5, 2, a Right move for you would have resulted in 2 rather than 3, if we assume that I would next go Right there.

PHILOSOPHER: I see.

LOGICIAN: Mind you, the theorem provides no underpinning of your belief that I will play τ. Indeed, τ may go totally against my known preferences. But the rationalization becomes more convincing if we can think up some plausible story of why I might want to act according to τ. And this is sometimes possible in ways different from BI. Look once again at our earlier example. *(Points at the whiteboard:)*

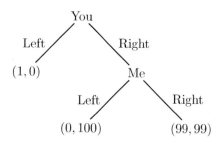

Think of why I might believe that you will choose Right in this game. Here
is a plausible story. If a player has run risks for the "common good" by doing
the other player a favor, he should not be punished for that, but rewarded,
the argument goes. In this particular example, I run the risk of losing one
point in playing Right. Hence you owe me at least that much—and you
should reward me by choosing an outcome where I do not lose that point.
This story is worked out in [20] and [23], by the way, where a candidate for
a general alternative to BI is put forward in terms of *Returning Favors*.

PHILOSOPHER: Maybe we should then look at *BI-style reanalysis* and *Returning Favors-style reanalysis* as two different ways of making sense of the
same behavior? Surely these are just extreme cases of rationalizing given
strategies in games.

LOGICIAN: Yes, indeed. And I suppose the moral is that we could devise
procedures manipulating both my preferences and beliefs. But instead of
rationalizing what has happened already, we can also try to do something
about the initial situation we find ourselves in. Look at our running example
again. What could I possibly do to break out of the scenario we are in, and
change it in my favor?

PHILOSOPHER: Well, I suppose you could make a promise to the other
player. Or rather, "I" could make a promise to "You", if you see what I
mean. "I herewith solemnly promise that I will not go Left when you have
gone Right." That should do the trick, if we suppose you know that I am
honest. I mean, if we suppose "You" knows that "I" is honest. Well, you
know what I mean.

LOGICIAN: Do you mean "'You' knows what 'I' means"? But I shouldn't
tease you, for you are quite right.

GAME THEORIST: As the KGB officer said, we can always force people to
be honest. Let us say that my promise puts such a high punishment on my
choosing Left that this branch disappears from the game tree. This would
give the following new game:

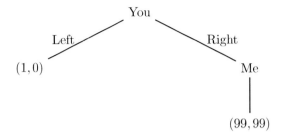

I suppose the general question becomes how to model a process where games can change because of certain actions?

COMPUTER SCIENTIST: Dynamic logics of information update. I knew it. I saw it coming.

LOGICIAN: How perceptive you are! A binding promise is like a public announcement $!\varphi$ of a true assertion φ. To be precise here, we should work again with game models $\mathbf{M}$, not just games. Details are given in [18, 19].

COMPUTER SCIENTIST: A public announcement φ restricts the current $\mathbf{M}, s$ to a model $\mathbf{M}|\varphi, s$ of just those worlds in $\mathbf{M}$ which satisfy φ. One can then analyze effects of making announcements on agents' beliefs in dynamic epistemic or doxastic logics which involve valid "reduction axioms" such as:

$$[!\varphi]B_i\psi \;\leftrightarrow\; \varphi \to B_i(\varphi, [!\varphi]\psi).$$

Here $[!\varphi]\psi$ expresses that ψ holds after public announcement φ, and $B_i(\cdot, \cdot)$ is used for conditional belief. Note that the axiom pushes the $[!\varphi]$ operator past the belief operator.

LOGICIAN: In our game scenario, a promise announces an intention in a game, which restricts the possible reachable nodes. For a complete logic for game-changing by promises and announced intentions, one needs a language over game models which describes players' moves, preferences, and beliefs. A good test on whether the right expressive power has been achieved is definability of the BI solution. There is already an extensive literature on this: [18, 43, 115, 25]. Never mind the details.

GAME THEORIST: I suppose that if you make the base logic strong enough you can prove completeness by reduction, just as in the case of public announcement logic. Let me guess:

There is a complete logic of public announcements over extensive games of perfect information which consist of a standard static base logic plus a complete set of reduction axioms for announcement modalities over the relevant move and preference modalities of the game language.

Am I right?

LOGICIAN: Yes, but maybe the more interesting issue concerning behavior is how public announcement of intentions changes what we know about the effects of strategies in a game. Strategies can be defined as programs in a dynamic logic over extensive games [19], which can then define a modality $\{\sigma\}\varphi$ saying that strategy σ only leads to nodes satisfying condition φ. Now we can also give reduction axioms for reasoning about the effects of strategies in the changed game.

COMPUTER SCIENTIST: Reduction axioms again. Push the promise through the strategy operator, and you are done. So the axiom for the changing power of a promise A should be something like "$[!\varphi]\{\sigma\}\psi$ is equivalent to $\{\sigma\}[!\varphi]\psi$." Am I right?

LOGICIAN: Absolutely right. This all uses good old propositional dynamic logic [185]. The result uses the insight that propositional dynamic logic is closed under domain relativization. It applies to reasoning about the new BI-strategies in our earlier games changed by a promise.

PHILOSOPHER: I guess this gets us at procedural conceptions of rationality, as following the right procedure to improve one's situation. But how about issuing threats, not just promises?

COMPUTER SCIENTIST: We can handle that by substitution. Just a matter of replacing carrots by sticks. That shouldn't cause any technical difficulties. There may be ethical implications, but we feel we can safely leave such matters with you.

(They all smile at the philosopher.)

Chapter 10
What is Protocol Analysis?

Francien Dechesne, Jan van Eijck, Wouter Teepe, Yanjing Wang

The following is a transcript of one of the discussion sessions that took place during the Workshop on Games, Action and Social Software *at the Lorentz Center in Leiden. The discussion theme was set by the workshop organizers: "Is logic useful for the analysis of protocols, and if so, how?" The theme has attracted the usual protagonists, plus a cognitive scientist and a specialist in computer security.*

LOGICIAN: The workshop organizers have asked me to chair this session. I suppose the first thing we should establish is that everyone present here understands the question at hand in the same way.

PHILOSOPHER: Well, I could definitely use some clarification. A *protocol* is generally understood to be some set of rules or conventions, but that is very broad. I'm afraid I do not have a clear picture of what is meant by *protocol analysis*. Could anyone explain this to me?

COGNITIVE SCIENTIST: In cognitive science, protocol analysis is the name of an experimental method for gathering so-called intermediate state evidence concerning the procedures used by a human to compute a function. More in particular, subjects are trained to think aloud as they solve a problem, and their verbal behavior forms the basic data to be analyzed.

PHILOSOPHER: This sounds as if the analysis is understood as *reconstructing* or mimicking the protocol that is (assumed to be) used by this human. Do I see this correctly? Maybe you could give a more concrete example.

COGNITIVE SCIENTIST: Well, standard examples of protocols we analyze are the mechanisms people use to solve brainteaser problems. You can think of the following "crypt-arithmetical problem": *(Writes on the whiteboard:)*

$$
\begin{array}{cccccc}
D & O & N & A & L & D \\
G & E & R & A & L & D & + \\
\hline
R & O & B & E & R & T \\
\end{array}
$$

Let it be given that $D = 5$. How do you solve this?

COMPUTER SCIENTIST: May I? Let us see. If $D = 5$ then $T = 0$, from the last column. From the first column we know that $G + 5 = R$, so $R \geq 5$. From the second column we then get that E has to be 0. This gives $A = 5$ from column four, and there has to be a carry to column three. Looking at the fifth column, we see that $L = 2$ would give $R = 5$ and $G = 0$. Let's pursue this. In column three, we could set $N = 1$, which yields $B = 7$, as there was a carry from column four. The value of O is not constrained. Let's set it to 1. We are done:

$$
\begin{array}{cccccc}
5 & 1 & 1 & 5 & 2 & 5 \\
0 & 0 & 5 & 5 & 2 & 5 & + \\
\hline
5 & 1 & 7 & 0 & 5 & 0 \\
\end{array}
$$

But this solution is far from unique. As remarked, we could have picked any other value for O to get a solution. Also, we could have chosen $L = 3$, which would have given $R = 7$ and $G = 2$, again for different values of O. Or $L = 4 \ldots$

PHILOSOPHER: Yes, I think we get the point. In cognitive science, the next step of what you call protocol analysis would be to analyze this verbal description of how our computer scientist solved the puzzle.

COGNITIVE SCIENTIST: Yes, we would now use this so-called *verbal protocol* to infer the subject's problem space.

PHILOSOPHER: What do you mean by "problem space"?

COGNITIVE SCIENTIST: The problem space is a set of rules that are used to transform knowledge states concerning the problem.

PHILOSOPHER: So these are just postulated?

COGNITIVE SCIENTIST: That's right. Once one has a suitable problem space, one can proceed to create a problem behavior graph, supposed to reflect state transitions as subjects search through the problem space in their attempts to solve the problem.

COMPUTER SCIENTIST: I see what you mean. So a problem space is just a labeled transition system viewed as a search space. If you give me a finite search space I can give you any number of solution algorithms for your problem.

COGNITIVE SCIENTIST: Yes, and the task of protocol analysis is to pinpoint the particular search algorithms that reflect how humans do it. Finally, one can compare the verbal protocol to the computer simulation, to validate the assumptions that led to the simulating program. Once validated, the simulating program provides a rich description of the processing steps performed by the human subject. Two classic books dealing with the subject are [89] and [163].

LOGICIAN: OK, I think this interpretation of term "protocol analysis" is clear now. But I have the feeling the term has quite a different meaning in computer science, is that right?

SECURITY ANALYST: Indeed, protocol analysis in computer science refers to a quite different activity. In computer security, we are concerned with the design and specification of communication protocols, and with checking whether they fulfill the given goal and/or satisfy the desired properties.

Any protocol that is designed to satisfy some kind of *security* property, can be called a security protocol. Such properties may be about trust, or about fairness (making sure that agents can't cheat), but for this discussion, maybe it's best to restrict ourselves a bit. A more narrow class of security protocols would be the *communication* protocols (i.e., sets of rules for sending and receiving messages), in which it is ensured that particular pieces of information are kept *secret* from certain parties, or in which it is ensured that you're talking to the agent you intend to talk to: *authentication.*

LOGICIAN: So security protocols are formal constraints on communication patterns that are meant to ensure some agents get to know something while outsiders remain in the dark, or that ensure that you know whom you're talking to. It sounds as if the protocols ensure certain epistemic properties of the communication. This relates to our central question, whether logic can be useful for protocol analysis. It seems we have a perfect working place here for epistemic logic: the logic for reasoning about knowledge.

COGNITIVE SCIENTIST: I am sorry, but I don't really understand. I have trouble with vague formulations like "get to know something" and "outsiders". What is it that should be analyzed? The protocol? Properties of the protocol, properties of the parties participating in the protocol?

PHILOSOPHER: Actually, there was a talk at this workshop addressing such questions, by Francien Dechesne and Yanjing Wang. It was about how security protocols can be analyzed, and a link was made with dynamic epistemic logic. As an example of a security protocol, they mentioned the Needham-Schroeder public key authentication protocol. Maybe it's good to use that example to clarify the terminology a bit?

COGNITIVE SCIENTIST: That's a good idea, for I missed that talk, I am afraid. What is this Needham-Schroeder protocol supposed to do? And how does it achieve its purpose?

SECURITY ANALYST: Before we state the actual protocol, we need some preliminary notions and assumptions. For one thing, we assume that every agent a owns a private (secret) key to decrypt messages that were encrypted with the publicly available key PK_a. By the way, does everyone know how public key encryption works?

COMPUTER SCIENTIST: Shall I explain? Public key encryption is a nice example of how work in pure mathematics (in this case, number theory) may suddenly and unexpectedly turn out to have high practical relevance. Public key encryption is based on the existence of mathematical operations that are very difficult to reverse. For example, multiplication of two large prime numbers is easy, but finding the prime factors of a very large number is extremely difficult: if I tell you, for instance, that 7879 and 5113 are primes, then it is very easy for you to calculate their product. But suppose instead of this I tell you that 40285327 is the product of two primes, and challenge you to produce these primes ...

COGNITIVE SCIENTIST: But if you give me one factor, it is easy to find the other. So I guess the key is supposed to be some number or maybe other piece of information that makes the reversal operation very easy to do?

COMPUTER SCIENTIST: You got it. And it should be understood that for really large numbers, without the key, sophisticated guesses or even supercomputers would be of no help. No known method for finding the prime factors of a number is substantially better than trial and error.

SECURITY ANALYST: Yes, then with some tricks, for example by applying the RSA algorithm [197] we could have one-to-one functions f on the natural numbers with the property that computing $f(N)$ is easy if you know the "public key", even for very large N, while computing $f^{-1}(M)$ for large M is extremely difficult without knowing the "secret key".

Actually, for our analysis, we don't have to go into all the mathematical details. We can leave that to the specialized mathematicians, the cryptographers. In security *protocol* analysis it is the custom to keep the mathematics behind the encryption outside the model. This is called the *black box approach* to cryptography. It is enough to just assume that such keys exist.

LOGICIAN: I see. So, the relevant part is that we may assume the existence of some "practically unbreakable" encryption functions, that allow anyone to encrypt a message—using the public key of the intended receiver—but only allows the possessor of the secret key to decrypt it.

SECURITY ANALYST: Right. Let me now write down the Needham-Schroeder protocol. Its purpose is to make sure that two agents who are communicating with each other can identify their correspondent. It assumes that the private keys are kept secret, and the public keys are available for all, so that every agent can create messages that can be read by one and only one agent. Here it is: *(Writes on the whiteboard:)*

$$
\begin{array}{llll}
\text{Message 1} & a \rightarrow b: & \{n_a, a\}_{\text{PK}_b} \\
\text{Message 2} & b \rightarrow a: & \{n_a, n_b\}_{\text{PK}_a} \\
\text{Message 3} & a \rightarrow b: & \{n_b\}_{\text{PK}_b}
\end{array}
$$

Here n_a is a so-called *nonce* ...

COGNITIVE SCIENTIST: Nonce? Sounds like nonsense ...

SECURITY ANALYST: In a sense it is *non-sense*. A nonce is a very big arbitrary number that a has privately generated. It is assumed that it is impossible for others to have a clever guess. How such numbers can be generated is also left to the cryptographers.

COGNITIVE SCIENTIST: But still there's one thing rather unclear to me. Why doesn't the first message simply consist of a public-key encoded $\{a\}_{PK_b}$? Why the nonce? I mean, it's now encrypted, right?

SECURITY ANALYST: Well, this nonce serves as a kind of time stamp. It was generated just for the purpose of this particular message, as a kind of challenge for b. It is a better challenge than a's name, which may be rather easy to guess.

LOGICIAN: Let us see. So the first message that a sends to b consists of a pair of a nonce n_a and the name of a, encrypted with the public key of b. These public keys are there for grabs, remember. But only b can decrypt this and get hold of n_a and a. Now b creates his own nonce n_b, and sends the pair of the two nonces n_a and n_b back to a, encrypted with a's public key.

PHILOSOPHER: Presumably, this is meant to prove to a that this message is indeed from b. Only a can decrypt this, so the final message, where a sends n_b back to b encrypted with b's public key, is supposed to prove to b that he is indeed talking to a. But how can we be certain that the protocol is secure?

SECURITY ANALYST: This is the interesting but tricky field of verification of security protocols. For example, the Needham-Schroeder protocol was first proved secure using a special "logic of authentication", but later it was found to contain a security hole after all.

LOGICIAN: *(Looks challenged, and thinks out loud:)* But then this logical analysis did not adequately cover the essentials of the protocol. I mean, it is not so clear what verification of the protocol means. What, exactly, are the properties we should check? Informally, the protocol should ensure that a and b know with whom they have been interacting. I guess this means that they should both know the values of n_a and n_b. Moreover, it should be known to a and b that no one else knows the values of n_a and n_b. I suppose one would need epistemic logic to check such properties ...

SECURITY ANALYST: *(Interrupts:)* The attack on the Needham-Schroeder protocol was detected ten years ago, using process-theoretic tools [144]. The protocol itself is from as early as [162]. The "correctness proof" was given in [44], in the paper which introduced the logic of authentication, which was baptized *BAN-logic* after the authors. To their credit one should say that, even if their proof was flawed, their paper initiated the now active field of verification of security protocols. By the way, Needham himself once described security protocols as "three line programs that people still manage to get wrong". Well, he was right in this particular case.

LOGICIAN: I am curious, both about the logic and about the attack.

SECURITY ANALYST: About the logic ... You'll be interested to learn that it reasons about *beliefs* in a very abstract way, by specifying inference rules for that. But I would say that it has no sensible semantics.

LOGICIAN: Well, that makes it hard to talk about soundness and completeness, I guess.

SECURITY ANALYST: Lowe's attack, however, is easily explained. Assume a initiates a session with c, whom she trusts. So a sends $\{n_a, a\}_{\mathrm{PK}_c}$. Instead of responding as specified by the protocol, c passes the message on to b, encoded with b's public key. b now thinks he is talking to a and sends $\{n_a, n_b\}_{\mathrm{PK}_a}$ back. This is intercepted by c and forwarded to a later. Now a still thinks she is running the protocol in interaction with c, so she responds with $\{n_b\}_{\mathrm{PK}_c}$. To conclude the protocol with b, c decrypts this message and encrypts it with b's public key to forward the nonce to b. So b ends up with the mistaken belief that he is talking to a, while he is in fact talking to c: *(Writes on the whiteboard:)*

Message 1	$a \rightarrow c$:	$\{n_a, a\}_{\mathrm{PK}_c}$
Message 1'	$c(a) \rightarrow b$:	$\{n_a, a\}_{\mathrm{PK}_b}$
Message 2	$b \rightarrow c(a)$:	$\{n_a, n_b\}_{\mathrm{PK}_a}$
Message 2'	$c \rightarrow a$:	$\{n_a, n_b\}_{\mathrm{PK}_a}$
Message 3	$a \rightarrow c$:	$\{n_b\}_{\mathrm{PK}_c}$
Message 3'	$c(a) \rightarrow b$:	$\{n_b\}_{\mathrm{PK}_b}$

When I write $c(a)$ I mean c masquerading as a. This compromises the protocol, for it is clear that after this session b mistakenly believes that b and a are the only ones who know n_a and n_b. Also, a has the mistaken belief that a and c are the only ones knowing these nonces.

COMPUTER SCIENTIST: This is all going much too fast. Can we go back to the very first line of the Needham-Schroeder protocol, please? *(He points at the first line of the original protocol, still on the whiteboard:)*

$$\text{Message 1} \quad a \rightarrow b: \quad \{n_a, a\}_{PK_b}$$

This says that agent a sends a message to b consisting of the nonce n_a and the name a, but encrypted by b's public key. Now a sends to b ...

SECURITY ANALYST: That is not the whole story. In the analysis of security protocols we always assume that there could be some bad guys who are trying to gain information or spoil communication. In an actual run according to the protocol, an eavesdropper might also receive this message. But assuming that the eavesdropper does not have b's private key, he does not really learn anything from it.

COGNITIVE SCIENTIST: "Not really learn anything" is too vague for me.

PHILOSOPHER: And what do you mean by an actual run "according to the protocol"?

SECURITY ANALYST: *(Sighs.)* OK. *(Turns to Cognitive Scientist:)* "Not really learn anything" means that if the eavesdropper tries to guess the content of the decrypted message, there is no algorithm using the encrypted message that is significantly faster than an algorithm that just performs random guesses. Please don't ask me to write down the definitions, they are long, technical, and boring.

LOGICIAN: But wait. I think the eavesdropper does learn something! At least he now knows that there was a message being sent intended for someone.

SECURITY ANALYST: Yes, but does it mean anything useful to him?

LOGICIAN: Well, that depends on the circumstances. He may learn from it that a run is going on, for instance. Maybe it is useful for him to reason about other stuff in the remaining run. I feel dynamic epistemic logic could help here to express such subtleties, and then it may become visible whether it can be useful ... *(Smiles and drifts away in thoughts.)*

PHILOSOPHER: Interesting indeed, but what about my question? What do you mean by "according to the protocol"?

SECURITY ANALYST: Ah, I meant that the pattern of the actual actions matches the protocol specification.

PHILOSOPHER: Ahem, that is still not completely clear. You specified action patterns from an outsider's perspective. But what about the agents' perspective? How do they know what they should do to arrive at a run "according to the protocol"?

COMPUTER SCIENTIST: Maybe we should require that the protocol specification also contain the preconditions for agents to do a certain action according to the protocol. Then we know what are the possible runs.

SECURITY ANALYST: I see your point. Actually, for traditional security protocol verification, using model checking, a run generator—which produces all the possible runs according to the protocol specifications—is crucial. The preconditions for the actions are always implicitly assumed to arise from some kind of pattern matching. For example, as presented in [53], the author assumes that trusted agent b will send message $\{V, n_b\}_{\text{PK}_a}$ whenever he reads message $\{V, a\}_{\text{PK}_b}$ according to the Needham-Schroeder protocol. Here V is just a variable which can be instantiated in a specific run.

COGNITIVE SCIENTIST: Okay, that sounds reasonable. After all, the agents themselves can't see that V is indeed the nonce n_a generated by a. It shouldn't be in the preconditions of the actions. I would expect names of agents would sometimes be variables as well.

SECURITY ANALYST: Yes. In fact we call the names "roles" in the protocol specifications since in the actual runs any number of agents can be involved in multiple sessions. One particular agent can be acting the a role in one session but the b role in another session.

COMPUTER SCIENTIST: Yet another complication.

SECURITY ANALYST: I am afraid it cannot be helped. However, the variables we introduced give us executable protocol specifications for every agent. The possible runs—or the possible action sequences—are the sequences in which every action's precondition was satisfied after the execution of the previous action.

LOGICIAN: Let us go back to the attack. I am still not fully satisfied there. For example, in the description of the attack, the agents look a bit gullible. If I were b, I wouldn't have believed that what I just received was straight from a. And if I had seen something going on between a and c, I might even have discontinued the run. In other words, if I knew about the possible attack, I would be suspicious upon receiving the message $\{a, n_a\}_{\mathrm{PK}_b}$. It seems that you assume all the agents have so much faith in the protocol that they suspend their own judgment.

SECURITY ANALYST: I see what you mean. But maybe you should bear in mind that an agent need not be human. Think of the agents as communicating processors. They don't have reasoning power, or a will of their own.

PHILOSOPHER: *(Towards the logician:)* If you give the agents unlimited reasoning power, as you seem to suggest, they turn into a kind of perfect logicians. Which means that they will be able to find out about possible attacks beforehand, by analyzing the protocol as you would analyze it yourself. Or in the way Lowe analyzed the Needham-Schroeder protocol. Just imagine. You then assume that if there exists an attack, they will discover it, and then they refuse to conduct any run: "We know we are under threat of attack". And then all security analysts will lose their jobs ... *(smiles)*

LOGICIAN: But at least we have to make explicit what the reasoning and observation powers of the agents are. Maybe for different situations we need different assumptions.

COMPUTER SCIENTIST: It seems to me that our discussion has revealed quite a list of tacit assumptions. Why don't we try and make a list?

COGNITIVE SCIENTIST: Yeah!

SECURITY ANALYST: Well, we did not yet discuss assumptions about the bad guys. A model where such a bad guy is assumed to exist is called an *intruder model* or *threat model*. An intruder model that is well-known is the so-called Dolev-Yao model [68]. In this model it is assumed that the intruder has complete control over the communication channel. That is, he can intercept every message, delete messages at will, and insert messages into the communication channel. Of course, the model is supposed to be realistic about what intruders can do and cannot do. It is assumed that the intruder cannot work magic. An intruder can only insert messages that can be construed in polynomial time on the basis of the information he already possesses.

PHILOSOPHER: So, if I look at the first message of the Needham-Schroeder protocol, the $a \rightarrow b$ only means that it prescribes a to send some message, but there is no guarantee that b gets the message, nor, if b gets some message, that he can be sure that the message he receives originates from a. Is that correct?

SECURITY ANALYST: Yes. But we do assume that the encryption works as it should: the message sent there can only be decrypted by agent b. Recall that we treat the cryptographic primitives as perfect black boxes [207]. Thus, hashes, encryption, decryption and what-have-you all exist, and work as they should. We don't worry about the mathematical foundations of their existence, or about details of their implementation. By the way, this does not mean that cryptographic primitives are not interesting: For example the definition of what a cryptographic hash should do has been in a constant flux over the last twenty years. I won't go into details here, but I recommend reading [231, chapter 3] for a nice wrap-up of this history.

COGNITIVE SCIENTIST: Hello? I thought you were all doing exact sciences. Now I am surprised how much is still under debate, and how dubious your verification methods are. Like this BAN-logic, which has no semantics and which proves flawed protocols correct. Deep maths is not a guarantee for maturity, or is it? By the looks of it, your discipline is still in its infancy. Just like ours, in fact.

COMPUTER SCIENTIST: We're not even finished yet with the list of assumptions. In the Needham-Schroeder protocol, the claim of authentication relies on the fact that the nonces n_a and n_b are only known to a and b, respectively. But why wouldn't a or b disclose these nonces?

SECURITY ANALYST: Well, they don't. And yes, that is another assumption for the trusted agents. So the claim is in fact conditional if we spell out the types of the agents as follows: If both agent a and b are trusted then they can identify each other after any run of the protocol.

LOGICIAN: The list of assumptions keeps growing. What worries me more is that the list of quantifications is also rapidly growing.

PHILOSOPHER: Yes, indeed, it is.

COGNITIVE SCIENTIST: What do you mean? Quantifications over what?

LOGICIAN: Well, first, if a principal sends an encrypted message, everybody who does not possess the decryption key deems any other message possible. Second, the bad guy or the so-called intruder of this Dolev-Yao model can do anything anytime. He can insert messages, almost any message, and he can delete messages that are sent.

SECURITY ANALYST: Yes, we have to be careful to keep our model manageable. To answer your first point: we can assume trusted agents that only do pattern matching to pick up the right messages. And I do agree with your remark about quantifications: if we need to take into account all the possible behaviors of non-trusted agents, the model grows huge! Another thing to bear in mind, by the way, is that the fewer assumptions you make, the more general will be your correctness proof . . .

PHILOSOPHER: Now let's finally make a list of all the aspects of the modeling we discussed.

LOGICIAN: Well, this is just preliminary, of course: *(Stands up and walks to the whiteboard and writes:)*

- **Protocol description**
    - executable protocol specification for each agent (who should do what under what preconditions);
    - initial distribution of information and kept secrets (e.g. the information about the names of participants, the public/private keys);
    - requirements (what facts should be true at the end of the protocol or even in the middle stage of a run of the protocol?)

- **Assumptions**
    - primitives (what cryptographic primitives are used?)
    - intruder model (what can the intruder do?)
    - trusted agent model (how do they behave, reason and observe?)
    - communication model (how the messages are sent and received, related to agents' observations.)

COGNITIVE SCIENTIST: Well, you are the logician, what do you make of all these questions?

LOGICIAN: The challenge is to find a logical system that fits these situations like a glove. Actually, I do have some ideas for such a logic already . . .

PHILOSOPHER: That's great! But for now I think we should call it a day. May I invite you all to a delicious dinner at NIAS?

Chapter 11
Dynamic Epistemic Logic
for Protocol Analysis

Francien Dechesne, Jan van Eijck, Wouter Teepe, Yanjing Wang

The next day, the participants in the discussion on protocol analysis reconvene. This time, they have an in-depth exchange of ideas on possible uses of epistemic logic.

LOGICIAN: Yesterday we concluded that there are many things that need to be formalized for the analysis of security protocols. After a good night's sleep, I have the feeling that this may be a nice field of application for some kind of *dynamic* epistemic logic. It is about updates of knowledge after the passing of messages, and the protocols are designed to fulfill requirements in terms of knowledge or belief.

COMPUTER SCIENTIST: Yes, that sounds good, but how does one get started? I guess we should avoid going down the road of BAN-logic.

LOGICIAN: We definitely want to have a clear semantics. So why don't we take possible worlds semantics, as for modal logics, as the starting point? We then have a set of *possible worlds*, on which there is also a valuation function that gives the truth value for each primitive proposition. For each agent, his uncertainties about the real world are modeled by an *accessibility* relation on those worlds. A world that is accessible for an agent from a given world, is held to be *possible* by that agent in that world. For an agent to know φ, means that φ holds in each world that he considers possible from the *actual* world.

SECURITY ANALYST: But I see a complexity problem popping up in this semantics with respect to the cryptographic primitives. For example, suppose that we model all possible values that nonces could have. If the nonces don't have an upper bound, or even if the agents just don't know they have an upper bound, we would have to put an infinite number of possible worlds in our model. For each nonce whose value you don't know, there is then an infinite number of possible worlds you can't distinguish ...

LOGICIAN: Yes, I've been pondering that. But I think I have a nice solution! Suppose the actual value of the number n is N. Then one should lump together all worlds where n is different from N. So two worlds are enough to represent your uncertainty about N.

COMPUTER SCIENTIST: I see. I propose we call your new-style worlds *condensed worlds*. Instead of a single valuation, a condensed world has a non-empty set of valuations. I suppose this will work, but it seems rather awkward. Suppose one wishes to check whether $n = M$ is true in a condensed world. Then you may not get a single answer.

LOGICIAN: Still there is no need to go for a logic of partiality. Remember that what we have done till now is essentially a succinct representation of the huge possible worlds space. When we evaluate a formula we just need to split the condensed world to get relevant information. Here we take the dynamic approach. We replace evaluation in condensed worlds by updating with an appropriate *evaluation action model*. Let me draw some pictures. Here is the situation where you don't know the actual value N of n:

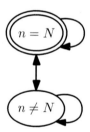

And here is an action model for checking whether the value is M or not:

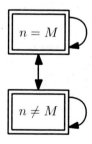

Notice that the equalities and inequalities in the boxes are the preconditions for the corresponding actions. An action can only happen on the worlds which satisfy the precondition of it.

Then the result of updating the condensed model with the action model is the following condensed Kripke model:

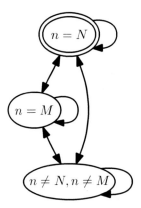

COMPUTER SCIENTIST: I see what you are getting at, and I will explain this general method of updating to the others in a while [12]. It makes the semantics pretty complicated when you want to evaluate a complex modal formula on a condensed world. Anyway, suppose it is well-defined, then I see another useful update action: valuation expansion. I suppose generating a nonce can be seen as a combination of first expanding the valuations in our representation with a new register, and next filling the register with a value.

LOGICIAN: That's right. Let us try our hand at the analysis of the Needham-Schroeder protocol. We start with a situation of blissful ignorance, with an empty list of valuation registers. Assume there are three agents a, b, c.

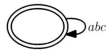

The first thing that happens is that a generates a nonce n_a. This consists of valuation expansion followed by generating the value. The effect of valuation expansion:

Private generation of value N for the new register is represented by the following action model:

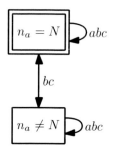

Updating with this gives a situation where only a knows the value of the nonce:

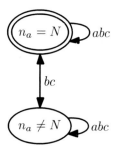

COGNITIVE SCIENTIST: The only difference between the last two pictures is that in the first I see boxes and in the second ovals. Can anyone explain, please?

COMPUTER SCIENTIST: The ovals represent worlds in a Kripke model and the boxes represent actions that take place and that transform Kripke models. This is called "action update". It was invented by Baltag, Moss and Solecki [12]. Action update is a product operation: Worlds in the updated Kripke model are pairs consisting of an old world and an action. Arrows in the updated Kripke model relate pairs where both the world component and the action component were related by the same arrow.

COGNITIVE SCIENTIST: And I suppose the actual worlds after the updates are those pairs of worlds and actions where the world was an actual world before the update and where the action was an actual action. For the double boxes indicate the actual actions, don't they?

COMPUTER SCIENTIST: Yes, you got it.

SECURITY ANALYST: Now how about the action of sending the nonce to b? There is also the issue of encryption with the public key of b. How should we represent that? And a is also putting her own name inside the message.

LOGICIAN: First, we need to create appropriate registers.

COMPUTER SCIENTIST: Register expansion again. Can we agree to use the obvious conventions for naming the registers? Then registers a and $\{n_a, a\}_{\mathrm{PK}_b}$ need to be created. Here is the effect of valuation expansion:

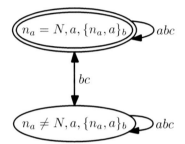

LOGICIAN: Let us suppose that the actual value of a equals A, and the actual value of $\{n_a, a\}_{\mathrm{PK}_b}$ equals M.

COGNITIVE SCIENTIST: What do you mean by the value of a?

LOGICIAN: Think of A as the number that represents the name of a, maybe the encoding of a's name in ASCII. It is just a number that everyone recognizes as the name of a. Agent a decides to use her name A to sign a message. This means that a can distinguish the true value of the register a from other possible values, and the other agents cannot. And similarly for M. M is the number that results from encoding the pair consisting of the nonce number N and the name A with b's public key. One can say that M equals the number $\{N, A\}_{\mathrm{PK}_b}$, where $\{\cdot\}_{\mathrm{PK}_b}$ now stands for computing with the public key encryption function for b. Again, since a generated this, she knows about it. Here is the update model for this:

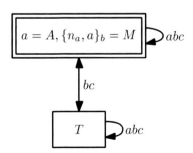

COGNITIVE SCIENTIST: I see. So this expresses that a generates a message for the pair consisting of n_a and her own name, encrypted in the public key of b.

COMPUTER SCIENTIST: Now notice that M means something for b, since it is supposed to be a result of encryption in b's public key. But to the others M means nothing. So the act of making the encrypted message public can be neatly encoded in an update action, as follows:

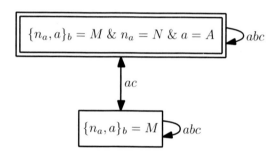

What this says is that b is the only agent who uses the number M in register $\{n_a, a\}_{\mathrm{PK}_b}$ to find the correct register contents for n_a and a, namely N and A.

LOGICIAN: Yes, that's right. In the action model, the actual action provides the link between the encoding M and the plain text that it encodes, but other agents (in our example, a and c) confuse this with the update where nothing happens.

COMPUTER SCIENTIST: Note that the action model could be decomposed into an action model for private communication of the implication

$$\{n_a, a\}_{\mathrm{PK}_b} = M \Rightarrow n_a = N \wedge a = A$$

to b, plus a public announcement of $\{n_a, a\}_{\mathrm{PK}_b} = M$.

LOGICIAN: That's right. What matters is that b is the only agent that can combine the two actions and derive $n_a = N \wedge a = A$ by modus ponens.

COGNITIVE SCIENTIST: Which means that the others do not get the message. In the case of a this makes no difference, as the message originates with her. But the point is that c will not get informed.

LOGICIAN: Indeed. Now look at the result of updating the previous Kripke model with these two action models (Figure 1).

PHILOSOPHER: But wait a minute. It is not clear to me yet how to read this picture. Doesn't the fact that $\{n_a, a\}_{\mathrm{PK}_b} = M$ is true in all worlds

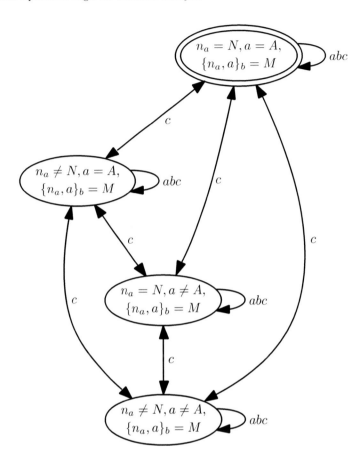

FIGURE 1.

imply that c knows that $\{n_a, a\}_{\mathrm{PK}_b}$ equals M, in other words that M is the result of applying b's public key to the values of n_a and a?

COMPUTER SCIENTIST: That would be a mistake. Please recall that the register naming scheme is just a convenience. To c, M is just a number, and $\{n_a, a\}_{\mathrm{PK}_b}$ is just a register to store this number. If c could use M for computing A and N then the c-indistinguishability arrows would be absent from the picture. Having the number M stored somewhere does not help c at all.

PHILOSOPHER: Ah, now I see.

COMPUTER SCIENTIST: I hope it is clear now how this should go on, at least in principle. By the way, calculating these updates by hand is madness. Fortunately there is an implementation of a powerful dynamic update logic: the version described in [24]. It is called DEMO [85].

LOGICIAN: Yes, I have heard of this. It is an epistemic model checker, right? It has been used for checking the so-called dining cryptographers protocol [84]. It would be useful to extend this into a tool for a wider range of protocols.

COMPUTER SCIENTIST: I like your idea of the condensed worlds very much. However, the model is still essentially infinite. If my understanding of the possible worlds semantics for knowledge is correct, you are forced to represent all possible ways of making $n = N$ false to represent the agent's ignorance that the value of n equals N. What this means is that you need to represent all possibilities $n = M$ where $M \neq N$, since there is no particular value for M that is of special interest.

SECURITY ANALYST: Actually, I don't think you need to talk about those possible values for things like nonces, under some strong assumptions about the cryptographic primitives. Suppose we assume that the agents can't make effective guesses about the value of a nonce, then either they know the value or they don't. You can reformulate the relevant part, whether an agent *knows* a value, or stated differently (non-epistemically!): whether you *possess* some piece of information or not. After yesterday's discussion, I remembered I saw a nice way of modeling this in a paper by Ramanujam and Suresh [188]. This is in the context of some temporal logic, and I think it was inspired by Paulson's work [179].

LOGICIAN: OK, I see the point. So an agent either "has" a nonce, or he doesn't have it. That leaves the actual value totally implicit. And "a has nonce n_a" is actually a proposition, without any epistemic operators ...

SECURITY ANALYST: Yes, that's what I mean! Formally, we can build these propositions using a predicate on agents a and messages m: $a \cdot \textbf{has} \cdot m$. On top of the propositions $a \cdot \textbf{has} \cdot m$, we can build up a full dynamic epistemic logic, with the possible world semantics as usual. For example, we can express "a knows that b has the key k" with the formula $K_a(b \cdot \textbf{has} \cdot k)$ in our language.

LOGICIAN: Ah, now it's getting very interesting! There is a problem expressing this using epistemic operators and values. If we formalize "a knows b knows k" as $K_a K_b(k = N)$, this would necessarily imply also that $K_a(k = N)$ in the classical setting. But this is very problematic! For agent a is assumed to know that agent b knows the value of his own private key, and this is common knowledge, but agent a does *not* know the value of b's private key. That is the essential feature of this type of encryption.

PHILOSOPHER: Doesn't this have to do with the *de dicto–de re* distinction? I would say a better way to express that "a knows that b knows the value of k" would also involve a quantification: $K_a(\exists N K_b(k = N))$, as opposed to $\exists N K_a K_b(k = N)$. The disadvantage of such quantification is that it makes the modeling even more complicated ... I like this idea of separating "real" knowledge—knowledge of facts—from "possession of bits of information." By the way, this discussion reminds me of Plaza's formalization of agents knowing the value of the two secret numbers in the sum-and-product puzzle [184]. Let's continue in this direction!

LOGICIAN: Intuitively, I would say indeed that $K_a(b \cdot \mathbf{has} \cdot k)$ should not imply $a \cdot \mathbf{has} \cdot k$. But how does the evaluation of the propositions of the form $a \cdot \mathbf{has} \cdot m$ work formally? In possible worlds semantics, every world comes with a valuation for the basic propositions. So I guess we need to extend these valuations in some way?

SECURITY ANALYST: Yes, we could do so by assigning in each world, to each agent i, a set of messages, to which we will refer as a's *information set* in that world. The elements of this set represent the keys he possesses (like his private key), the nonces he generated, and the messages he received. The proposition $a \cdot \mathbf{has} \cdot m$ is then defined to be true in that world, if either m is in i's information set, or m can be constructed by a from the elements in his information set.

COMPUTER SCIENTIST: You could think of the messages as terms generated as follows: *(Writes on the whiteboard:)*

$$m ::= a \quad | \quad n \quad | \quad k \quad | \quad \{m\}_k \quad | \quad (m, m')$$

PHILOSOPHER: I guess $\{m\}_k$ stands for a message m encrypted with key k. But what is (m, m') supposed to mean?

SECURITY ANALYST: Just pairing of messages. Now, for example, if you have some message m and a key k in your information set, you should be able to construct $\{m\}_k$. So we have some rules determining which messages an agent can construct from his information set: *(Writes on the whiteboard again:)*

$$\frac{\{m\}_k \quad \overline{k}}{m} \qquad \frac{m \quad m'}{(m, m')} \qquad \frac{(m, m')}{m} \qquad \frac{(m, m')}{m'} \qquad \frac{m \quad k}{\{m\}_k}$$

PHILOSOPHER: So now we can say that $a \cdot \mathbf{has} \cdot m$ is true if the message m is in the closure of a's information set under these rules... Quite nice!

LOGICIAN: *(To himself:)* And then it can easily be the case that b actually has the key k in all worlds a considers possible, but a still doesn't possess k herself. So, indeed, $K_a(b \cdot \textbf{has} \cdot k)$ does not imply $(a \cdot \textbf{has} \cdot k)$.

COGNITIVE SCIENTIST: That sounds reasonable, but how do you model the communication between agents? I mean, the actions in the protocol are all communicative actions.

LOGICIAN: For this we can use the action models again. Let me give you an example of the action model to get a flavor. Suppose there are three agents a, b, c, and c is the special name for an intruder. The action model "a sends b the message m" would be like: *(Draws on the whiteboard:)*

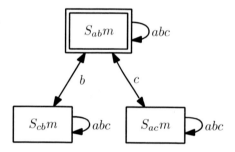

COMPUTER SCIENTIST: Let me see ... So the actual action is "a sends m to b successfully", indicated by $S_{ab}m$ in the picture. But b is not sure whether he received it from a or from the intruder c, and a is not sure whether the message she sent got intercepted by c or not.

LOGICIAN: That's exactly right.

SECURITY ANALYST: I guess the precondition for each action is that the sender "has" the message m?

LOGICIAN: That's right. Moreover, we have a "postcondition" for each action as well. For example, the postcondition for $S_{ab}m$ should be that b learns m but both a and c learn nothing. We just need to update the information set of b in the worlds that satisfy the precondition of $S_{ab}m$ by adding the message m.

SECURITY ANALYST: OK, I can sense the general direction. Still, these action models seem rather ad hoc to me.

LOGICIAN: Yes, I agree that there is still a lot that we need to make clear. For example: what is it exactly that the agents observe when communication takes place? This depends on assumptions we make about the channels, whether it is observable that messages are passed among agents, and between whom. Such things are crucial for building action models.

PHILOSOPHER: I am beginning to wonder whether this Needham-Schroeder protocol is the best test case for dynamic epistemic logic. Could anyone come up with a more convincing example maybe?

LOGICIAN: Of course, there is the famous muddy children example [15]. I guess you all know that?

SECURITY ANALYST: Is that a protocol? I don't think I know it . . .

LOGICIAN: Here's how it goes: Among n children, there are k (which is at least one) of them with mud on their foreheads. They can see each other but not themselves. Now their father confronts them and says aloud: 'At least one of you has mud on his forehead. Will all the children who know they have mud on their heads please step forward?' First, none of the children step forward. When the father repeats his question, he will still get no response until he asks the question for the kth time. Then, miraculously, all muddy children step forward.

SECURITY ANALYST: Hey, I did know this problem, but I know it as the *unfaithful wives problem*.

PHILOSOPHER: That must be the politically incorrect version.

LOGICIAN: If you care for political incorrectness you should also look at the *unfaithful husbands* variation [160]. Well, the reasoning always amounts to the same, and nowadays everyone knows it. I suppose I could convince all of you that a dynamic epistemic analysis can be used nicely to explain what is going on. There are similar problems, for example "Product and Sum" and "Russian cards", that have also been analyzed using these logical techniques [65, 64].

COMPUTER SCIENTIST: Ahem, to me these examples don't sound like protocols at all. They don't *prescribe* actions to fulfill a certain goal. Instead, they seem to *describe*, or explain if you wish, how smart logically thinking agents could solve puzzles about knowledge and ignorance.

COMPUTER SCIENTIST: And didn't we decide that protocol analysis was about checking whether some given requirements are fulfilled after each possible run of the protocol? In the above cases, I don't see directly what the requirements are. And how would you check them, in practice?

SECURITY ANALYST: A possibly better example that comes to my mind is the so-called "Dining Cryptographers Protocol" [46], which is a way of doing an anonymous broadcast. Three cryptographers are dining out and at the end of the evening they are informed that their bill has been paid. Moreover, they know that either one of the cryptographers has paid for the dinner, or otherwise the National Security Agency (NSA) has. The cryptographers want to achieve common knowledge on whether it was the NSA that paid or one of them, in the latter case without revealing which individual footed the bill. By flipping coins and announcing bits, this can be achieved. An epistemic analysis is in [84] and in Chapter 13 (p. 194).

COMPUTER SCIENTIST: However, this still sounds like an epistemic puzzle to me: Initially, the agents have some uncertainties about the facts, but the facts themselves are already established. Through making announcements following a certain pattern and in accordance with the epistemic states of the agents, the agents get to know the desired facts. In terms of the protocol, the communicative actions have epistemic preconditions and the requirements to be fulfilled after the protocol are also purely epistemic.

SECURITY ANALYST: Yes, you have a point. Moreover, there is a crucial element in security protocol analysis that is missing in these puzzles.

COMPUTER SCIENTIST: Let me guess: These puzzles don't really have *runs*.

SECURITY ANALYST: Exactly! In these puzzles, there is usually one (and only one) sequence of actions and it leads to the desired outcome. In that sense, I would say they are not really protocols as we usually understand them. There are no intruders or compromised players. In the analysis of security protocols on the other hand, we consider all possible sequences of actions, which could also result from interleavings of several instantiations of the same protocol. Think for example of Lowe's attack on the Needham-Schroeder protocol, where two instantiations of the protocol were smartly connected by the intruder.

COMPUTER SCIENTIST: I do not see yet how we can generate all possible runs in this dynamic epistemic framework.

COGNITIVE SCIENTIST: In those puzzles, you assumed implicitly that the agents attended a course on epistemic logic and can reason with it in a perfect way, and even that this assumption itself is common knowledge among the participants. Such assumptions may be too strong for protocol analysis in general. You shouldn't rely on the reasoning power of agents unless the preconditions of the actions require some kind of epistemic reasoning.

PHILOSOPHER: And you assume that not only the protocol but also the epistemic reasoning are common knowledge among agents.

LOGICIAN: Ahem, these are very useful insights, thanks a lot! Anyway, you never get anywhere if you don't start somewhere. It would be a perfect starting point if we can find a real protocol not only *about* knowledge but also having epistemic preconditions for actions. A good indication of the epistemic nature of a protocol could be when the requirements to be achieved by the protocol involve nested modal knowledge operators. I feel that the strengths of epistemic logic would really come to the fore in such cases.

COMPUTER SCIENTIST: You will have to actively look around to find such protocols. Standard protocols like Needham-Schroeder definitely don't seem to fit in the category.

SECURITY ANALYST: Yes, it may not be easy to find such protocols in the practice of computer communications. With these subjective perspectives, they look too complicated.

PHILOSOPHER: Still, there might be communication scenarios between humans that require this kind of analysis, maybe? Indeed, why don't you try to find real-life scenarios and make up the protocols that fit yourselves?

LOGICIAN: Good idea! Would you guys give me some suggestions?

PHILOSOPHER: Did you go to Wouter Teepe's talk in this workshop? He talked about this funny scenario that might be interesting to you.

COGNITIVE SCIENTIST: All I remember is that Wouter talked about gossiping. Always interesting, I suppose . . .

PHILOSOPHER: His example story went like this. Geertje tells her friend Wouter that she is pregnant. A few days later, Wouter meets the secretary at the coffee corner. The secretary looks expectantly at Wouter. It seems she wants to gossip with Wouter about something, perhaps Geertje's pregnancy. However, as a good friend of Geertje, Wouter promised her not to disclose the secret. So Wouter can start gossiping about Geertje's pregnancy only if he is sure that the secretary also knows the secret. The question is: Is there a protocol that will allow Wouter to find out whether he can safely start his gossip?

LOGICIAN: That looks promising. Let us try to list the requirements: *(Writes on the whiteboard:)*

- After the protocol execution, Wouter knows whether the secretary has the secret.

- If the secretary did not have the secret, neither does she after the protocol execution.

- If the secretary has the secret, she knows Wouter has it too after the protocol execution.

Security Analyst: Maybe we should also require that no one else learns the secret and no one else learns whether Wouter and the secretary share a secret.

Logician: We can formalize such requirements in a straightforward way in our epistemic language. And I can see that the actions of the protocol must have some sort of epistemic preconditions since the secretary should respond to Wouter according to the information she has.

Computer Scientist: Yes, actually Wouter himself gave several protocols of such scenarios in his thesis [231].

Security Analyst: And I think they are real protocols which are quite useful in the cases when you need to compare information without leaking it.

Computer Scientist: In fact, maybe I should have spoken up earlier, but in my view there is one type of logics that is very suitable for protocol analysis, but which we hardly discussed: temporal logics! Model checking of those logics is very well developed in computer science. There are several mature model checking tools around, and also some standards and languages for the modeling of protocols. Maybe a framework combining the best of both worlds is also worth investigating.

Logician: Yes, there are many promising directions. Anyway, the application of dynamic epistemic logic in protocol analysis deserves to be pursued. I am quite confident it will turn out to be useful at least for some of the cases.

Cognitive Scientist: That sounds hopeful. Unfortunately I need to dash now to catch my train.

Security Analyst: May I join you? *(The security analyst and the cognitive scientist amble off together towards the bus stop.)*

Computer Scientist: I hope they won't gossip about us . . .

Logician: Let them gossip. *(Looking smugly at the philosopher.)* At least *I* do not have anything to hide.

Philosopher: I already gathered that you frown upon my behavior at yesterday's NIAS dinner. Ah, the wonderful Beaujolais they served! I must admit that I do not remember much of what transpired. Well, as long as our two colleagues use that fellow Wouter Teepe's protocol for their gossiping, they will not learn anything new about *me*, either.

COMPUTER SCIENTIST: Indeed, ignorance is bliss.[8] *(Looks dreamily into the distance.)*

---

[8] The theme of ignorance as bliss is developed further in the chapter 'Eating from the Tree of Ignorance', starting on p. 183.

Chapter 12
Battle of the Logics

Barteld Kooi and Rineke Verbrugge

A concern of the organizers of the workshop on 'Games, Action and Social Software' is that although everyone is keen to use logic for the analysis of key concepts in this area, it is not so clear which logic or which tools from logic to use for investigating games, actions and social software. For this reason, they have organized a discussion session on the theme "Battle of the Logics: Temporal Logic, Dynamic Logic, Game Logic, Logic for Belief Revision ... Are There too Many?" Participants in the discussion are logicians of four different stripes: a Temporal Logician, a Dynamic Logician, a Philosophical Logician, and a Mathematical Logician. As always, the Computer Scientist is also present. A Multiagent System Designer who uncharacteristically does not know a lot about logic has just been referred to the four logicians for advice.

MULTIAGENT SYSTEM DESIGNER: As a multiagent system designer, I am usually not that concerned with logic. Of course I use a bit of logic every now and again. A good programmer cannot do without it and should have a good understanding of logic, but I am more concerned with the features and the desired behavior of the system I am designing, than with logical aspects of multiagent systems. Even when I am looking for a logic to support me in the design process, I notice that there is a whole bunch of logics that I could use: temporal logic, dynamic logic, belief-desire-intention logic, which is usually called BDI, and so on. Since there are so many logicians here, I am sure that you could point me in the right direction and tell me what logic I should be using.

TEMPORAL LOGICIAN: I think you will want to use temporal logic. As Fagin, Halpern, Moses and Vardi have shown in their wonderful book *Reasoning about Knowledge* [90], extensions of temporal logic are best suited to reason about multiagent systems. The approach is very straightforward.

As you will acknowledge, a multiagent system can best be represented as a distributed system of computer processors. These processors can be in different *local states* at different times. Together the local states constitute a *global state* of the system. You, as a designer, will have limited the number of global states that are allowed to occur and also which sequences of global states are allowed to occur. We call these sequences of global states *runs*. Formally, a multiagent system can best be thought of as a set of runs. I would even argue that a multiagent system simply *is* the set of runs of the system. We can then interpret a logical language with temporal operators on these runs, and with a little effort we can also interpret epistemic operators on them, and possibly other propositional attitudes. So, temporal logic with such a semantics of interpreted systems is the way to go.

DYNAMIC LOGICIAN: Although I agree that temporal logic is a good approach to modeling *some* multiagent systems, I would not advise you to stick to just one logic. As you said, there are lots of approaches. At first this might seem somewhat unfortunate. After all, if logicians cannot even agree on one system for one application, then the whole enterprise must be flawed. However, you can also see this as an advantage. Apparently there are so many aspects of multiagent systems, and so many questions one might ask about social software or intelligent interaction in general, that one logic might not be enough. I have heard Johan van Benthem compare this situation to the mathematics of space, where geometry and topology are not seen as competitors. They are complementary approaches to the mathematics of space [1]. In the same way, different logics for multiagent systems can complement each other, together giving a rich perspective on intelligent interaction.

TEMPORAL LOGICIAN: Come on. We cannot expect our poor Multiagent System Designer to wade through the entire literature of logics for multiagent systems. This colleague is asking us for some very specific advice, and we should give it. Temporal logic is the best way to go.

DYNAMIC LOGICIAN: If you insist, I will join you in your battle of the logics then. Besides temporal logics, our Multiagent System Designer might do well to consider using dynamic logic. In fact, dynamic logic might appeal more to programmers than temporal logic would. After all, the constructs in the dynamic language are very much like a programming language. There is a great textbook by Harel, Kozen and Tiuryn on dynamic logics [114].

COMPUTER SCIENTIST: Why use logics of action when game theory provides all that is needed for analyzing what goes on when rational agents interact? But I suppose the Game Theorist has not been invited to this "Battle of the Logics" ...

PHILOSOPHICAL LOGICIAN: No, we allow ourselves to be myopic today and to talk about logic, just this once. We have talked about possible uses of logic in game theory on another occasion (see Chapter 9).

DYNAMIC LOGICIAN: Please let me continue my explanation of dynamic logic then. In the language of dynamic logic, there are modal operators corresponding to programs. To inductively build up these programs, there are usually some atomic actions α, as well as tests $(?\varphi)$, which correspond to a program that tests whether a formula φ is true. Then there is sequential composition $(\pi; \pi')$, which simply says first do π, then do π'. You also have non-deterministic choice $(\pi \cup \pi')$, which allows either to execute π or π'. And last but not least, there is iteration (π^*), which tells you to execute π zero or more times. Sometimes, an intersection operator $\cap$ is also used; it is defined semantically by the intersection of the two accessibility relations.

TEMPORAL LOGICIAN: Aha, so intersection is a bit like the operator for distributed or implicit knowledge in the logic of knowledge: if two agents would pool all their knowledge, their implicit knowledge is what they would know. For example, if I know that p and you know that p implies q, then we implicitly know that q. The semantics of implicit knowledge is also based on the intersection of the agents' accessibility arrows, just like your intersection operator for programs, and the completeness proof for the resulting logic is a bit tricky because this intersection is not characterizable by modal axioms.

DYNAMIC LOGICIAN: Exactly, the same problem also holds for dynamic logic with intersection. Incidentally, the dynamic language might seem somewhat far removed from programming languages, but you can easily represent an 'if p then π else π'' construction as $(?p; \pi) \cup (?\neg p; \pi')$, and a 'while p, do π' construction as $(?p; \pi)^*; ?\neg p$. This logic is my personal favorite, and I recommend you to take a look at it, also for specifying and verifying your multiagent systems.

PHILOSOPHICAL LOGICIAN: You seem to be glossing over a very important philosophical point that is relevant to the current discussion. "Useful" is a *relational* concept. One cannot discuss the usefulness of an object, without specifying the purpose for which it is to be used: One cannot say that a car is useful on its own. However, if one wants to go from A to B, a car might be very useful. It is these simple philosophical points that seem to complicate discussions between non-philosophers all the time. A basic course in philosophy should be mandatory in any academic program. This would save us a lot of wasted time. So, what would you like to use these logics *for*?

MULTIAGENT SYSTEM DESIGNER: Well, obviously, to help me design, implement and analyze systems of interacting agents, because that happens to be my job. In fact, I have many applications in mind. Perhaps a suitable logic could help me design a multiagent system by providing a nice logical language to write down a specification of desired system behavior. Perhaps logic could help me verify that the system I have designed indeed has the desired properties I had in mind while making it. Perhaps logic could also warn me not to try to implement impossible systems, such as a decision method for the provability of formulas in predicate logic.

MATHEMATICAL LOGICIAN: Perhaps it would be nice to ask ourselves more generally what logics are supposed to be good for. When you look at the historical roots of formal logic, you see that modern logic arose from a desire to provide a firm foundation for mathematics. Think about the so-called logicist program of Frege and Hilbert's Program, where the aim was to found mathematics on logic. Alas, Hilbert's Program in its original guise failed on two counts: Gödel's incompleteness theorems showed that the supposed foundations, which at that time were represented by Russell and White-head's axiomatization of arithmetic in *Principia Mathematica*, were incomplete, and that such systems could not even prove their own consistency. Second, Turing and Church proved that first-order logic is undecidable. Still, Hilbert's Program has proved to be very fruitful for mathematical logic, and nowadays many interesting revisions of Hilbert's Program are around, that try to justify ideal mathematics by restricted means. For example, people like Feferman, Kreisel, Friedman and Simpson have shown that a lot of scientifically applicable mathematics can be based on weak subsystems of analysis, which are reducible to finitary mathematics [214].

COMPUTER SCIENTIST: So, logicians have by no means lost their interest in very precise mathematical proofs. And now we even have computational proof assistants as powerful as Coq, a direct descendant of Automath. Isn't it fascinating that a group of researchers has recently succeeded in constructing and checking a completely formal proof of the four color theorem in Coq [105, 106]?

PHILOSOPHICAL LOGICIAN: That's all very well, but do not forget that logic started with Aristotle who had a somewhat broader view of logic than just mathematics. He was thinking about argumentation and science in general. If you want go back to the real historical roots of logic, you will see that its purpose is twofold. On the one hand, logic is a normative tool to assess the validity of inferences. On the other hand, due to its precision it clarifies and explicates intuitions one has about complex concepts.

MULTIAGENT SYSTEM DESIGNER: This is a bit too abstract for me. May we turn to a specific type of logic? In my field I have heard a lot about logics for beliefs, desires and intentions, BDI logics for short. Could you clarify for me what use these logics would have for me?

TEMPORAL LOGICIAN: BDI logics are simply extensions of branching time temporal logic as it was developed in theoretical computer science to investigate distributed systems. The founders of BDI logics wanted to formalize the concept of an agent. You could view BDI logics as a formalization of work done in philosophy on intentions and planning [190].

PHILOSOPHICAL LOGICIAN: In philosophy, intention has been the subject of study for years. It seems that people in artificial intelligence are always reinventing the wheel, because this is exactly what Michael Bratman proposed [40, 41]. He said that if one has an intention to do something in the future, one forms a partial plan, that one can fill in along the way. For example, if one wants to go to New York, there are many ways to get there. So, one forms some sort of highly abstract plan: For example one might want to travel by air rather than by sea. Some things one may leave to the very last minute before one starts executing the plan. One may for example decide to take a taxi to the airport, but one would probably not have selected a particular taxi in advance. It is quite clear that intentions and plans are very closely connected.

TEMPORAL LOGICIAN: Yes, and Bratman's is exactly the work upon which BDI logic is based. So the researchers in artificial intelligence have bought Bratman's very nice wheels instead of reinventing them. You can view BDI logics as providing a specification for the implementation of real agents.

MATHEMATICAL LOGICIAN: So can someone explain the basics, please?

TEMPORAL LOGICIAN: Just think of the branching time logic CTL, computation tree logic. At each time point, the tree can branch to several successors according to different events taking place, or atomic actions if you like. In the language, you use temporal operators like inevitably (on every branch), optionally (on some branch), eventually (at some future point on the current branch), next, and until. Now Rao and Georgeff's idea was to combine this with operators for beliefs, goals and intentions. In the model, this would lead to a number of time trees, where for example the agent believes a formula at a time in the current tree if that formula holds in all belief-accessible time trees at the corresponding point in time. So, it's just as you would expect. If you want to have obvious axioms in your system that say things like "if you intend something, then you also desire it", this corresponds to a semantic property such as "every desire-accessible world has a subtree that is an intention-accessible world".

MULTIAGENT SYSTEM DESIGNER: I find it hard to believe that such an abstract logic has anything to do with working systems. If BDI logic really is about this notion of agency, it is a philosophical exercise.

DYNAMIC LOGICIAN: Well, BDI logic can be used for planning and that's really relevant for artificial intelligence. BDI logics are on the supply side of social software. They provide social procedures. They do not aim to describe reality, but they are going to help make things reality by providing specifications that can be implemented.

PHILOSOPHICAL LOGICIAN: Why don't you give us a concrete example?

TEMPORAL LOGICIAN: A well-known automobile factory has constructed a prototype of a conveyor belt system for car manufacturing [126] based on a BDI architecture. The usual method of manufacturing cars is that a central controller pre-plans the whole production process for a day, but then you lose a lot of time if one of the machines breaks down during the day, as often happens. Instead, Jennings and his colleagues designed a decentralized control system. All machines and all manufactured parts were conceptualized as agents with their own objectives, such as "get myself to the end of the manufacturing line after a specified set of operations has been performed on me". Then constant negotiations among different agents took place, following the Contract Net Protocol, where machines bid for the opportunity to carry out operations on the parts [202]. All these objectives and outcomes of the task allocation protocols were represented as agents' desires and intentions. It turns out that the BDI-based decentralized system is much more flexible and robust in the face of an uncertain dynamic environment than the usual centralized one.

MULTIAGENT SYSTEM DESIGNER: That's a really neat application, I'm impressed! I will look up that conveyor belt paper and see if I can build upon Jennings' neat work. Still, isn't the notion of agency in BDI logics too much like the notion of a player from game theory to be of practical use?

DYNAMIC LOGICIAN: Indeed there are close connections between multi-agent systems and game theory, and what goes on in games can also be captured in dynamic logics [18]. I do not want to go too deeply into games here as we have already talked about them elsewhere (in Chapter 9), but let me remind you that the notion of agency is one of the key concepts to be analyzed in both fields.

MATHEMATICAL LOGICIAN: I once attended a lecture on BDI logics and remember being surprised by the high number of different aspects that were mixed in one logic. It might have been the case that this was due to the area still being so young, but I would consider it unwise to develop a logic that is so rich in language and semantics. These rich systems might seem attractive when you want to write things down in your logic, but any metalogical result is very hard to obtain. I prefer simple systems with small languages, with which one can obtain beautiful results.

PHILOSOPHICAL LOGICIAN: Again it seems a question of the purpose of one's enterprise. To me, it seems as though in mathematical logics the axiomatization of a logic comes first. Because one desires a certain elegance of axiomatization, one consequently makes the language very poor. I remember certain mathematical logicians whose preferred fragment of propositional logic only contained implication and absurdity. Of course, this language is truth-functionally complete, and proofs with induction on the language are less cumbersome, but in this way, other philosophically important logical operators are ignored. When I develop a logic, the language simply contains logical operators for those concepts I deem important.

TEMPORAL LOGICIAN: Maybe you should start with model theory instead of language. Indeed, a logic is used for reasoning about certain structures. You should first capture these structures, then you can decide on the language. Remember that there are lots of ways to represent time. One can have branching time or linear time, or one can have interval based models [88, 26]. Once you fix your models, you can interpret all sorts of languages on them. But the models come first.

MATHEMATICAL LOGICIAN: Hey, what are you all quibbling about? Doesn't every well-trained logician know that once you have a sound and complete system, there is a one-to-one correspondence between syntax and semantics?

DYNAMIC LOGICIAN: Of course we all know that, and I guess my colleagues here were just getting a little carried away talking about private tastes. In fact, I also think of the models first, and language and axiomatization later. This is not because I think the models are somehow fundamental. They just give me the best intuitions in developing a logic. I can well imagine that this works differently for other people, though.

COMPUTER SCIENTIST: Actually, there is one perspective from which your quibble between models and deductions is important, and that is feasibility. Halpern and Vardi describe this very well in their paper *Model Checking vs. Theorem Proving: A Manifesto* [111]. In good old-fashioned artificial intelligence, an agent's knowledge was represented as a knowledge base, a collection of formulas. An agent was said to know something if it was provable from his knowledge base. But as the fathers of AI, and especially McCarthy, found that first-order logic was the logic for knowledge representation, this meant that the theorem-proving approach led to undecidability. In the model-checking approach, in contrast, you only need to check whether a given formula holds in a database, and that problem takes up memory space only polynomial in the size of your data: it is in PSPACE.

TEMPORAL LOGICIAN: In my field, there are also such striking cases where model checking is much more efficient than theorem proving. For example, if you want to verify a finite-state program, let's say a communication protocol, with respect to some specification that can be expressed in a branching time logic. Then the theorem-proving way would be that you first completely characterize your protocol by a temporal formula: You just need to describe all possible transitions in all possible global states. Then you need to check whether this description implies your specification. Unfortunately, checking this is not tractable because the validity problem for branching time logic is EXPTIME-complete.

MULTIAGENT SYSTEM DESIGNER: Sorry, guys and girls, all this complexity stuff with PSPACE- and EXPTIME-complete goes way over my head.

COMPUTER SCIENTIST: OK, so let me fill you in on the four most famous complexity classes. Computer scientists are interested in classifying problems by how much computational resources, like time and memory, they take to solve, as a function of the length of the input of the problem. Problems that take up time polynomial in the length of the input are in the class P, and those problems are usually said to be tractable. For example, think of the problem whether a certain valuation satisfies a given propositional formula—this corresponds to checking a single row in a truth table, which can clearly be done in linear time. The next important class is called NP for non-deterministic polynomial time. This class includes problems that can be described as "guess a polynomially short potential solution, and then check in polynomial time whether this guess indeed forms a solution". A typical example of a problem in NP is satisfiability for propositional formulas, abbreviated as SAT: guess a valuation, and then check in linear time whether it indeed satisfies the formula. Now the interesting thing is that there are no problems in NP that are essentially more difficult than satisfiability: Cook proved already in 1971 that each problem in NP can be easily translated to a suitable instance of SAT. Such problems like SAT that are in NP and are also among the hardest in NP, are called "NP-complete". As you probably know, it is still unknown whether P and NP are really different. If they aren't, that could have serious repercussions for public key cryptography (see Chapter 13).

MULTIAGENT SYSTEM DESIGNER: And if you prove it one way or another, the Clay Mathematics Institute will give you a million dollars, right?

COMPUTER SCIENTIST: Right, but being a Buddhist, the money doesn't interest me much. Let me tell you about two other relevant complexity classes. One is called PSPACE, and contains those problems that can be solved using memory space polynomial in terms of the input. A typical example is the model checking problem for predicate logic that I just mentioned for databases. Another one is the satisfiability problem for the most common modal logics [34, Chapter 6]. Both of these problems are in fact PSPACE-complete, again in the sense that all other problems in PSPACE can be reduced to them. It is immediately clear that NP is included in PSPACE, because short guesses and polynomial checking of them can never take up more than polynomial space. But again, nobody has yet found out whether NP and PSPACE are really different classes.

MULTIAGENT SYSTEM DESIGNER: Now I wonder how EXPTIME fits into this picture. Surely exponential time is really more difficult than polynomial time?

COMPUTER SCIENTIST: Indeed it is, and that's in fact the only equivalence among the four complexity classes P, NP, PSPACE and EXPTIME that has been disproved. The simple thing we know is that PSPACE is included in EXPTIME—this is done by a nice proof, which you can look up in classical textbooks on complexity theory, such as Papadimitriou's [174]. A typical problem in EXPTIME is the satisfiability problem for propositional dynamic logic, where satisfying a formula that includes the Kleene star operator may require tree models of exponential depth [34, Chapter 6].

DYNAMIC LOGICIAN: So, just to sum up all relations: P is included in NP, which is included in PSPACE, which is in turn included in EXPTIME, and the only inequality that has been proved is the one between the two extremes P and EXPTIME.

MULTIAGENT SYSTEM DESIGNER: Wow, so much is still unknown in complexity theory! Doesn't that mean that computer science has been built on quicksand?

COMPUTER SCIENTIST: You could view it that way, but personally I rather think that these problems are at the heart of computation and show the depth of my subject.

DYNAMIC LOGICIAN: I think we can now safely return to our earlier discussion of theorem proving versus model checking for finite-state programs such as communication protocols with respect to specifications that are represented by branching-time formulas.

TEMPORAL LOGICIAN: Thank you for getting us back to this main branch of our discussion. In the early eighties, Clarke and Emerson found out that you could represent a finite-state program by a Kripke model. The worlds of the Kripke model represent possible global states of your program, and the accessibility relations represent possible transitions. The great thing is that the Kripke model does not get out of hand: it is just about the same size as your program. Now checking whether your program satisfies the specification amounts to checking whether the specification holds at the world in your Kripke model that corresponds to the initial global state. And you can do this in time just linear in the sizes of the specification formula and your Kripke model [111]!

COMPUTER SCIENTIST: Unfortunately I have to temper your enthusiasm about this low complexity a bit. In model checking problems, the model is often assumed to be part of the input, so a seemingly attractive complexity result like "linear time in terms of the size of the input" is sometimes misleading, as these models can be very large in practice [121].

PHILOSOPHICAL LOGICIAN: I think that the complexity of a logic should also be viewed in relation to its *use*. For example, in the context of cryptography, high complexity is a feature, not a bug.

MULTIAGENT SYSTEM DESIGNER: I am of course not a logician, but, returning to the question where to start, I think I would start on the language instead of the model. There are just properties that you want to express. I do not want some very small language in which it takes a lot of work to express some basic concepts.

DYNAMIC LOGICIAN: Ah, but that is exactly what can get me excited: A very simple language with great expressivity. I agree with our Mathematical Logician that having language and semantics that are rich might make metalogical results difficult to obtain. Even worse, it could be that the system "does" things that are incorrect, but you are unaware of this because the system is too complex. I am reminded of what Albert Visser once said in a talk on logic and linguistics: Logicians prefer small and correct theories, and linguists prefer big and incorrect theories. That is to say, when a logician tries to capture an aspect of natural language, he or she develops a dedicated system for a small fragment of natural language. Linguists, on the other hand, try to capture all of natural language in their system. They are bothered that the fragments that the logicians use for describing parts of natural language do not capture *all* of natural language. But their wish to cover everything leads them to adopt theories that contain inconsistencies, which in the eyes of logicians is committing mortal sin after mortal sin.

MATHEMATICAL LOGICIAN: I see what you mean. Just like the linguists you mentioned, computer scientists sometimes seem to construct logics that can express everything you want, but the semantics and axiomatization might be mistaken here and there.

COMPUTER SCIENTIST: I object! No one in his right mind could claim that contributions to conferences such as Logic in Computer Science present shaky semantics and axiomatizations. Use of logic in computer science is often very subtle and we can compete with the best of mathematical logicians in our use of abstract structures like locales, quantales and co-algebras. I think you have ample reason to tone down your arrogance. Mathematical logic has never been viewed as mainstream mathematics, and there has been only little contact between mathematical logic and the natural sciences. On the other hand, you can hardly over-estimate the role of logic in computer science. Just think of the relations between logic and complexity, the use of predicate logic as database query language, the influence of type theory on programming language research, and the use of modal logics in multiagent systems. You should definitely read the classic paper *On the unusual effectiveness of logic in computer science* [108].

MATHEMATICAL LOGICIAN: Ahem, sorry about that.

MULTIAGENT SYSTEM DESIGNER: To go back to the previous point, I feel sympathetic towards the linguist perspective, and start with all the expressivity that you need. After all, even as a programmer, first you build a system and then you try to debug it.

COMPUTER SCIENTIST: Now wait a minute, that is not the state of the art in software development at all! Nowadays we start with requirements and specifications, we use logic to check these specifications, and we let the implementation process go hand in hand with unit testing and specification-based random testing. For almost all aspects of this process, logic is highly relevant.

MULTIAGENT SYSTEM DESIGNER: Point taken. What I was worried about is, what good is a logical system that at best will only do part of what I want it to do?

DYNAMIC LOGICIAN: I understand your concerns. But in that case, instead of taking the risk of developing an incorrect theory, you can follow a piecemeal approach. You first create dedicated systems that do only part of what you really want and then you extend and combine systems. Initially we only focus on aspects that are interesting for us. Dynamic epistemic logic, for instance, is only about information change [66]. It does not capture anything else. This is also a valid approach.

PHILOSOPHICAL LOGICIAN: Of course a piecemeal approach assumes that a problem can be thought of and solved in an analytic fashion. This is a very old philosophical discussion, of which I am afraid none of you are aware. One can imagine that there are problems that can only be solved as a whole. That is to say, there can be a need for holism. A system that only deals with some aspects of the problem will in that case always be dreadfully misguided.

DYNAMIC LOGICIAN: Can you give an example of this?

PHILOSOPHICAL LOGICIAN: The notion of obligation is very much connected to the notion of action. One is usually obliged to do something, to take an action. And the obligation is met when a certain action has taken place, and afterwards there may not be an obligation anymore. Therefore a philosophically sound deontic logic needs to be grafted on a logic of action. The work of John Horty is a nice example of this [123].

DYNAMIC LOGICIAN: But deontic logic and the logic of action have developed separately. A holistic approach might have been too difficult initially. Moreover, as has recently been shown, the notion of knowledge is also very important for the notion of obligation [173]. Yet, epistemic logic was very fruitfully developed on its own.

PHILOSOPHICAL LOGICIAN: I will admit it, but in order to grasp a concept in full, one cannot leave out crucial aspects.

MATHEMATICAL LOGICIAN: Even if an analytic approach is possible, it may not be straightforward at all. Given two different logics, it seems highly non-trivial to combine them into one logic.

TEMPORAL LOGICIAN: It is indeed. When you investigate the complexity of combinations of logics, you might like to turn to general results on the transfer of the complexity of satisfiability problems from single logics to their combinations: isn't a combination of a few PSPACE-complete logics, with some simple interdependency axioms, automatically PSPACE-complete again? However, it turns out that the positive general results that do exist (such as those in Edith Spaan's Ph.D. thesis [219]) apply mainly to minimal combinations, without added interdependencies, of two NP-complete systems, each with a single modality.

DYNAMIC LOGICIAN: Even more dangerously, I've heard of some very negative results on the transfer of complexity to combined systems. Listen to this: there are two "very decidable" logics whose combination, even without any interrelation axioms, is undecidable. For the first logic, let's take a weak variant of dynamic logic with two atomic programs, both deterministic. Take the sequential operator ; and the intersection operator ∩ as only operators. Satisfiability of formulas is in EXPTIME, just like for propositional dynamic logic itself. For the second logic, take the logic of the global operator A (Always), which just means what you would think, namely that the formula it is applied to is true everywhere throughout the Kripke model. Satisfiability for this logic is in NP. Blackburn and Spaan have shown that the minimal combination of the two logics is not only *not* in EXPTIME, but even undecidable in any finite time. This goes to show that we need to be very careful with any assumptions about generalizations of complexity results to combined systems [35, 34].

MULTIAGENT SYSTEM DESIGNER: But those are just artificial examples made up to achieve horrendous undecidability results. Let us stick to a realistic multi-modal logic such a BDI combination of the standard logics for beliefs, goals and intentions, and add some reasonable interdependencies, such as the axiom that having an intention implies having the corresponding goal.

TEMPORAL LOGICIAN: That combination turns out to be PSPACE-complete, so no better or worse than its individual component logics [80].

COMPUTER SCIENTIST: Here I agree with you, the situation is not so bad. You may also be interested in Gabbay's *fibring* as a general approach to combining logics. I will try to tell you roughly what it is, but you all should really read his book about it [99]. Given two logics, let us say linear temporal logic and epistemic logic, the language of their fibring is obtained by combining all atomic symbols and operations from both of them. As for deduction, you suppose that the two given logics have the same type of deductive system (for example, both a Hilbert style one, or both a tableau system). Then in the fibring, you can freely use inference rules from both. If the two original systems were schematic, this means that the inference rules can be applied to formulas including symbols from the "other" language, and fibring them makes sense. The semantics is quite complicated, so you should just look it up in the book, but you could think of a fibred model as a cloud of points. At each point you can extract a model of the first logic and a model of the second one, so in our example you would be able to extract a time line as well as a model of epistemic logic.

TEMPORAL LOGICIAN: I do not really see the point of combining systems. Why would you want to model everything at the same time? And why should everything be in the language? It might be fine to have temporal models for multiagent systems with knowledge and just interpret an epistemic language on those models. There is nothing wrong with that.

MATHEMATICAL LOGICIAN: I only know of one situation where the models can be uniquely described by the logic: propositional logic with only finitely many propositional variables. In that case the language is not only truth-functionally complete, but also expressive complete in the sense that for every model, there is a formula that is true in exactly that model and in no others. For other logics the models are much richer than the logical language can describe. Modal logics cannot distinguish bisimilar models for instance, but bisimilar models are not isomorphic.

MULTIAGENT SYSTEM DESIGNER: What are bisimilar models?

DYNAMIC LOGICIAN: Do you know what a Kripke model is?

MULTIAGENT SYSTEM DESIGNER: Yes.

DYNAMIC LOGICIAN: Good. A bisimulation is a relation between two Kripke models.

The concept of bisimulation was independently developed in automata theory, modal logic, and non-well founded set theory. Davide Sangiorgi has a nice paper on its history [203]. The idea is that two structures are bisimilar if their "behavior" is somehow the same. In automata theory that means that two automata accept the same language, in modal logic it means that two models satisfy the same formulas and in non-well-founded set theory it means that two sets are identical.

A bisimulation between two Kripke models is a relation between the worlds of the two Kripke models. Such a relation has to satisfy three requirements in order to be a bisimulation. First of all, if two worlds w and w' are linked by the relation, then they have to satisfy the same propositional variables. Secondly, for each accessible world v from w, i.e. by the accessibility relation in the one Kripke model, there is an accessible world v' from w' in the other model such that v and v' are also related. This is called the *forth* condition. Thirdly, for each accessible world v' from w', there is an accessible world v from w such that v and v' are also related. This is the *back* condition. Let me draw you a picture for the forth condition.

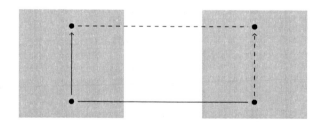

We have one model on the left and one on the right. If the two worlds below are linked and there is a world accessible on the left, then there is a world accessible on the right such that those accessible worlds are also linked. The "if" part is the normal lines, the "then" part is the dashed lines. The picture for the back condition looks like this.

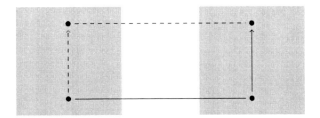

The relation is called a bisimulation because what can be done on the left can be done on the right and simultaneously what can be done on the right can be done on the left. The two models simulate each other simultaneously.

Modal logic cannot distinguish bisimilar models in the sense that they satisfy the same formulas. So in that sense, the models are much richer than the logic can describe.

MULTIAGENT SYSTEM DESIGNER: I would not like that kind of situation. Why would you want rich models and a poor language? There seems to be something out of balance in that case.

COMPUTER SCIENTIST: Not at all. This is not a *defect*, this is a *virtue*. This is how process theorists look at modal logics. Processes are about choice and sequence, and one and the same process can be pictured in different ways. Take the process X of making a choice between doing a and b, and next performing X again. One can picture this as

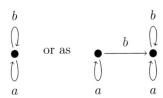

Both pictures describe the same process. These pictures happen to be bisimilar. So the "real process" is the class of all pictures that are bisimilar to the first picture.

MULTIAGENT SYSTEM DESIGNER: I see what you mean. But how is it a virtue that different pictures can represent the same process?

COMPUTER SCIENTIST: The notion of process captures the essence of the picture. It tells us what is important and what is not.

DYNAMIC LOGICIAN: In modal logic it tells you when two models are not essentially different.

TEMPORAL LOGICIAN: This depends on the logical language of course. It is quite easy to distinguish the two structures above using first-order logic.

DYNAMIC LOGICIAN: It might be better to view this as something of a range of possibilities. On one extreme a feature of the models can be entirely captured such as the propositional case that our Mathematical logician mentioned earlier. At the other end of the spectrum, the extra structure cannot be captured in the language at all. There might be good reasons to be on one side of the spectrum or the other, or somewhere in the middle.

TEMPORAL LOGICIAN: I don't think we should have a general discussion about this. Why don't you give us a specific example?

DYNAMIC LOGICIAN: Indeed, so let's consider the case of AGM-style belief revision versus the dynamic doxastic logic of Segerberg [139]. Although both systems deal with the same phenomena, they have a very different methodology when it comes to something being inside or outside the language. The basic ingredients of belief revision are so-called belief sets. These are simply logically closed sets of either propositional or first-order formulas. Then there are operations on these belief sets that correspond to changes in belief. Dynamic doxastic logic arose out of the idea to internalize these operations in a logic, so to view the operations on belief sets as modal operators in an extended logic.

PHILOSOPHICAL LOGICIAN: I must say that I really appreciated the original AGM paper [2]. I do not see what extra insight is gained by internalizing belief change operators.

DYNAMIC LOGICIAN: In their paper, Leitgeb and Segerberg argue that one of the main advantages is that by putting everything in the language you can nest belief operators and change operators [139]. In this way you can explicitly formalize beliefs about changes, as well as changes of belief. I agree that this is a great advantage. Rather than formalizing belief change, you formalize reasoning about belief change.

TEMPORAL LOGICIAN: This reminds me of the two different schools in addressing the effects of communication in multiagent systems. There is the famous school of Fagin, Halpern, Moses and Vardi [90] on the one hand, where the semantics are based on interpreted systems. These are in turn based on a temporal structure such as linear or branching time, with added epistemic structure reflecting agents' observational powers. Such interpreted systems work wonders when you want to model processes that arise when a protocol is followed through time. Of course the corresponding language of Epistemic Temporal Logic (ETL) combines epistemic and temporal operators.

The other school is called Dynamic Epistemic Logic (DEL). There, the epistemic events such as public announcements are included in the language. In order to describe communicative processes, you then have to compute so-called product updates in stages, starting from an initial situation.

COMPUTER SCIENTIST: As a computer scientist, I really appreciate the work from the Halpern school: they think as computer scientists and give many examples of how logic can be used to specify and analyze protocols for communicating systems. In fact, one of my favorite papers of all time is Joe Halpern and Lenore Zuck's *A little knowledge goes a long way*. They introduce the concept of a knowledge-based algorithm and give an extremely nice and convincing logical analysis of such computer science classics as the alternating-bit protocol. It seems to me that the DEL examples, which often involve puzzles or simple card games, have much less of a "real life" flavor.

TEMPORAL LOGICIAN: I keep wondering whether our two schools are really so different as some authors claim.

DYNAMIC LOGICIAN: You have timed your question very well indeed. Recent work by Van Benthem, Pacuit, Gerbrandy and others shows that if you look at it the right way, you can find very interesting analogies between ETL and DEL. Rather than reducing one framework to the other, these authors aim to merge them. This program has already led to some interesting results and techniques, such as a new kind of modal correspondence theory which relates properties of DEL protocols to corresponding ETL properties. Also they have proved some completeness theorems for ETL model classes generated by DEL protocols. So instead of remaining rivals, these logicians now use ideas from our DEL school to add fine structure to ETL [27].

TEMPORAL LOGICIAN: But aren't ETL-style logics much more complex than DEL?

DYNAMIC LOGICIAN: To be sure, another article that embodies the temporal-dynamic unification program is aptly named *The tree of knowledge in action: Towards a common perspective* [28]. It explores complexity issues around epistemic logics from both the temporal and the dynamic point of view. At first sight the ETL view on branching time gives rise to models that quickly get out of hand. Especially if the added epistemic structure enables some grid-like structure to be encoded, for example because of properties like Perfect Recall and No Miracles, undecidability may result. Van Benthem and Pacuit go on to use ETL-style methods to investigate the complexity of some DEL-like logics that live close to the edge of undecidability. For example, the result by Miller and Moss that the dynamic epistemic logic of public announcement with program iterations is undecidable may be contrasted with the fact that adding temporal "past" operators to DEL does not destroy decidability. Also in this case, methods from one camp are fruitfully used to chart the complexity of logics from the other camp.

MATHEMATICAL LOGICIAN: As the paper by Van Benthem and Pacuit suggests, it seems that there is still a certain amount of strife between temporal and dynamic camps, though. I remember that Johan van Benthem compared this situation with the start of computability theory. There were several approaches, from recursive functions through lambda calculus to Turing machines. Rather than bicker and argue about which approach was the best, the logicians at the time proved that these definitions were equivalent and embraced Church's Thesis that every effectively calculable function is general recursive [28].

DYNAMIC LOGICIAN: And rather than weakening their own position, their joint forces strengthened the field enormously because it turned out that the notion of computability is quite stable. Indeed, "seeing differences may make for short-term gains, seeing analogies leads to a long-term common cause" [28].

PHILOSOPHICAL LOGICIAN: I do not think such a grand unification can ever be achieved in the case of logics for intelligent interaction. There are simply too many systems and they seem quite incomparable. Moreover I think it is nonsensical to aim to achieve unification. It will only give us a few extra theorems, but no better understanding of the concepts involved.

TEMPORAL LOGICIAN: There is a danger if one never compares systems. A lot of time will be wasted if different people work on essentially the same problem, because they are blind to the fact that the systems they use are essentially equivalent. The book by John Horty *Agency and Deontic Logic* for instance uses branching time temporal logic and I think his approach fits in very nicely with the temporal logics that are used in computer science [123]. It would be very useful if the people working on logics for "seeing to it that" and the people working on computation tree logic would compare notes.

DYNAMIC LOGICIAN: I've heard that Broersen, Herzig and Troquard have started doing so: they found some nice first results on the connection between Alternating-time temporal logic and STIT logic [42].

TEMPORAL LOGICIAN: Indeed, today we have hardly discussed alternating-time temporal logic (ATL), but I think it is also a worthwhile approach for specifying multiagent systems [121]. If temporal logics tell you *when* you will be happy, and dynamic logic can express *how* it is done, ATL can speak about *who* will achieve this state for you. This seems to be quite an essential aspect when you are interested in intelligent interaction.

MULTIAGENT SYSTEM DESIGNER: I wish there were a map of the logics of intelligent interaction, showing what the connections between different approaches are and charting in what ways some of them are equivalent. Then I would, depending on the purpose, be able to use one of those systems off the shelf.

DYNAMIC LOGICIAN: Let a thousand flowers and trees of knowledge bloom in the logical landscape! Our task is to be both gardeners and cartographers, so that everyone can find his way.

Chapter 13
Eating from the Tree of Ignorance

Jan van Eijck and Rineke Verbrugge

Jan and Rineke are having a discussion while making preparations for their farewell talk at NIAS. They have already sent out a title and an abstract.

RINEKE: Have you seen the instructions for the NIAS lectures? They frighten me a bit, really. Listen to this: NIAS talks should combine scientific depth with general accessibility; they should be geared at the general NIAS audience, but they should definitely be more than just superficial overviews.

JAN: I suppose we should not only talk about ignorance but we should also presuppose ignorance. Ignorance about logic, that is. Can you show me our abstract again, please?

RINEKE: Here it is (Figure 1).

The title is certainly intriguing enough. Strictly between you and me: What exactly did you have in mind when you proposed it?

JAN: I would like to explain the concepts of common knowledge and lack of common knowledge to our audience, and analyze some examples where ignorance is bliss. In particular, I would like to explain that if I manage to keep information about my personal life out of the public view, I am helping others to protect their own privacy as well. Together we can reap the fruits of this. Ignorance is bliss, for knowledge can be exploited. Ignorance can also be exploited, of course, but this is well-known.

RINEKE: It is indeed often the case that your ignorance proves your innocence. This is because many obligations are knowledge based. A doctor who does not know that a patient is sick does not have a legal or moral obligation to treat that patient. This is all very nicely analyzed in [173].

JAN: The other day, Rohit Parikh came up with an amusing example of the reverse. A case where to prove innocence would have involved showing

Eating from the Tree of Ignorance

Jan van Eijck & Rineke Verbrugge

In this talk, we will first introduce some examples of contexts, such as negotiations, where participants need to reason about others' knowledge and ignorance. Based on these examples, we will then introduce a logical model that can be used to reason about knowledge and ignorance: epistemic logic. This logic turns out to be well-suited for modeling social types of knowledge, for example common knowledge, which forms the basis of conventions such as "everybody drives on the right". Limitations of the idealized logical point of view on knowledge will also be given.

Many social interaction protocols are designed to preserve certain kinds of ignorance. Anonymity and privacy boil down to guaranteed absence of knowledge. We will analyze a number of interaction protocols with tools from epistemic logic. Finally, we will argue that certain types of ignorance may be beneficial for the individual ignorant agents, for a group, or even for society at large.

FIGURE 1.

that one did know. Some policewoman, posing as a teenaged girl, engaged a middle-aged man in erotic discussions over the web. The man was convicted under some kind of "protection of children" act and sent to prison for five years. But the policewoman was not in fact a minor, and had the man been able to prove that he knew he was chatting with an adult woman, he would not have been convicted. So it was his ignorance about the true identity of his date—the fact that he did *not* know she was not a child—which created an obligation not to chat about sex. The obligation would have vanished had he known about the true identity of the person he was chatting up.

RINEKE: An intriguing case, certainly. It revolves around what others know about what we know. But some people may just not care about what others know.

JAN: If we want to analyze such cases for our public, we'll need to give them some background on reasoning about knowledge, and in particular epistemic logic.

RINEKE: Okay, I'll do that by starting with some contexts that they're all familiar with, negotiations. It turns out that in the Camp David negotiations between Israel and Egypt in 1979, which were mediated by Carter, both

Sadat and Carter made some strange mistakes that where based on their lack of reasoning about the knowledge of the others. It was Carter's role in the negotiation to devise proposals that were then separately critiqued by Begin and Sadat, after which Carter would present a new proposal, until a proposal would be accepted by both parties. Did you know that already on the second day Sadat, who trusted Carter as a friend, presented a letter to Carter? This epistle outlined Sadat's fallback position, detailing all his possible concessions [169]!

JAN: I hope that Carter did not misuse this knowledge later?

RINEKE: Well, not intentionally, but accidentally he let slip to Begin that he had received such a letter from Sadat, even if he did not spill the beans about its precise contents to Begin. After that, Begin, who was a savvy negotiator, started to offer inconsequential concessions and to expect large concessions from Egypt, and Carter never caught on that Begin was pushing him to move in the direction of Sadat's fallback position. In addition, Begin took care to make it common knowledge that the Knesset would never accept an Israeli concession on Palestinian self-government on the West bank and the Gaza strip, and after that the whole issue was more or less left out of the negotiation.

JAN: I suppose that Sadat never caught on?

RINEKE: No, he did not, and neither did the rest of the world, until quite recent analyses. The way that the Sinai issue was resolved by giving it back to Egypt while demilitarizing it, was even presented as a prime example of good 'win-win' negotiation in handbooks such as *Getting to Yes* by Ury and his Harvard colleagues. I could show our public some epistemic formulas summing up the situation: Carter knew that Sadat was prepared to make a concession on that issue ($K_C p$), and Begin knew that Carter knew ($K_B K_C p$), but Sadat didn't know that Begin knew that Carter knew ($\neg K_S K_B K_C p$).

JAN: Will you also introduce possible worlds semantics in the lecture?

RINEKE: Definitely, maybe first starting with a simpler example, such as the model with two states illustrating that our NIAS fellow Anne-Marie doesn't know whether it is raining right now in Damascus.

JAN: Then you could go on with a model of something more complicated, such as the wise persons puzzle.

RINEKE: That's a good idea. I'll tell them that there are two wise persons, Abelard (A) and Heloise (H). It is publicly known to everyone that there are three hats: two red ones and one white one. The king puts a hat on the head of each of the two wise persons, who cannot see their own hat but can see the other person's hat (and they both know this).

JAN: This is all easily captured by a Kripke model.

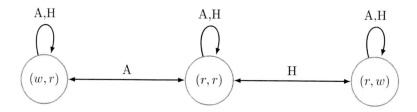

RINEKE: That's right. Then I'll go on with the story: the king asks Abelard and Heloise sequentially if they know the color of the hat on their own head. The first person, Abelard, says that he does not know; the second person, Heloise, says that she knows.

I'll show the model after Abelard's admission of ignorance, and explain how cutting away accessibility arrows corresponds to eliminating ignorance:

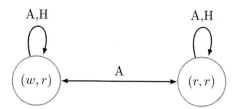

JAN: I think by this point the public should be able to derive the color of Heloise's hat.

RINEKE: I will do my best for that! After introducing the possible worlds semantics for common knowledge, I will tell the public something about people's cognitive limits in reasoning about other people's knowledge and ignorance, that I told you about before [92, 238].

JAN: Let us now go back to the issue of public and private information, and finally to ignorance as bliss.

RINEKE: There is a saying "The innocent have nothing to fear", suggesting that only those with criminal intentions should worry about personal information getting public.

JAN: I don't know where you got that from, but I think it is very dangerous. The distinction between the public and the private sphere is fundamental in Western democracies. It is also in the Universal Declaration of Human Rights, in article 12. I looked it up.

> No one shall be subjected to arbitrary interference with his privacy, family, home or correspondence, nor to attacks upon his honour and reputation. Everyone has the right to the protection of the law against such interference or attacks.

I take it that an attack on privacy is an attempt at finding out facts about my private sphere that I choose to keep out of public view. Lines between the public and private spheres are drawn differently in different countries. Those who have lived in the UK know that even British quality newspapers publish stories about naughty vicars. Dirty stories about public figures do appear in the Dutch press as well, but usually not in the quality papers.

RINEKE: In some countries individual privacy may conflict with freedom of speech laws. Such laws may require public disclosure of information which would be considered private in other countries and cultures.

JAN: Let's talk about procedures for preserving anonymity and privacy, then. Sending emails without cc:s (possibly with encryption). Or: Sending letters in closed envelopes (maybe with a seal). Such procedures are meant to keep the contents of the messages private. Third parties should remain ignorant of the message contents.

RINEKE: Another example is discreetly finding out if you share a secret with someone, without disclosing the secret if you are not. The other party should not find out the secret if she does not already know it.

JAN: That's all rather run of the mill. A more sinister example would be organizing a secret society on a need-to-know basis. This is meant to prevent the membership list of the society from becoming common knowledge. Even members should remain (partly) ignorant about who are their fellow members.

RINEKE: Here is an example that our NIAS audience is very familiar with. The reviewing process of scientific papers is meant to preserve anonymity. Authors should remain ignorant of the identity of the reviewer, in the interest of objectivity.

> **Dr A:** "By the way, were you one of the reviewers of my paper?"
>
> **Dr B:** "I am sorry, but I think we should not discuss this matter. Maybe I was, maybe I was not. I am not going to tell you, for I believe in anonymity of reviewing."
>
> **Dr C, who actually was not a reviewer:** "Well, if I had been I would of course not have been allowed to tell you. But in fact I was not."
>
> **Dr D, who actually was a reviewer:** "No, I did not review your paper."
>
> **Dr D to Dr B:** "In fact I did review that crap, but of course I couldn't tell poor Dr A."

FIGURE 2.

JAN: Anonymous reviewing has a long tradition. I would like to talk about the dangers of compromising the anonymity of reviewing. Here is my slide (Figure 2).

RINEKE: I guess the moral of the story would be that it is really hard to preserve anonymity. You shouldn't even tell your colleagues that you did *not* review their paper, as Dr C innocently does. I wish all of us were Dr. B's ...

JAN: But the need for privacy protection has increased enormously in the electronic communication age. It should be possible to anonymously cast an electronic vote. The software should be designed in such a way that others should not be able to detect your vote.

RINEKE: Modern software designs can even do better: It is possible to anonymously cast a receipt-free vote. The idea is that not only should others not be able to detect your vote, you should not be able to prove your vote. The vote is kept private even when the voter wishes to reveal it. This property is required in a setting with vote-buyers or coercers, where the voter might be tempted or forced to reveal his vote.

JAN: Privacy protection is big business these days: there is no shortage of programs for hiding my identity when I surf on the Internet: Anonymizer, IDecide, Disappearing, Hushmail, Zip Lip, Zero Knowledge, ... All these programs routinely use public key encryption, by the way.

RINEKE: We should explain to the public how that works.

JAN: Yes, that is a nice challenge. Suppose I tell them that 40285327 is the product of two primes, and challenge them to produce these primes. Let us say I allow them the use of a pocket calculator. I am not going to hand out calculators, of course, but it should not be difficult to convince them that this is a hard task.

RINEKE: You should list some attempts at solutions, and explain why the outcomes of the trial attempts do not yield information that can be used to improve the guesses.

JAN: Yes, let us say I give them some calculation results:

$$\frac{40285327}{7} = 5755046.71428571$$

$$\frac{40285327}{509} = 79146.025540275$$

$$\frac{40285327}{5333} = 7553.97093568348$$

$$\frac{40285327}{5347} = 7534.19244436132$$

RINEKE: Of course, you will have to explain to them that the four numbers 7, 509, 5333, and 5347 are all primes. More generally, you have to tell them that there are reasonably efficient ways of finding out whether very large numbers are primes.

JAN: Yes, of course. And finally I tell them that 7879 and 5113 are primes, and I demonstrate to them how easy it is to calculate their product:

$$
\begin{array}{r}
7879 \\
5113 \quad \times \\
\hline
23637 \\
78790 \\
787900 \\
39395000 \quad + \\
\hline
40285327
\end{array}
$$

RINEKE: That should drive home the moral that multiplication of two large prime numbers is easy, but finding the prime factors of a large number is very difficult. No known method for finding the prime factors of a number is substantially better than trial and error.

---

1. Choose two large random prime numbers p and q,

2. Compute $n = pq$.

3. Compute the totient $\varphi(n)$ of n.

   This is the number of positive integers i with $i \leq n$ and $\gcd(i, n) = 1$ (i co-prime to n).

   From p, q prime it follows that $\varphi(n) = (p - 1)(q - 1)$.

   Example: $\varphi(15) = 8$, for $1, 2, 4, 7, 8, 11, 13$, and 14 are co-prime to 15.

4. Choose an integer e with $1 < e < \varphi(n)$ and e co-prime to $\varphi(n)$.

   Release e as the public key exponent.

5. Compute d to satisfy $de = 1 + k\varphi(n)$ for some integer k. I.e., $de = 1 \pmod{\varphi(n)}$.

   Keep d as the private key exponent.

FIGURE 3.

JAN: I could flash a slide (Figure 3) with the RSA (Rivest, Shamir, Adleman) algorithm for public/private key generation [197].

RINEKE: It is not necessary to explain every detail. But the slide makes clear that as long as p and q remain secret, it does no harm to make n and e public.

JAN: I will just give an example of how this is used. Alice transmits her public key (n, e) to Bob and keeps the private key d secret. Bob then wishes to send message M to Alice. First he turns m into a number smaller than n. Next he computes cipher c given by $c = m^e \pmod{n}$ and transmits c to Alice. Alice can recover m from c by using her private key d, as follows: $m = c^d \pmod{n}$. From m, Alice can recover the original message M.

RINEKE: The main point about public key cryptography, and the reason why it works so well, is that it is asymmetric.

JAN: There is a nice analogy to explain this: the simile of a padlock. Anyone can lock it, but only someone with the key can unlock it. If Bob has an open padlock and Bob knows that Alice is the only one with a key to it, Bob can send a secure message to Alice by putting the message into a box, locking the box with the padlock, and sending the locked box to Alice. For locking an open padlock you don't need the key, remember.

RINEKE: That certainly explains why sending around public keys can do no harm. It is like sending about open padlocks, with a message on each padlock about who has the key to it. You should also explain how public key encryption can be used for authentication.

JAN: You mean, digital signatures? Unfortunately, this is where the padlock analogy breaks down. Digital signatures depend on the fact that the public key and the private key are inverses of each other. So a message encrypted with a private key can be decrypted with the corresponding public key. If you know that I am the only one who has the private key, then you can check that the encrypted message "This is my digital signature. Regards, Jan" really originates with me. Simply apply my public key to it and check if the expected plaintext comes out.

RINEKE: But you have to be careful. This explanation may still confuse people. You have to make clear that what matters is that a message encoded with your private key can be decoded *only* with your public key. No other key will fit.

JAN: That's right. Your conclusion that the message must come from me depends on this.

RINEKE: And on my assumption that your private key has not fallen into the wrong hands, of course. I suppose you could go on with explaining the effects of secret messages by showing the effects on Kripke models.

JAN: Yes, I have slides for this. Suppose p is a secret: Alice knows p, but Bob and Carol do not. They do not even suspect that Alice knows.

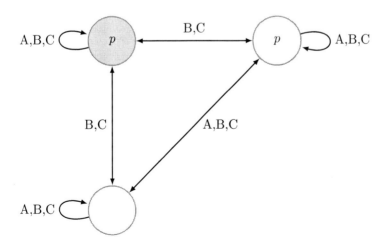

RINEKE: Now the audience will certainly ask 'Why does this look so much more complicated?'

JAN: Yes, I will have to explain that the picture not only models the fact that Alice knows that p, but also that Bob and Carol do not know whether Alice knows or not. Bob and Carol cannot distinguish the actual situation (pictured in grey) from a situation where p is true but where Alice does not know this (the situation on the right in the picture) or from a situation where p is false but Alice does not know this (the situation at the bottom in the picture).

RINEKE: And I suspect that the situation gets even more complicated when Alice tells Bob the secret?

JAN: Indeed, it does. For now Carol is the only one who does not know p, but Carol still does not know that the other two know. Here is a picture. This time I have left out the loop arrows at the individual nodes.

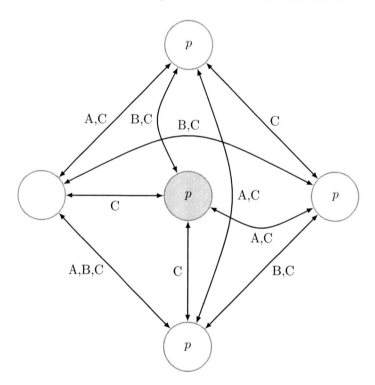

RINEKE: Wow. How did you manage to construct that?

JAN: Well, it is a redrawing of a picture that was generated by my DEMO epistemic modeling tool [85]. Here is the original picture. This will give the audience a chance to apply what they learnt from you.

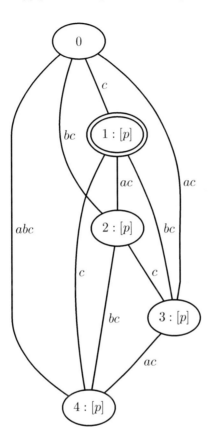

RINEKE: There is also the well-known puzzle about a situation where neither A nor B knows whether p. Then they meet; B asks whether p, and A truthfully answers, 'Yes, I know'.

JAN: You mean the case where A has the additional piece of information that if p is not the case, then B knows that not p? The case of the chair of the program committee who has been told by his secretary that all authors of rejected papers have been notified. When Doctor B meets Professor A, then B's question 'Has my paper been accepted?' reveals to A that the answer must be 'Yes', for A reasons that otherwise B would have known. Here is a picture:

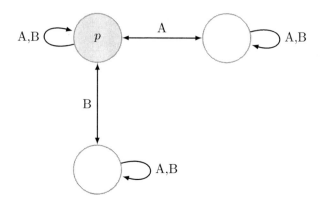

RINEKE: Another example you should certainly mention is the protocol of the dining cryptographers [46].

JAN: Chaum's famous protocol to protect privacy. Yes, I am sure they will love it. Three cryptographers are eating out. At the end of the dinner, they are informed that the bill has been paid, either by one of them, or by NSA (the National Security Agency). They want to find out whether NSA paid or not. They also want to respect each other's rights to privacy: In case one of them has paid the bill, her identity should not be revealed to the two others.

RINEKE: Why is it important not to use a trusted outsider or a ballot box?

JAN: Methodological reasons. How can one convince oneself that a protocol is secure? The computer science approach is to make very strong assumptions about the presence of bad guys and about their capabilities. The use of a trusted outsider makes a protocol vulnerable. Traffic over an electronic network can reveal information, so it has to be assumed that all conversations can be overheard. Chaum's proposal demonstrates that the thing still can be done.

RINEKE: I remember that each cryptographer tosses a coin with each of his neighbors, with the result of the toss remaining hidden from the third person. You can do a demonstration for the audience, with real coins hidden behind menus.

JAN: That should make it easy to explain why each cryptographer has a choice between two public announcements: That the coins that she has observed agree or that they disagree. This is a public statement about private information: the others both hear it, but they cannot check the truth of the statement. And then the protocol is simply this:

- If she has not paid the bill she will say that they agree if the coins are the same and that they disagree otherwise;

- if she has paid the bill she will say the opposite: she will say that they agree if in fact they are different and she will say that they disagree if in fact they are the same.

RINEKE: But why does this solve the problem?

JAN: We should let the audience find out, really. But that may be a bit tough on them. OK, note that as far as coin agreement is concerned there are just two possible situations. Either all coins agree (all heads or all tails), or two of the coins agree and the third one is different. Now assume nobody is lying about the agreement of the two coins she can see. Then if all coins are the same there will be no statements of disagreement, and if one of the coins is different there will be two statements of disagreement. So, if no one has picked up the bill there is an even number of disagreement statements. If one of the three is lying about what she observes, one of the statements will change. So if one of the three paid the bill, there will be an odd number of disagreement statements.

RINEKE: It is clear why this calls for an epistemic analysis. To show that the procedure is secure one should show that the identity of the payer really is kept secret.

JAN: I prepared a slide for that. I analyzed the situation with the DEMO model checker [85], as follows. I started out from the assumption that no one knew anything, and where this ignorance was common knowledge. Next, I updated with the public announcement of 'at most one cryptographer paid', so that this also became common knowledge.

RINEKE: Yes, for public announcements of factual information always generate common knowledge. We discussed these matters before (p. 119).

JAN: Next, I updated with the information that every participant knew whether she had paid or not. This is obvious, but it has to be spelled out. Next, update with the results of the coin tosses, update with appropriate group announcements of the results of the coin tosses, and update with appropriate public announcements about coin (dis)agreement, and Bob's your uncle.

RINEKE: Then you show the picture.

JAN: Here is my slide (Figure 4). Of course, I will have to explain that q_i means that coin i shows heads, and p_j that participant j has paid the bill.

When I discussed the protocol some weeks ago, in a talk for an ILLC work-

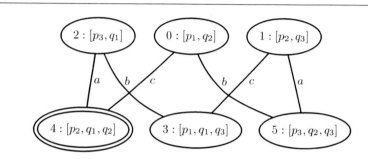

- Cryptographer 2 paid, coins $1, 2$ show heads.
- $\neg K_a p_2, \neg K_c p_2$
- $C_{\{a,b,c\}}(\neg K_a p_2 \wedge \neg K_c p_2)$.
- $K_b(q_1 \wedge q_2 \wedge \neg q_3)$

FIGURE 4.

shop in Amsterdam, Valentin Goranko made an instant proposal for a version of the protocol that could be used to check how many out of N dining cryptographers have made contributions to the bill, without revealing their identities. Let someone start by whispering a number M larger than N into the ear of her left-hand neighbor. The neighbor then whispers a number to his left-hand neighbor, and so on. The ones who did not pay pass on the same number they heard, but the ones who paid increase the number by one. After one round, the initiator of the protocol hears the number K, and she knows that $K - M$ people contributed to the bill. In the course of a second round everyone finds out, by comparing the number they heard the first time with the number they heard the second time.

RINEKE: Brilliant.

JAN: But not quite as good as Chaum's original proposal. Assuming that every conversation can be overheard this is an insecure procedure.

RINEKE: This audience will certainly be very interested in social networks and coordinated action. We should make sure we have enough time to discuss that as well.

JAN: I have prepared an example based on a nice description from [47]. Here are two social networks, where the individual members think the same and have the same intentions, but where the results are radically different.

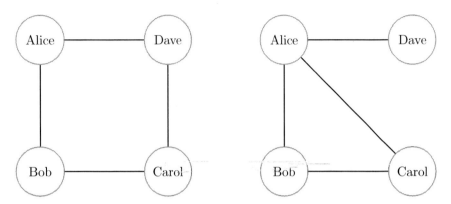

The links picture the communication channels. In each picture, everyone thinks: "If I know for sure that at least two other people are going to take action, I will join in." In each picture, everyone communicates this intention to their neighbors.

RINEKE: And then the point is that it makes a difference whether I am in touch with the neighbors of my neighbors or not.

JAN: Indeed. Because knowing that my neighbor will join if at least two other people join is not enough *for me* to be sure that he will join in. He can be sure about *me*. But how about his *other* neighbors?

RINEKE: So in fact, in the situation on the left no one joins in, and in the situation on the right, where three people have links to the neighbors of their neighbors, these three people join in. Shouldn't we also mention examples where we don't yet have a full analysis? Otherwise, they might think that we have exhausted our subject at the end of our project.

JAN: How about Olmert's nuclear slip-up? This is really puzzling to me. Here is the relevant quote from the Internet (Figure 5).

Clearly, even if everyone has individual knowledge that φ, public announcement of φ still has an epistemic effect. But that was not quite the case here. Twenty years ago, an Israeli dissident, Mordechai Vanunu, gave full disclosure of the Israeli nuclear program. This then became public knowledge, we must assume. The pictures he took were in the *London Sunday Times*, in 1986. In Vananu's own words, he was sentenced to 18 years in jail for "revealing something that everyone knew already"—or in our parlance, for turning general knowledge, "everyone knows", into common knowledge. Still, this seems to be not quite the same as an official public statement by

> Ehud Olmert, the Israeli Prime Minister, faced calls for his resignation today after admitting — in an apparent slip of the tongue — that Israel has got nuclear weapons.
>
> But Israeli officials tried to push the cat back into the bag, denying that Mr Olmert had made any such admission and falling back on the Jewish state's policy of "nuclear ambiguity".
>
> Widely considered the Middle East's sole nuclear power, Israel has for decades refused to confirm or deny whether it possesses the atomic bomb. Mr Olmert appeared to break that taboo in an interview with a German television station as he began a visit to Berlin.
>
> TimesOnline, 12 December 2006

FIGURE 5.

the Israeli prime minister that 'Israel is a nuclear power'.

RINEKE: And what is even more puzzling is how they think they can wiggle out of it again, by denying that Olmert had said what he said. Can public exposure be undone? By erasing the information from the minds of those who heard the interview?

JAN: That's a puzzle for sure.

RINEKE: I am curious what our colleagues from the humanities and social sciences will have to say about all those intriguing dilemmas that we discussed today.

JAN: Me too. You know, I've begun to look forward to our farewell lecture and the discussions with our NIAS fellows.

RINEKE: Only a pity that it is really meant as a farewell, and that our project will be over soon. There's still so much we could do! *(Looks wistfully.)*

Chapter 14
On Collective Rational Action

Jan van Eijck

A sociologist is visiting, on a mission to discuss the problem of collective rational action. The other participants are our familiar protagonists: logician, computer scientist, philosopher. Two other project visitors, an economist and a game theorist, have joined the discussion out of curiosity. The computer scientist has brought his laptop, with wireless Internet connection.

SOCIOLOGIST: Nice project you've got going here guys. A pity your project description fails to mention sociology as a relevant discipline. After all, the problem of collective rationality is a key issue in my field.

COMPUTER SCIENTIST: When the project description talks about "the social sciences", it is also meant to encompass sociology, of course. We are very glad you are visiting us, and you're most welcome to join our discussion.

PHILOSOPHER: The problem of collective rationality has been a key issue in philosophy for more than two millennia. Aristotle discusses it at length, in the *Politics*.

COMPUTER SCIENTIST: *(Looking at his laptop:)* Wait, let me google for a quote. Ah, here it is, from Book II of the *Politics*. *(Points at the screen:)*

> For that which is common to the greatest number has the least care bestowed upon it. Every one thinks chiefly of his own, hardly at all of the common interest; and only when he is himself concerned as an individual. For besides other considerations, everybody is more inclined to neglect the duty which he expects another to fulfill; as in families many attendants are often less useful than a few [4, paragraph 403, Book II].

SOCIOLOGIST: Why, that is the earliest reference to the bystander effect that I've ever heard of! This effect has been empirically studied in the late sixties [56]: solitary people usually intervene in case of an emergency, whereas a large group of bystanders may fail to intervene—everyone thinks that someone else is bound to have called the emergency hotline already, or that someone else is bound to be more qualified to give medical help.

LOGICIAN: The most dramatic instance I've read about was in an article by Pacuit, Parikh and Cogan, which provided a logical analysis of how one's obligations depend on one's knowledge and vice versa. They applied this idea to the intriguing case of Kitty Genovese, who was stabbed to death in 1964 while 38 neighbors watched from their windows but did nothing [173].

SOCIOLOGIST: Actually, three social psychologists have recently shown that this Kitty Genovese story is not supported by fact, but it is more like a parable [145]. Nonetheless, I think it remains an important warning.

GAME THEORIST: Whatever the case may be, the more general problem that Aristotle mentions has made it to the game theory textbooks as "The Tragedy of the Commons", after an essay by Garrett Hardin [113]. Hardin, who died in 2003, was a microbiologist and ecologist, and "The Tragedy of the Commons" is his most well-known essay. Still well worth reading, by the way.

SOCIOLOGIST: Yes, I know the story. If I'm not mistaken, it goes like this. Imagine a village with village greens open to all. Each farmer will try to keep as many cattle—let's say goats—on the common meadows as possible. As long as the numbers of farmers and goats stay low in relation to the carrying capacity of the land, this arrangement works fine. But there will come a time of prosperity: farmers and goats start to multiply. At some point each extra goat will lead to a marked deterioration of the greens. Still the mechanism of individual rationality will act as an encouragement for farmers to keep adding goats.

GAME THEORIST: That's right. Here's the tragedy in a picture [103]. *(Draws on the whiteboard:)*

Value of grazing
an extra goat
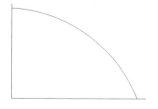

Total number of goats

PHILOSOPHER: How does that explain what goes on?

GAME THEORIST: On the far left you see the situation where there is still plenty, on the far right the situation where the meadows are completely destroyed. The picture shows that as we move to the right, the detrimental effect of adding extra goats keeps increasing. The value of each individual goat gets less and less, until it reaches zero.

COMPUTER SCIENTIST: If you want a modern version of the problem, look at the emission of carbon dioxide into the atmosphere. The Fourth IPCC Assessment report is available as a draft on the Internet. Listen to what they say:

> The climate system tends to be overused (excessive GHG concentrations) because of its natural availability as a resource whose access is open to all free of charge. In contrast, climate protection tends to be underprovided. In general, the benefits of avoided climate change are spatially indivisible, freely available to all (non-excludability), irrespective of whether one is contributing to the regime costs or not. As regime benefits by one individual (nation) do not diminish their availability to others (non-rivalry), it is difficult to enforce binding commitments on the use of the climate system [130, 129]. This may result in "free riding", a situation in which mitigation costs are borne by some individuals (nations) while others (the "free riders") succeed in evading them but still enjoy the benefits of the mitigation commitments of the former [199, p. 102].

PHILOSOPHER: What do they mean by GHG concentrations?

COMPUTER SCIENTIST: Green house gasses: carbon dioxide and methane. Mainly carbon dioxide, the bubbles in your Perrier water. We've started pumping it into the atmosphere in large quantities since the beginning of the industrial age, when we started burning fossil fuels in earnest. And IPCC is the International Panel on Climate Change that is trying to assess the damage.

PHILOSOPHER: But it's not really clear, yet, how dangerous this is, is it?

LOGICIAN: What do you mean, "not clear"? There's no doubt that the planet is warming. And climatologists on the IPCC agree that it is highly likely that the increased concentration of carbon dioxide causes global warming [199]. If you want to read up on the issue you should visit their website, or if you are short of time, read Marc Maslin's *Global Warming, A Very Short Introduction* [147]. Maslin also addresses what the skeptics say. Believe me, more scientific agreement than this you are not going to get.

SOCIOLOGIST: Yes, expecting every single scientist to agree would be quite unreasonable. Compare this to the question of whether smoking causes lung cancer. This is commonly accepted as scientific fact. Insurance companies use it to adjust their fees for smokers. But if I search the Internet it's not at all difficult to find mavericks who deny the connection.

PHILOSOPHER: But surely on the issue of global warming there are believers and dissidents. Al Gore's film *An Inconvenient Truth* gives a voice to the believers. A much less well-known documentary, *The Great Global Warming Swindle*, was shown on British television by Channel 4.

LOGICIAN: Please, be reasonable. Scientific opinion has gravitated to the conclusion that global warming is real, that it's man-made, and that it's dangerous. Obviously, the public does not want to hear this. So there's a huge demand for denial. And there will always be journalists, scientists and documentary makers that cater for this demand. And, to add insult to injury, right-wing political groups such as the Republican Party in the US actively promote biased media coverage of the scientific discussion about global warming [157]. In the Netherlands we have science journalist Simon Rozendaal [135]. In the US there are Fred Singer [215] and Richard Lindzen [141]. Then there is the Danish skeptical environmentalist, Bjørn Lomborg [142]. The public laps it up, of course.

COMPUTER SCIENTIST: Hang on! Singer is not a scientist but a lobbyist.

SOCIOLOGIST: And Lomborg is not denying the reality of global warming, or that it is man-made. He is skeptical about the proposed solutions. But otherwise I agree. It is only natural to prefer a comforting lie to an inconvenient truth.

LOGICIAN: It may be natural, but it ain't rational. Not long ago, in a public lecture, I mentioned global warming as an example of a phenomenon calling for collective rational action. A distinguished professor from the University of Amsterdam urged me not to worry. The earth had seen higher temperatures and greater atmospheric concentrations of carbon dioxide during the Cretaceous period, she said.

GAME THEORIST: What, a hundred million years ago? Well, the whole scene looked a lot different then. Dinosaurs may have liked it hot, but there were few mammals. If you take such a broad perspective then, indeed, we need not worry. The earth is a tough old lady, she will surely get over what we did to her, in a few million years. And given that there are so many of us it is unlikely that no humans will survive, so the human species is also not in immediate danger. But whether civilization as we know it will survive, that is a different matter [143].

LOGICIAN: Global warming is what Edward Tenner calls a revenge effect of industrialization, an unintended consequence [232]. Revenge effects are everywhere. Building new roads solves a short-term problem but generates more traffic congestion in the long run as it causes suburbia to spread. Large-scale use of antibiotics causes emergence by natural selection of antibiotic-resistant bacteria. RSI is a revenge effect of office automation. And so on. Only this time the consequences might be more serious than usual.

COMPUTER SCIENTIST: *(Listening to the conversation while crawling the Internet:)* Yes, I found it! The Royal Society, probably the most respected and certainly the oldest learned organization in the world, issued a press release to respond to *The Great Global Warming Swindle*. This is what Martin Rees, their president, said:

> Global temperature is increasing. This warming threatens the future health and wellbeing of many millions of people throughout the world. This is especially true of those in the developing countries who are the least able to adapt and who are likely to be the worst affected. Many factors play a part in global warming but there is significant scientific evidence that greenhouse gas emissions, particularly CO_2, are responsible for most of the temperature rise. If present trends continue the projected climate change will be far greater than that already experienced. Greenhouse gas emissions are something that we can and must take action on.

The Royal Society. Press release, 9 March 2007

LOGICIAN: So there you have it. Do we want to side with the scientists, or with the mavericks? That seems to be the question.

PHILOSOPHER: I beg your pardon. Professor Hendrik Tennekes, former head of the Royal Netherlands Meteorological Institute (KNMI), is not a maverick. He is deeply worried about the arrogance of climate scientists, who erroneously think they can predict the climate [166].

COMPUTER SCIENTIST: Tennekes has turned against KNMI. He calls his former colleagues "civil servants" who are telling their politician-masters what they want to hear.

PHILOSOPHER: Well, he is in a position to speak his mind, isn't he? I mean, he has retired, there is nothing at stake for him. His former KNMI colleagues have to keep their institute running. They know that the policy makers that provide their funding want climate forecasts, so it would not be prudent for them to admit that their computer models are flaky or fake. On the other hand, the fact that we are breaking weather record after weather record should worry Tennekes too. The winter of 2007 was the mildest one in the last three centuries [235].

LOGICIAN: I am not sure what Tennekes is playing at. He may have an axe to grind. He claims he was forced to retire because of his unfashionable views on the topic of climate change [236].

COMPUTER SCIENTIST: There have been attempts to discredit the scientific findings, by lobby groups indirectly linked to Exxon-Mobile [154, 156]. Not a new trick. Philip Morris tried the same before, to discredit a report on the dangers of passive smoking [156].

LOGICIAN: Martin Rees has urged scientists to get more involved in public debate, to speak out against minority "maverick" views [164]. Only those who understand how science works—and I suppose that includes all of us— can appreciate the difference between peer-reviewed papers in top-ranking scientific journals and mere pamphlets on the Internet. We are skilled in distinguishing false from true in scientific matters, and I believe that this skill comes with responsibilities. We can see that there is a consensus on climate change. The scientific consensus is that there is global warming, that it is to a large extent anthropogenic, and that it is dangerous.

PHILOSOPHER: Maybe this whole discussion about climate change misses the point. Nobody can deny that we are putting great strain on our living environment. Or that we should limit our use of fossil fuels. Even if CO_2 in the air is not a problem, the supply of fossil fuels is limited, and our economy is hooked on it. And this addiction creates huge political problems, because the main natural gas and oil reserves happen to be in politically unstable regions.

SOCIOLOGIST: Or maybe regions where enormous fuel reserves are detected have a tendency to become politically unstable because dominant powers move in from elsewhere to get a share of the pie.

PHILOSOPHER: The Arab peninsula was a backward region well before oil was detected there. And when huge natural gas reserves where found in the Netherlands and Norway, this did not cause any destabilization, or did it?

SOCIOLOGIST: Never mind. Jared Diamond suggests that the collapse of a civilization always has something to do with mismanagement of natural resources [62]. The environment is our common meadow, and it is about to be depleted. We are at the limits of growth, and the public doesn't want to hear it.

ECONOMIST: *(With a wry smile:)* Only economists and fools believe in continued exponential growth in a finite world, right?

COMPUTER SCIENTIST: That's completely right, yes. *(With a side glance at the sociologist:)* I believe the socialization procedures for social scientists are different from those for computer scientists. For sure, every first year economy course has an explanation of exponential growth at some point, and a story about what the prisoner's dilemma predicts for cases where individual interests are at odds with the common interest.

ECONOMIST: The students quickly understand which side their bread is buttered on: Future employers are not a bit interested in limits to the growth of their market share.

LOGICIAN: In the fields of logic and computer science the situation is dramatically different. We also explain to our students what an exponential function is, but with us the message is that they should never ever forget. If an algorithm is exponential in the size of the input, then this is a fundamental limitation that no investment in hardware will cure. Different socialization, indeed.

COMPUTER SCIENTIST: Formal sciences have an additional benefit. They prepare you for the view that there are insights that are "for all eternity", so to speak. Expressive formal languages are undecidable: You can use them to state questions that no computer can answer. No computer scientist in his right mind would ever dream of wanting to refute Turing and Church. Sociologists seem to think that because their subject matter is empirical, any insights in social reality have to be refutable by further evidence.

SOCIOLOGIST: Social phenomena have both empirical and formal aspects. I do not deny that a mathematical look at social reality might reveal eternal truths. In fact, one of my favorite books gives examples of this. *(Shows and opens a copy of a book by Mancur Olson, [170]:)* Let me quote:

> But it is not in fact true that the idea that groups will act in their self-interest follows logically from the premise of rational and self-interested behavior. It does not follow, because all of the individuals in a group would gain if they achieved their group objective, that they would act to achieve that objective, even if they were all rational and self-interested. Indeed unless the number of individuals in a group is quite small, or unless there is coercion or some other special device to make individuals act in their common interest, rational, self-interested individuals will not act to achieve their common or group interests.

> [170, p. 2]

COMPUTER SCIENTIST: Ahem—less optimistic about the emergence of an optimal outcome than Adam Smith's famous invisible hand, the hidden mechanism that fuses actions motivated by individual interests into a self-regulating social mechanism. Another well-known quote that should be easy to find on the Internet. *Smith benevolence butcher* should be enough for Google. Yes, there it is:

> It is not from the benevolence of the butcher, the brewer or the baker that we expect our dinner, but from their regard to their own interest. We address ourselves not to their humanity but to their self-love, and never talk to them of our necessities but of their advantages. Nobody but a beggar chooses to depend chiefly upon the benevolence of their fellow-citizens [216, Book 1, Chapter II].

ECONOMIST: Smith never wanted to defend self-interested behavior; he just wanted to argue that it is not necessarily bad. You may care to know that Smith also wrote a *Theory of Moral Sentiments* [217], where he extols the virtue of selflessness. Also, when he died, most of his wealth went to charity. Hardly the act of a selfish man.

GAME THEORIST: In game theory, as in economics I suppose, maximization of individual interest is used as a means of abstraction. It turns out that one can explain quite a lot about human behavior by assuming that every individual is pursuing his own interest. What that says about human nature is beside the point for now. But what is interesting, is that the theory of individual rationality sometimes yields funny results. Most game theory books have a chapter on the prisoner's dilemma. See for example [103] or [225]. The dilemma illustrates that perfect individual rationality may lead to a non-optimal outcome. Should one keep silent or betray the other, that is the question. *(Draws on the whiteboard:)*

	B Keeps Silent	B Betrays
A Keeps Silent	six months in jail for each	10 years in jail for A B goes free
A Betrays	A goes free 10 years in jail for B	2 years in jail for each

SOCIOLOGIST: That's consistent with what Olson has to say.

COMPUTER SCIENTIST: Yes, we all know the example. Betrayal pays off, whatever happens. Suppose I am prisoner A. If B keeps silent I get six months if I also keep silent, and I am free if I betray. So it is in my interest to betray. And if B starts talking, I get ten years if I keep silent, but only two years if I also talk. So again it is in my interest to betray. But what is the big deal? Why are you guys going on and on about this?

LOGICIAN: I suppose we should first establish why this is a dilemma.

GAME THEORIST: Usually, in strategic situations, it is important to predict what others will do. Not so here: Whatever B does, it is always in A's interest to betray. This shows that betrayal is what is called a dominant strategy. You are *always* better off by betraying. The other guy reasons as you do. He will also betray you.

LOGICIAN: So here is the dilemma: By both acting rationally, namely by defecting, the two prisoners are worse off than if they had both stayed silent.

GAME THEORIST: That's correct. The prisoner's dilemma is a non zero-sum game where defection yields a Nash equilibrium that is not an optimal solution. It is not a Pareto optimum.

COMPUTER SCIENTIST: Pareto optimum? Nash equilibrium? Can you remind us of the definitions, please?

GAME THEORIST: We discussed all these notions extensively in our discourses on Social choice theory and on Game theory, logic, and rational choice. But as a reminder, a *Pareto optimum* is an outcome that cannot be improved upon without hurting at least one player. A *Nash equilibrium* is a set of strategies (one for each player) such that no player has an incentive to unilaterally change her action.

COMPUTER SCIENTIST: I see. The point is that to get at a better outcome, both prisoners have to change strategies at the same time, and there is no other way.

GAME THEORIST: OK. Now let's change this to an $N + 1$ prisoner game. I am in prison. There are N other prisoners. They all, like me, have the choice between keeping silent or talking, to incriminate the others in order to get a lighter sentence. I do not know what they are going to do. What do I do? *(Draws on the whiteboard again:)*

	Number of Others Keeping Silent										
	0	1	2	3	4	5	6	7	8	9	10
I keep silent	−2	−1	0	1	2	3	4	5	6	7	8
I betray	−1	0	1	2	3	4	5	6	7	8	9

Look at the picture, which gives the case for $N = 10$. Whatever the others do, it is *always* in my interest to betray. The more of the others keep silent, the better for me. I suppose the question is this: If *you* are in this situation, would you keep silent or talk?

COMPUTER SCIENTIST: Can we assume there are no repercussions?

GAME THEORIST: Assume that the other prisoners will never know that it is because of *you* that they are serving these long jail sentences.

COMPUTER SCIENTIST: Then I would betray them.

PHILOSOPHER: Shame on you.

COMPUTER SCIENTIST: Why make this a moral issue? *"Es ist eine Krankheit, das schlechte Gewissen, das unterliegt keinem Zweifel, aber eine Krankheit, wie die Schwangerschaft eine Krankheit ist."*

PHILOSOPHER: You are quoting Nietzsche, aren't you? "Bad conscience is an illness, there is no doubt about it, but an illness in the same way that pregnancy is an illness." That is from the *Genealogy of Morals* [165, p. 19]. What Nietzsche is trying to say is that it is others who instill a conscience in us.

COMPUTER SCIENTIST: Like a pregnancy, a conscience is at least partially caused from outside. And it is always a good idea to try and find out in whose interest the moral behavior is that others have instilled in me. In the $N + 1$ prisoner's dilemma it is in my interest to instill a conscience in the other prisoners, so they all stay silent, and I get maximum benefit from betraying them all.

PHILOSOPHER: There is also an evolutionary argument against moral behavior. Those without conscience have an advantage if they convince others to act on their conscience. It increases their likelihood of survival. And the wimps that let themselves be talked into following their conscience are at a disadvantage with respect to those without one.

SOCIOLOGIST: This would predict that moral behavior has to die out, in the long run. But does it? Not what we see, is it?

PHILOSOPHER: How can anyone tell? Maybe all we see is an appearance of morality. Of course, in the struggle for survival it is an advantage to *appear* moral and altruistic. As Machiavelli aptly remarked, many people live by appearances anyway, and if one wants to have one's way with people it is wise to take this fact of life into account.

GAME THEORIST: Anyway, in Garrett Hardin's essay [113] there is a nice analysis of the moral appeal as a double bind. A double bind is a contradiction between an overt and a hidden message. In the case of the tragedy of the commons, the overt message is: You are bad, bad, bad if you thrive at the expense of the community. But the hidden message is quite different.

COMPUTER SCIENTIST: You are silly, silly, silly, if you let yourself be talked into carrying the burden of others.

PHILOSOPHER: The upshot of this seems to be this. When hearing a moral appeal, find out who is talking. In particular, find out whether they have an interest at stake.

COMPUTER SCIENTIST: Never believe anyone who has something to sell.

LOGICIAN: That rules out a lot of people, and maybe too many. But there is a Dutch saying that may help: *"Als de vos de passie preekt, boer pas op je kippen."* When the fox takes up preaching, farmer watch your chickens.

ECONOMIST: How does one recognize foxes?

LOGICIAN: Simple. Their moral appeals are always aimed at preventing the institution of a binding regulation. Binding regulations would go against their interests.

PHILOSOPHER: That's right. Foxes are always in favor of giving both foxes and chickens free range.

SOCIOLOGIST: But now we are faced with an empirical problem. According to the game-theoretic analysis we have seen so far, behavior that is in the collective interest will not easily emerge. In many cases that is what we actually see. In the early Middle Ages, the farmers in West European coastal villages were quite ineffective at fighting off the Nordic invaders. Once the Erics and Olavs had disembarked, they should have been at a disadvantage against a well-organized collective of determined farmers. But for a long, long time these farmers did not get their act together.

GAME THEORIST: Well, that is only in accordance with the findings of game theory, isn't it?

PHILOSOPHER: I don't agree that the Vikings were at a disadvantage. Just imagine: they arrived in ships that needed at least twenty men to handle, in heavy weather. Cooperation was of the essence, and "One for all and all for one" must have been natural to them. Not so for the farmers, who had perhaps only learnt to be surly and mind their own business.

SOCIOLOGIST: Game theory predicts that *no* collective ever gets their act together. But this is contradicted by what we see in actual life. What we see is that suddenly the collective structures emerge that allow successful coping with emergencies. How can we explain that this happens?

LOGICIAN: What is needed is emergence of common knowledge and common intention. The issue of common knowledge we have discussed at length already (see Chapter 8). The theme of collective action is quite hot in theories of multi-agent interaction these days. In [74] there is a nice overview.

SOCIOLOGIST: But let me ask again. How do common knowledge and collective intention arise in the first place?

LOGICIAN: As I said, we have talked about common knowledge before. Basically, there are just two ways: public announcement and common experience. Mind you, public announcement is also a kind of common experience. All of us hear the same proclamation, and we are aware of the fact that we are all hearing it.

SOCIOLOGIST: And collective intentions?

LOGICIAN: Collective intentions have a clear motivational component, so a public announcement or a common experience does not suffice. After all, a collective intention among a team means that its members not only intend to do their best to achieve the goal as part of the team, but they also need a mutual intention, which means that they all intend that they all intend that they all intend ... and so on, ad infinitum, to achieve the goal together. Often a team leader will need to persuade each individual potential team member, in order to create such a heavy-duty mutual intention. After that, the team leader can indeed use a public announcement to create a common knowledge or common belief about this mutual intention. Finally, after both these kinds of communication, the collective intention is in place and the team can start to work [63].

SOCIOLOGIST: Communication and ostentation certainly play a role in the emergence of collective social structures. The way in which the care of the poor got organized in medieval Europe is a nice example. The clergy played a role in this, and they may have liked to believe that people started to contribute to collective charities out of a moral sense instilled by the Church. But in fact what the clergy did was much more effective. They created a communication structure where everyone knew how much everyone else was contributing to poor relief. Making a contribution to the collective soon became a matter of honor. One might say that collectives come into being as a result of common knowledge and common action [228].

LOGICIAN: In modern logical theories of the effects of communication, one can study the difference in effects between private acts of communication and public events. These differences turn out to be vast. And in the logic of action, there is an agreement that effective collective action can never be the sum of individual actions. At least three ingredients seem needed: (i) common knowledge of the moral stature of those influencing the group, (ii) common knowledge of what is the interest of the group as a whole, (iii) common knowledge of the collective willingness to take action. I suppose social structures for this are all structures that foster the sense of community.

PHILOSOPHER: Some societies were much more effective at this than others. Picture the life in a Greek city state, on a festival day. The whole city would gather for a day at the theater, for three tragedies and a comedy, in a place where everyone can see that everyone is there, to be part of the same overwhelming experience. A very powerful way to shape a community and keep it together.

LOGICIAN: You are a romantic. But you are right, going to the theater is much more civilized than watching ferocious animals slaughter innocent Christians, as the Romans were fond of doing.

PHILOSOPHER: Which in turn is only slightly worse than watching hooligans disturb football matches, I suppose.

SOCIOLOGIST: It is clear that you are not great admirers of popular culture. Perhaps we should return to our main question. How does collective rational action emerge? That is not an easy one to explain. Charles Darwin himself believed he had a ready explanation [57]. He cheerfully applied the principle of natural selection to groups, assuming that groups compete just like individuals and that the features that make some groups more successful than others—altruism, courage, selfless acting in the interest of the community—were perfected through natural selection of the most successful groups. But this explanation simply cannot work. For within such communities, the free riders who make use of the spirit of self-sacrifice of others are at a huge evolutionary advantage.

GAME THEORIST: That's completely right. Modern evolutionary game theory has analyzed some interesting solutions though, which I will explain in a while [167].

COMPUTER SCIENTIST: (Who is running Google queries all the time:) Wait, wait, I have found an online version of Darwin's *Descent of Man*. Chapter 5 discusses precisely this issue. Listen, here it is:

> But it may be asked, how within the limits of the same tribe did a large number of members first become endowed with these social and moral qualities, and how was the standard of excellence raised? It is extremely doubtful whether the offspring of the more sympathetic and benevolent parents, or of those who were the most faithful to their comrades, would be reared in greater numbers than the children of selfish and treacherous parents belonging to the same tribe. He who was ready to sacrifice his life, as many a savage has been, rather than betray his comrades, would often leave no offspring to inherit his noble nature. The bravest men, who were always willing to come to the front in war, and who freely risked their lives for others, would on an average perish in larger numbers than other men. Therefore,

it hardly seems probable that the number of men gifted with such virtues, or that the standard of their excellence, could be increased through natural selection, that is, by the survival of the fittest; for we are not here speaking of one tribe being victorious over another [57, Chapter 5].

SOCIOLOGIST: *(Dryly:)* Darwin is quite eloquent in expressing the refutation of his own explanation. How does the chapter go on to refute the refutation?

COMPUTER SCIENTIST: Well, he talks about men developing foresight, and learning that giving aid commonly meant receiving aid in return. And more importantly, about successful tribes learning to use praise and blame to regulate the behavior of the tribe members.

A man who was not impelled by any deep, instinctive feeling, to sacrifice his life for the good of others, yet was roused to such actions by a sense of glory, would by his example excite the same wish for glory in other men, and would strengthen by exercise the noble feeling of admiration. He might thus do far more good to his tribe than by begetting offspring with a tendency to inherit his own high character [57, Chapter 5].

PHILOSOPHER: To me, this sounds more like cultural selection than natural selection. Surely, if both these mechanisms are at work, they have to be quite different. Darwin presents cultural selection as a kind of minor variation on natural selection. Very strange.

SOCIOLOGIST: What we are looking for is a mechanism that explains how the tragedy of the commons can be avoided. It seems to me that the Darwin quote does not provide that.

GAME THEORIST: Let me give you the common understanding in game theory. Most game theorists do not buy Darwin's account of group selection. Rather, to get out of the tragedy, they devised mechanisms that make altruism pay. Two mechanisms for that are kin altruism and reciprocal altruism. The first was eloquently defended in a famous book by George Williams [241]. It tries to explain the emergence of altruistic behavior by assuming that "altruistic genes" (genetic treats that cause cooperative behavior) favor families that have them over families that do not, on the assumption that the altruistic behavior is limited to next-of-kin. The theory of reciprocal altruism, first proposed by Robert Trivers [234], explains the emergence of collaboration because it pays off, for the individual. A game-theoretic version of this argument was later given by Robert Axelrod [9].

PHILOSOPHER: Aha, I see. You guys simply explain altruism away as a rather special kind of egoism. Immanuel Kant would have been shocked: to him, altruistic behavior emerges from application of the golden rule or categorical imperative—"treat others as you would like to be treated yourself"— a commandment of reason. For Kant, doing things because you *like* doing them, or even worse, because they serve your interest, could never be moral behavior.

GAME THEORIST: Axelrod studied a version of the prisoner's dilemma where the same two players repeatedly interact, the so-called iterated prisoner's dilemma. He even organized iterated prisoner's dilemma tournaments, where colleagues were asked to propose strategies for this game. It then turned out that a very simple strategy, tit for tat, devised by Anatol Rapoport, was the most successful [191].

SOCIOLOGIST: I suppose what makes the iterated prisoner's dilemma so different from the simple prisoner's dilemma is the fact that there are other consequences besides the immediate payoff. Other players will remember how you treated them, and can retaliate in later installments of the game. The tit for tat rules are very simple. Always collaborate, unless provoked. When provoked, retaliate immediately. Be quick to forgive.

COMPUTER SCIENTIST: That's interesting, for it neatly sums up how I handle my colleagues. I don't mind if they treat me the same, but I doubt whether that is an application of Kant's categorical imperative.

SOCIOLOGIST: If you are sure that this is your last encounter with a particular player you can get away with being selfish. People with long experience in business are understandably wary when dealing with colleagues on the brink of retirement. These guys may be tempted to play you a departure trick, knowing that you cannot get back at them.

GAME THEORIST: In modern times, binary reciprocity is just the simplest kind of helping one another. Societies thrive best if there is *generalized reciprocity*, or paying it forward: If I scratch your back, you don't need to scratch mine, as long as you scratch someone else's. Recently, Nowak and Sigmund have published interesting research on such generalized reciprocity in evolutionary game theory. It turns out that two things help generalized reciprocity to emerge: shared information and a reputation mechanism by which an agent's social score depends on whether they are free riders or are paying it forward. Agents who are known to be free riders, are not helped anymore [167].

SOCIOLOGIST: In the Netherlands, Egas and Riedl conducted interesting experiments about such "altruistic punishments" via a public goods game on the Internet, in which almost a thousand people participated. It turned out that participants dealt out many more corrective punishments when it was cheap for themselves to do so and had high impact on the free-riders, than when it was expensive and had low impact [82].

PHILOSOPHER: *(To the sociologist:)* Surely, there are alternative sociological views on the emergence of group behavior. Wasn't Emile Durkheim, the founding father of your discipline, the one who said that the idea of society is the soul of religion?

SOCIOLOGIST: *(Quoting from memory:)* *"Car on sait aujourd'hui qu'une religion n'implique pas nécessairement des symboles et des rites proprement dits, des temples et des prêtres [...]. Essentiellement, elle n'est autre chose qu'un ensemble de croyances et de pratiques collectives d'une particulière authorité"* [79, p. 270].

COMPUTER SCIENTIST: Translation, if you please.

SOCIOLOGIST: *(Smiling:)* "For we know today that a religion does not necessarily imply symbols and rites in the narrow sense of those terms, or temples and priests. Essentially, it is nothing other than a body of collective beliefs and practices endowed with a certain authority." What Durkheim intends to say is that religion is what bonds people together in a community. Mind you, in the same essay he goes on to say that a "religion of individualism" is the only viable form of religion in modern society.

GAME THEORIST: David Sloan Wilson, in [242], tries to revive Darwin's argument for group selection, and identifies religion as the determining factor. Wilson is not a defender of religion. He is not blind to its dark side: the tendency to blend in-group morality with hostility towards outsiders. In fact, his analysis of religious practices as a set of group-forming operations that serve to enhance the survival value of the group squares well with this. But his book gives a minority report, although Robin Dunbar expresses some similar ideas about the importance of group cohesion and the role of religion in his *Grooming, Gossip and the Evolution of Language* [73]. Most game-theorists and evolutionary biologists still prefer kin altruism and reciprocal altruism as explanations of emerging group behavior.

SOCIOLOGIST: Durkheim and Wilson would have gotten along well. Durkheim was deeply aware of the fact that people need a community to belong to. In a truly groundbreaking work [78], he studied suicide rates in a great diversity of populations across Europe, and found a clear correlation between lack of social constraints—what Durkheim called 'anomie'—and likelihood to kill oneself. Durkheim drew the conclusion that people need obligations and constraints to instill their lives with structure and meaning.

People who are religious, married and with children are much less likely to kill themselves. Suicide, at first sight the most individual act one can imagine, is explained in terms of what links—or fails to link—an individual to society.

GAME THEORIST: Let's come back to "The Tragedy of the Commons". It may interest you what Hardin himself advocated as a solution. His recipe is what he called "mutual constraint, mutually agreed upon." He did believe in pledges, promises, laws and ... sanctions. Like Sigmund Freud, he was well aware that civilization comes at a cost; it invites or forces us to suppress part of our nature, in the interest of the community, and deep, deep down, civilized individuals do resent this [94]. But there is no other way.

PHILOSOPHER: Now apply this to the problem of global warming. This project has made quite a contribution to carbon dioxide emission, with flying in colleagues from around the world: the United States, New Zealand.

LOGICIAN: Do you think we should have set an example? What would be the point? I mean, if everyone else is blazing by in petrol guzzling SUVs, why should I be the only one to ride a bicycle? My solitary plodding along on my bike is not going to save the world. I am quite willing to give up my intercontinental flights and my car. Maybe even my house in France—it is getting too hot there anyway. But only on condition that others do the same.

SOCIOLOGIST: Preaching self-imposed abstinence or attempting to convert by setting an example are wastes of time.

LOGICIAN: Ahem—I admire those who are setting an example, but the trouble is there are too few of them. What we need is mutual constraint, mutually agreed upon. We individual citizens have to convince our governments that it is time to constrain us. This may sound paradoxical, but it makes sense. Not only that, but it is the only way.

PHILOSOPHER: Constrain us? How? By imposing a system of individual carbon dioxide emission rights [154]? My good man, we emit carbon dioxide every time we exhale. They can't forbid us to breathe.

LOGICIAN: First we need the insight that it is urgent to limit our ecological footprint, to live wisely on this planet. Next, we need to see that we have to be forced to live wisely, that we cannot do it without communities that support us and keep us on track. So we need to build and rebuild our communities, for they will have to impose the mutual constraints.

COMPUTER SCIENTIST: For all that to happen there has to be a universal sense of urgency, like the sense of urgency that was felt in the US after Pearl

Harbor. Not very likely.

PHILOSOPHER: One can see how the $N+1$ prisoner's dilemma now resolves itself. Suppose a group knows that they are a group, and that they are under mutual constraint, mutually agreed upon. Assume there are 11 prisoners, and the individual payoffs are as before: *(Points at the whiteboard:)*

| | | Number of Others Keeping Silent | | | | | | | | | |
	0	1	2	3	4	5	6	7	8	9	10
I keep silent	-2	-1	0	1	2	3	4	5	6	7	8
I betray	-1	0	1	2	3	4	5	6	7	8	9

Then the collective payoff of everyone keeping silent is $11 \cdot 8$, and the collective payoff of everyone defecting is $11 \cdot -1$, so we get:

Everyone keeping silent	88
Everyone incriminating each other	-11

LOGICIAN: Speaking about pledges: In the year 2000 there was an interesting *Unesco* initiative. The *Unesco Manifesto 2000* invites us to make a pledge to devote our honest efforts to fostering community sense and make our contribution to community building. One year after this call to action, 9/11 happened, and initiatives like this may have seemed pointless for a while. But for building communities one has to start with small steps. Anyway, have a look at http://www3.unesco.org/manifesto2000/. If it appeals to you, you are in the excellent company of the Dalai Lama and other winners of the Nobel Peace Prize.

GAME THEORIST: Expect to hear a lot more about pledges and contracts on environmental issues in the near future [104].

COMPUTER SCIENTIST: *(Starts googling immediately.)*

Chapter 15
Social Software and the Ills of Society

Jan van Eijck, Rohit Parikh, Marc Pauly, Rineke Verbrugge

PHILOSOPHER: Our project is drawing to an end, and our previous discussion has made clear that it will not be so easy for the social software enterprise to address, let alone cure, the ills of society. To get the discussion going, I would like to start today with a quote that I found in a collection of talks from the physicist Richard Feynman. It is from one of the pieces in *The Pleasure of Finding Things Out*, a digest of a talk on "The Value of Science". The talk starts like this:

> From time to time, people suggest to me that scientists ought to give more consideration to social problems—especially that they should be more responsible in considering the impact of science upon society. This same suggestion must be made to many other scientists, and it seems to be generally believed that if the scientists would only look at these very difficult social problems and not spend so much time fooling with the less vital scientific ones, great success would come of it.

> It seems to me that we do think about these problems from time to time, but we don't put full-time effort into them—the reason being that we know we don't have any magic formula for solving problems, that social problems are very much harder than scientific ones, and that we usually don't get anywhere when we do think about them.

> I believe that a scientist looking at nonscientific problems is just as dumb as the next guy—and when he talks about a nonscientific matter, he will sound as naive as anyone untrained in the matter [91, p. 141].

LOGICIAN: So the obvious starting question is: If one of the most eminent physicists of the twentieth century believes that he is as dumb as the next guy when it comes to curing the ills of society, who are we to think that we are smarter?

PHILOSOPHER: That's right. But maybe I should remind you that Feynman was not a great lover of philosophical reflection. In the same book, he says about the philosopher Spinoza that courage to take on the great questions does not help if one can't get anywhere with those questions.

LOGICIAN: Yes, Feynman was fond of saying that he was going to investigate the world without first defining it. And social software is as much about defining things as about investigating the social world.

COMPUTER SCIENTIST: But we are all "the next guy", aren't we? We all share a responsibility to inform ourselves about what ails society, and about what can be done. For I agree with Feynman that there are no specialists we can pass the buck to. So I am reading up on what I think is the most pressing issue that our society is facing, the prospect of climate change. But now my spouse has started to complain, telling me I should stop reading books on issues that I cannot do anything about, as it is bound to make me depressed. That's probably right. So what should I do?

PHILOSOPHER: Your spouse has a point. If you get depressed you will not be effective at anything, so your first duty to yourself, your family, and the world is not to get depressed.

COMPUTER SCIENTIST: Some of my friends claim they need the affluent lifestyle that modern industrial society affords in order not to get depressed.

PHILOSOPHER: Occasional shopping sprees as a cure for depression? You cannot be serious.

COMPUTER SCIENTIST: More like watching the water from the upper deck of *RMS Titanic* and thinking, hey it's rising fast, better order a few more bottles of champagne before it's too late.

LOGICIAN: I can think of some relevant thoughts. One is the puzzle of the peacock's tail, why it has such a big tail which serves no useful function. One commonly accepted explanation is that its function is to impress pea-hens, and until we change *their* nature, there is not much hope of changing peacocks. There is a tendency which humans have to consume much more than they need and this needs to be tamed.

PHILOSOPHER: What you are saying is that excessive desire—the tendency to consume more than one needs—causes problems. This sounds curiously familiar, for it is what the Four Noble Truths of Buddhism are also saying: there is suffering, suffering has a cause, the cause is desire, one can put an end to suffering by overcoming desire [131].

LOGICIAN: Another relevant thought is the tragedy of the commons where one party benefits at the expense of other parties, as we discussed in Chapter 14. India's hot climate has already become hotter and a glacier which used to feed the Ganges river is receding so that there might be eventually a period of drought.

PHILOSOPHER: Colder countries like the US which have caused global warming may even benefit as we may find coffee growing in Vermont at some stage.

LOGICIAN: Finally, I do not know if you know *The Road Less Travelled* by M. Scott Peck [182]. Peck is a psychotherapist; he talks about the tendency of most humans to believe that a problem will go away if one does nothing about it. Of course this is not the case.

COMPUTER SCIENTIST: *The Road Less Travelled* happens to be one of my favorites. Peck makes this useful distinction between neurotic behavior and character disorders. When people assume responsibility for problems that are not theirs—as when a child assumes that she is responsible for her parents' divorce—this is neurosis. So being neurotic is worrying about things one cannot change. Having a character disorder is refusing to take responsibility for what one can change. Neurotic behavior is generally easier to cure than character disorder, for neurotic people are used to taking charge.

LOGICIAN: Reminds me of the famous Alcoholics Anonymous prayer: O Lord, give me the serenity to accept the things I cannot change, the courage to address the things I can change, and the wisdom to see the difference.

PHILOSOPHER: Ah, Reinhold Niebuhr's serenity prayer. Anyhow, the ills of society look more like character disorders than neuroses to me, so if Peck is right they are difficult to treat. But does it make sense to ask the question a psychotherapist asks about his patients about society at large? How could a society or culture learn to take up responsibility for what it is doing to its natural environment? I wonder what would be the societal analogue of this?

LOGICIAN: Interaction with wise leaders, of course. Did you know that Angela Merkel is also a physicist by training? But to ensure that wise leaders are elected, we need wise citizens to elect them. So we should promote the teaching of wisdom. It seems to me that academic philosophy has badly neglected this task. To be a lover of academic wisdom is not at all the same as to be a lover of wisdom, or so it seems.

PHILOSOPHER: I will let that pass. Maybe we should focus on knowledge rather than wisdom. It strikes me that an important issue concerns the impact of scientific knowledge on society. Scientists tend to assume that scientific results speak for themselves, that they do not need scientists as effective messengers.

LOGICIAN: Yes, and that assumption is wrong. Getting a message across should be part of the job.

COMPUTER SCIENTIST: But one can understand why scientists—those shy types who have learned that questioning one's own results is the highest virtue—are not very good at that.

LOGICIAN: Still there are things we can and should do to improve science communication. Make communication skills part of every science curriculum. Encourage researchers to set aside part of their time for explaining to the public at large what their research means. Encourage scientists to make contributions to the public debate. Set up and improve training programs for science journalism at our universities.

PHILOSOPHER: And, to get back to your suggestion of wisdom teaching, maybe it interests you that educational psychologists with a training in philosophy are developing educational schemes for wisdom training. So they think it can be taught, and they may well be right, to a certain extent. Robert Sternberg [224] even gives lists of wisdom skills, with items like "learn to recognize your own interests, those of others, and those of institutions", or "learn to balance your own interests, those of other people and those of institutions", or "learn to integrate your own values in your thinking", or, and this may interest you: "learn to search for and then to try to reach the common good". And then Sternberg takes care to define the common good as a good where everyone wins, not only the ones with whom one identifies.

LOGICIAN: Yes, psychologists can be quite lucid sometimes about what it means to be mentally healthy. Not the same as wise, maybe, but close. When Sigmund Freud was once asked what a well-integrated individual should be able to do, his answer was very short: *Lieben und Arbeiten.* To love and to work. That sums it up, doesn't it?

PHILOSOPHER: When preparing for this session I came across another challenging quote, from the psychiatrist and culture critic Theodore Dalrymple:

> One might extend La Rochefoucauld's famous maxim that neither the sun nor death can be stared at for long, by saying that no member of the modern liberal intelligentsia can stare at a social problem for very long. He feels the need to retreat into impersonal abstractions, into structures or alleged structures over which the victim has no control. And out of this need to avoid the rawness of reality he spins utopian schemes of social engineering [54, p. 216].

LOGICIAN: Ahem—he sounds like a very angry man.

PHILOSOPHER: You bet he is angry. He has spent part of his working life as a prison doctor in Birmingham, where he has developed a very sharp eye for the tendency of many of his patients to deny responsibility for their own lives, to pass themselves off as victims, and for the social structures that let them get away with that.

GAME THEORIST: And he accuses social engineers of escapism. So should we go on doing science as usual or should we try to address the pressing issues of our times? I certainly sympathize with this dilemma, and feel it myself. I am willing to believe that social software can "make this world a better place", but I'm afraid I'm less optimistic that we have chosen the right profession to help with the climate problem. But I would be thrilled to be convinced otherwise.

COMPUTER SCIENTIST: OK, let me try to explain more clearly why I think social software should help. The problem about the climate problem, as I see it now, is that it is a call to arms that is *not* taken seriously by us, despite the fact that we can hear the clarions very clearly. And it seems to me that we don't need more climate science, but more understanding of the mechanisms that allow us to ignore the evidence that we are in grave danger. This is a problem of analysis of social processes, and if social software is about knowledge, incentives and logical structure, as we agreed earlier on in our discussions, then analysis of this problem is certainly on our agenda.

GAME THEORIST: But I think the economists are very able to develop incentive-compatible market mechanisms, for instance concerning fishing quotas or carbon dioxide emission trading. But what's lacking is the political will, and that also has a lot to do with psychology. The question of political will was hinted at by a letter to the *New York Times*. (*Unfolds his newspaper and starts reading:*)

> To the Editor:
>
> Often with the support of their own public officials, our competitors overseas are seizing on opportunities to develop the next generation of renewable energy technologies because they both offer a path to moderating climate change and produce handsome monetary profit.
>
> Sadly for the United States, domestic clean energy industries sputter along as public officials lean toward the special interests of big oil, coal, utilities and automobiles.
>
> 'The Capitol Energy Crisis,' by Thomas L. Friedman (column, June 24), is a civics lesson reminding us that it is still politics, and not technology, that remains our greatest challenge in confronting the global dilemma of our age.
>
> *New York Times*, June 24, 2007

COMPUTER SCIENTIST: Yes, this strongly suggests that it is the political will which is defective, and not the technology. In the mid 90's, General Motors introduced an electric car which sold well in California. California had a regulation that a certain percent of all cars had to be electric. Ten years later, the regulation had been abandoned and there was only *one* electric car left in California. What happened? The movie, *Who Killed the Electric Car*, gives an account of it.

PHILOSOPHER: A book you might enjoy is Jean-Pierre Dupuy's *Pour un catastrophisme éclairé* [77]. Dupuy, a philosopher at Stanford university, argues that the big problem is that while we know climate change is happening, we still do not believe it, the reason being that it is not inscribed in the future as certain, but just as a possibility. His book argues for adopting a new metaphysics, one that is suitable for approaching catastrophes as the climate problem.

COMPUTER SCIENTIST: I know that book. While I'm skeptical of this argument, it is certainly a very fascinating and innovative one. Also, reading it was very good for my French. The argument reminded me of the way of thinking of a physicist and philosopher from my student days in Groningen, professor H.J. Groenewold, who insisted that in assessing the danger of nuclear power one had to engage in a new calculus of probabilities, where a very small probability of a disaster of infinite magnitude would still lead to an unacceptable risk. But Dupuy's argument seems to be different, and I must confess I do not fully understand what he means by "the impossibility of believing that the worst will happen".

PHILOSOPHER: Yes, I am also a bit skeptical. Do we really need a new metaphysics to understand what is happening? It would seem to me that what we see at a global scale is a phenomenon that we are all quite familiar with at the level of the individual: not wanting to believe the evidence, because it would shatter our picture of reality. It is what some duped husbands do when they pretend not to see that their wives are unfaithful— Pierre Bezukhov's behavior towards his wife Elena in Tolstoy's *War and Peace*. It is what ineffective parents do when they refuse to act on the evidence that their children are on the road to disaster—Prince Kuragin's attitude towards his children, also in *War and Peace*. It is what Hamlet does when he refuses to act on the evidence that his mother and his uncle have murdered his father. World literature tells us all there is to know about self-delusion. But individually, not about self-delusion on a global scale.

COMPUTER SCIENTIST: Pierre gets redeemed in *War and Peace*, for he learns that he can act vigorously when overwhelming events come into play. Also, conveniently, Elena dies of a mysterious illness. Redemption also happens to Hamlet. The strong suggestion is that people get wise, not through "wisdom teaching", but through coping with the disasters in their personal lives.

LOGICIAN: In that case, reading more may just be a bad substitute for action, making you more depressed. It may be true that our research project cannot stop climate change, but what about getting our institutes to spend money for compensating carbon dioxide emissions on research trips, for example with Atmosfair or Greenseats? And I'm sure there's more innovative stuff one could think of.

COMPUTER SCIENTIST: That's funny. I tend to think about booking Atmosfair and Greenseats flights as particularly bad substitutes for action. I mean, the evidence suggests that we should be giving up intercontinental travel altogether.

GAME THEORIST: Agreed. I'd prefer to do both: Fly less and support Atmosfair. I just returned from a conference full of Europeans who decided that the next conference will be in Japan. That strikes me as ecological nonsense. By the way, a friend from Rome told me recently that this idea of paying for your carbon dioxide emissions is similar to the indulgences of the Catholic Church, paying to have your sins forgiven.

PHILOSOPHER: Very interesting thought. The original idea behind indulgences was, of course, that *past* sins could be compensated for by generous gifts to the Church. We all know that the practice went badly out of hand, with the introduction of indulgences for *future* sins. The protestants protested, and the Catholic Church has mended its ways. The take leave message after confession stresses this: "Go, and sin no more".

COMPUTER SCIENTIST: So it would seem to me that flying Greenseats is similar to buying indulgences for future sins. Truly a bad idea.

GAME THEORIST: Well, I thought it was a nice analogy, but here's another one from Catholic doctrine. The Church teaches abstinence before marriage, and to avoid the transmission of AIDS. But for all those who cannot be abstinent, maybe using condoms would still be better than getting AIDS.

COMPUTER SCIENTIST: I agree that one should be realistic in rules of behavior one wants to impose. Preachers of sexual abstinence seem to have missed a point about human nature. But are you implying that it is just not realistic to assume people are willing to give up travel by air, because the need for travel is as urgent as the need for sex?

GAME THEORIST: What I mean is that if we cannot give up flying then flying and compensating for the environmental effect is better than flying without compensation.

COMPUTER SCIENTIST: I am tempted to quote Oscar Wilde: We can resist anything but temptation. Booking Greenseats flights is a procrastination device, for it deludes us into thinking we are acting responsibly. And the reason we love it is that it allows us to go on doing what we all like best, which is flying around the world to spend pleasant time with colleagues at interesting international workshops.

LOGICIAN: But giving up intercontinental flights altogether? My goodness, let's hope we are all on the same continent when that happens.

GAME THEORIST: One thing we *can* all do as individuals is to become vegetarian. If everyone would stop eating meat, that would seriously lower methane emissions without having any of the negative economic consequences that lowering CO_2 emissions seems to entail.

COMPUTER SCIENTIST: Incidentally, the majority of our project participants already appear to be vegetarian. *(Looks ruefully at own steak.)*

LOGICIAN: I suppose that the social software perspective could come in when trying to find ways for governments to promote vegetarianism, say, by environmental taxes on meat, shifts in farm subsidies, and so on. Colleagues, let's get to work.

PHILOSOPHER: A variant of Niebuhr's serenity prayer may be applicable to us, social software enthusiasts. Our formal methods may be useful in contexts where there is the political will to solve the ills of society, for example to create security protocols with various beneficial properties, or to promote vegetarianism, as you suggest. Still, there remain scores of problems where our expertise will not help one iota as long as political will is lacking—formal negotiation theory alone cannot begin to solve the Middle East crisis at this stage of history. Let us hope that we will have the wisdom to see the difference.

Bibliography

[1] M. Aiello, I. Pratt-Hartmann, and J.F.A.K. van Benthem. What is spatial logic? In M. Aiello, I. Pratt-Hartmann, and J.F.A.K. van Benthem, editors, *Handbook of Spatial Logics*. Springer, Berlin, 2007.

[2] C.E. Alchourron, P. Gärdenfors, and D. Makinson. On the logic of theory change: Partial meet functions for contraction and revision. *Journal of Symbolic Logic*, 50:510–530, 1985.

[3] G.E.M. Anscombe. Modern moral philosophy. *Philosophy*, 33:1–19, 1958.

[4] Aristotle. *The Politics of Aristotle: Translated into English with Introduction, Marginal Analysis, Essays, Notes and Indices*, volume 1. Clarendon Press, Oxford, 1885. Translated and annotated by B. Jowett.

[5] Aristotle. *Ethics*. Penguin Books, 1958. Translated by J.A.K. Thompson.

[6] K. Arrow. *Social Choice and Individual Values*. Wiley, New York, 1951, second edition: 1963.

[7] Augustine. *Confessions*. Oxford University Press, 1992. With introduction and commentary by J.J. O'Donnell.

[8] R.J. Aumann. Agreeing to disagree. *Annals of Statistics*, 4(6):1236–1239, 1976.

[9] R. Axelrod. *The Evolution of Cooperation*. Basic Books, New York, 1984.

[10] J.W. Bailey. *Utilitarianism, Institutions, and Justice*. Oxford University Press, 1998.

[11] A. Baltag, L.S. Moss, and S. Solecki. The logic of public announcements, common knowledge, and private suspicions. In I. Bilboa, editor, *Proceedings of TARK'98*, pages 43–56, 1998.

[12] A. Baltag, L.S. Moss, and S. Solecki. The logic of public announcements, common knowledge, and private suspicions. Technical Report SEN-R9922, CWI, Amsterdam, 1999.

[13] A. Baltag, H.P. van Ditmarsch, and L.S. Moss. Epistemic logic and information update. In J.F.A.K. van Benthem and P. Adriaans, editors, *Handbook on the Philosophy of Information*, Amsterdam, 2008. Elsevier. To appear.

[14] J. Barkow, L. Cosmides, and J. Tooby, editors. *The Adapted Mind: Evolutionary Psychology and the Generation of Culture*. Oxford University Press, New York, NY, 1992.

[15] J. Barwise. Scenes and other situations. *The Journal of Philosophy*, 78:369–397, 1981.

[16] C.D. Batson, E.R. Thompson, G. Seuferling, H. Whitney, and J.A. Strongman. Moral hypocrisy: appearing moral to oneself without being so. *Journal of Personality and Social Psychology*, 77(3):525–537, 1999.

[17] J. van Benthem. Information update as relativization. http://staff.science.uva.nl/~johan/Upd=Rel.pdf, 2000.

[18] J. van Benthem. Games in dynamic epistemic logic. *Bulletin of Economic Research*, 53(4):219–248, 2001.

[19] J. van Benthem. Extensive games as process models. *Journal of Logic, Language and Information*, 11:289–313, 2002.

[20] J. van Benthem. Rational dynamics and epistemic logic in games. In S. Vannucci, editor, *Logic, Game Theory and Social Choice III*, pages 19–23, 2003.

[21] J. van Benthem. Rationalisations and promises in games. Handout, University of Beijing, October 2006.

[22] J. van Benthem. Patterns of intelligent interaction: games, action, and social software. *NIAS Newsletter*, 38:5–8, 2007.

[23] J. van Benthem. Rational dynamics and epistemic logic in games. *International Game Theory Review*, 9(1):13–45, 2007.

[24] J. van Benthem, J. van Eijck, and B. Kooi. Logics of communication and change. *Information and Computation*, 204(11):1620–1662, 2006.

[25] J. van Benthem, S. van Otterloo, and O. Roy. Preference logic, conditionals, and solution concepts in games. In H. Lagerlund, S. Lindström, and R. Sliwinski, editors, *Modality Matters*, volume 53 of *Uppsala Philosophical Studies*, pages 61–76. Department of Philosophy, Uppsala University, 2006.

[26] J.F.A.K. van Benthem. Temporal logic. In D.M. Gabbay, C.J. Hogger, and J.A. Robinson, editors, *Handbook of Logic in Artificial Intelligence and Logic Programming (Vol. 4): Epistemic and Temporal Reasoning*, pages 241–350. Oxford University Press, Oxford, UK, 1995.

[27] J.F.A.K. van Benthem, J. Gerbrandy, and E. Pacuit. Merging frameworks for interaction: DEL and ETL. In D. Samet, editor, *TARK '07: Proceedings of the 11th Conference on Theoretical Aspects of Rationality and Knowledge*, pages 72–81. ACM, 2007.

[28] J.F.A.K. van Benthem and E. Pacuit. The tree of knowledge in action: Towards a common perspective. In G. Governatori, I. Hodkinson, and Y. Venema, editors, *Advances in Modal Logic, Vol. 6*, pages 87–106. College Publications, 2006.

[29] A. Benz, G. Jaeger, and R. van Rooij. *An Introduction to Game Theory for Linguists*. Palgrave MacMillan, 2005.

[30] C. Bicchieri and E. Xiao. Do the right thing: But only if others do so. *Journal of Behavioral Decision Making*, 21:1–18, 2008.

[31] K. Binmore. *Fun and Games*. D.C. Heath, Lexington, MA, 1992.

[32] K. Binmore. *Game Theory and the Social Contract*. The MIT Press, 1994.

[33] D. Black. *The Theory of Committees and Elections*. Cambridge University Press, Cambridge, 1958.

[34] P. Blackburn, M. de Rijke, and Y. Venema. *Modal Logic*, volume 53 of *Cambridge Tracts in Theoretical Computer Science*. Cambridge University Press, Cambridge, 2001.

[35] P. Blackburn and E. Spaan. A modal perspective on the computational complexity of attribute value grammar. *Journal of Logic, Language and Information*, 2:129–169, 1993.

[36] S. Brams. Fair division. In B.R. Weingast and D. Wittman, editors, *Oxford Handbook of Political Economy*. Oxford University Press, 2005.

[37] S.J. Brams and A.D. Taylor. *Fair Division: From Cake-Cutting to Dispute-Resolution.* Cambridge University Press, 1996.

[38] S.J. Brams and A.D. Taylor. *The Win-Win Solution.* W.W. Norton, New York, 1999.

[39] A. Brandenburger and B. Nalebuff. *Co-Opetition: A Revolution Mindset that Combines Competition and Cooperation.* Doubleday, New York, 1997.

[40] M. Bratman. *Intention, Plans, and Practical Reason.* Harvard University Press, Cambridge, MA, 1987.

[41] M. Bratman. *Faces of Intention.* Cambridge University Press, Cambridge, 1999.

[42] J. Broersen, A. Herzig, and N. Troquard. Embedding alternating-time temporal logic in strategic STIT logic of agency. *Journal of Logic and Computation*, 16:559–578, 2006.

[43] B. de Bruin. *Explaining Games.* PhD thesis, ILLC, University of Amsterdam, Amsterdam, The Netherlands, 2004. *ILLC Publications* DS-2004-03.

[44] M. Burrows, M. Abadi, and R. Needham. A logic of authentication. *Proceedings of the Royal Society of London, Series A, Mathematical and Physical Sciences*, 426(1871):233–271, 1989.

[45] C.F. Camerer, G. Loewenstein, and M. Rabin, editors. *Advances in Behavioral Economics.* Princeton University Press, 2003.

[46] D. Chaum. The dining cryptographers problem: unconditional sender and receiver untraceability. *Journal of Cryptology*, 1:65–75, 1988.

[47] M.S.-Y. Chwe. *Rational Ritual.* Princeton University Press, Princeton and Oxford, 2001.

[48] H.H. Clark and C. Marshall. Definite reference and mutual knowledge. In A. Joshi, B. Webber, and I. Sag, editors, *Elements of Discourse Understanding*, pages 10–63. Cambridge University Press, 1981.

[49] N. de Condorcet. *Essai sur l'application de l'analyse à la probabilité des décisions rendues à la pluralité des voix.* Imprimerie Royale, Paris, 1785.

[50] K.S. Cook. *Trust in Society.* Russell Sage Foundation Publications, 2003.

[51] L. Cosmides. The logic of social exchange: Has natural selection shaped how humans reason? Studies with the Wason Selection Task. *Cognition*, 31:187–276, 1989.

[52] V. Crawford and J. Sobel. Strategic information transmission. *Econometrica*, 50:1431–1451, 1982.

[53] C.J.F. Cremers. *Scyther — Semantics and Verification of Security Protocols*. PhD thesis, Technical University Eindhoven, 2006.

[54] T. Dalrymple. *Our Culture, What's Left of It: The Mandarins and the Masses*. Ivan R. Dee, Chicago, 2005.

[55] A. Damasio. *Descartes' Error: Emotion, Reason, and the Human Brain*. Putnam, New York, 1994.

[56] J.M. Darley and B. Letane. Bystander intervention in emergencies: Diffusion of responsibility. *Journal of Personality and Social Psychology*, 8(4.1):377–383, 1968.

[57] C. Darwin. *The Descent of Man, and Selection in Relation to Sex*. John Murray, London, 1871.

[58] B.A. Davey and H.A. Priestley. *Introduction to Lattices and Order*. Cambridge University Press, Cambridge, second edition, 2002.

[59] R.J. Davidson. Affective style, psychopathology and resilience: Brain mechanisms and plasticity. *American Psychologist*, 55:1196–1214, 2000.

[60] R.J. Davidson. Well-being and affective style: neural substrates and biobehavioural correlates. *Philosophical Transactions of the Royal Society B*, 359(1449):1395–1411, 2004.

[61] D. Dennett. *The Intentional Stance*. The MIT Press, Cambridge, MA, 1987.

[62] J. Diamond. *Collapse: How Societies Choose to Fail or Succeed*. Viking Books, New York, 2005.

[63] F. Dignum, B. Dunin-Kęplicz, and R. Verbrugge. Creating collective intention through dialogue. *Logic Journal of the IGPL*, 9:145–158, 2001.

[64] H. van Ditmarsch, W. van der Hoek, R. van der Meyden, and J. Ruan. Model checking Russian cards. *Electronic Notes in Theoretical Computer Science*, 149(2):105–123, 2006.

[65] H.P. van Ditmarsch, J. Ruan, and R. Verbrugge. Sum and product in dynamic epistemic logic. *Journal of Logic and Computation*, 18:563–588, 2008.

[66] H.P. van Ditmarsch, W. van der Hoek, and B.P. Kooi. *Dynamic Epistemic Logic*, volume 337 of *Synthese Library*. Springer, 2007.

[67] K. Doets and J. van Eijck. *The Haskell Road to Logic, Maths and Programming*, volume 4 of *Texts in Computing*. King's College Publications, London, 2004.

[68] D. Dolev and A.C. Yao. On the security of public key protocols. *IEEE Transactions on Information Theory*, 29(2):198–208, March 1983.

[69] H.H.L.M. Donkers, J.W.H.M. Uiterwijk, and H.J. van den Herik. Selecting evaluation functions in opponent-model search. *Theoretical Computer Science*, 349(2):245–267, 2005.

[70] K. Dowding and M. van Hees. The construction of rights. *American Political Science Review*, 97:281–293, 2003.

[71] A.M. Duinhoven. Karel ende Elegast. http://www.dbnl.org/tekst/_kar001kare01_01/, 2001.

[72] A.M. Duinhoven and K. Eykman. *Karel ende Elegast*. Nederlandse Klassieken Reeks. Prometheus and Bert Bakker, Amsterdam, 1997. Translation in modern Dutch. The 1486–1488 version in Middle Dutch can be found in [71].

[73] R. Dunbar. *Grooming, Gossip and the Evolution of Language*. Faber and Faber, London, 1996.

[74] B. Dunin-Kȩplicz and R. Verbrugge. A logical view on teamwork. In J. van Eijck and R. Verbrugge, editors, *Games, Actions and Social Software*. College Publications. To appear.

[75] B. Dunin-Kȩplicz and R. Verbrugge. Collective intentions. *Fundamenta Informaticae*, 51(3):271–295, 2002.

[76] B. Dunin-Kȩplicz and R. Verbrugge. A tuning machine for cooperative problem solving. *Fundamenta Informaticae*, 63:283–307, 2004.

[77] J.-P. Dupuy. *Pour un catastrophisme éclairé*. Seuil, Paris, 2002.

[78] É. Durkheim. *Suicide*. Free Press, 1897/1951.

[79] É. Durkheim. *La Science Sociale et l'Action*. Collection SUP. Presses Universitaires de France, Paris, 1987.

[80] M. Dziubiński, R. Verbrugge, and B. Dunin-Kęplicz. Complexity issues in multiagent logics. *Fundamenta Informaticae*, 75:239–262, 2007.

[81] Umberto Eco. Towards a semiological guerrilla warfare. In *Travels in Hyperreality*, pages 135–144. Harvest Books, 1990.

[82] M. Egas and A. Riedl. The economics of altruistic punishment and the demise of cooperation. Tinbergen Institute Discussion Papers 05-065/1, Tinbergen Institute, June 2005.

[83] J. van Eijck. Discourse on social software — what is social software? *NIAS Newsletter*, 37:15–21, 2006.

[84] J. van Eijck and S. Orzan. Modelling the epistemics of communication with functional programming. In M. van Eekelen, editor, *Sixth Symposium on Trends in Functional Programming TFP 2005*, pages 44–59, Tallinn, 2005. Institute of Cybernetics, Tallinn Technical University.

[85] Jan van Eijck. DEMO — A demo of epistemic modelling. In J. van Benthem, D. Gabbay, and B. Löwe, editors, *Interactive Logic*, volume 1 of *Texts in Logic and Games*, pages 303–362. Amsterdam University Press, 2007.

[86] N. Elias. *The Civilizing Process, Vol. I. The History of Manners*. Blackwell, Oxford, 1969.

[87] N. Elias. *The Civilizing Process, Vol. II. State Formation and Civilization*. Blackwell, Oxford, 1982.

[88] E.A. Emerson. Temporal and modal logic. In J. van Leeuwen, editor, *Handbook of Theoretical Computer Science: Volume B: Formal Models and Semantics*, pages 995–1072. Elsevier, Amsterdam, 1990.

[89] K.A. Ericsson and H.A. Simon. *Protocol analysis: Verbal Reports as Data*. MIT Press, Cambridge, MA, 1984.

[90] R. Fagin, J.Y. Halpern, Y. Moses, and M.Y. Vardi. *Reasoning about Knowledge*. The MIT Press, 1995.

[91] R.P. Feynman. *The Pleasure of Finding Things Out*. Perseus Books, 1999. First Penguin Edition: 2000.

[92] L. Flobbe, R. Verbrugge, P. Hendriks, and I. Krämer. Children's application of theory of mind in reasoning and language. *Journal of Logic, Language and Information*, 17:417–442, 2008.

[93] P. Foot. *Natural Goodness*. Clarendon Press, 2001.

[94] S. Freud. *Das Unbehagen in der Kultur*. Internationaler Psychoana-
lytischer Verlag, Vienna, 1930.

[95] H. Freudenthal. (formulation of the sum-and-product problem).
Nieuw Archief voor Wiskunde, 3(17):152, 1969.

[96] H. Freudenthal. (solution of the sum-and-product problem). *Nieuw
Archief voor Wiskunde*, 3(18):102–106, 1970.

[97] M.F. Friedell. On the structure of shared awareness. *Behavioral Science*, 14(1):28–39, 1969.

[98] F. Fukuyama. *Trust: The Social Virtues and The Creation of Prosperity*. Free Press, 1996.

[99] D. Gabbay. *Fibring Logics*, volume 38 of *Oxford Logic Guides*. Oxford
University Press, 1998.

[100] G. Gamow and M. Stern. *Puzzle-Math*. Macmillan, London, 1958.

[101] J. Geanakoplos and H. Polemarchakis. We can't disagree forever.
Journal of Economic Theory, 28:192–200, 1982.

[102] A. Gibbard. Manipulation of voting schemes: A general result. *Econometrica*, 41:587–601, 1973.

[103] R. Gibbons. *A Primer in Game Theory*. Prentice Hall, 1992.

[104] N. Gingrich and T.L. Maple. *A Contract with the Earth*. Johns Hop-
kins University Press, 2007. Foreword by E.O. Wilson.

[105] G. Gonthier. A computer-checked proof of the four colour theorem.
Technical report, Microsoft Research, 2005.

[106] G. Gonthier. Formal proof—the four-color theorem. *Notices of the
American Mathematical Society*, 55(11):1382–1393, 2008.

[107] J. Haidt. The new synthesis in moral psychology. *Science*,
317(5827):998–1002, 2007.

[108] J.Y. Halpern, R. Harper, N. Immerman, P.G. Kolaitis, M.Y. Vardi,
and V. Vianu. On the unusual effectiveness of logic in computer science. *The Bulletin of Symbolic Logic*, 7(2):213–236, 2001.

[109] J.Y. Halpern and Y. Moses. Knowledge and common knowledge in a
distributed environment. In *Proceedings of the 3rd ACM Symposium
on Principles of Distributed Computing (PODS)*, pages 50–61, 1984.

[110] J.Y. Halpern and Y. Moses. Knowledge and common knowledge in a distributed environment. *Journal of the ACM*, 37(3):549–587, 1990.

[111] J.Y. Halpern and M.Y. Vardi. Model checking vs. theorem proving: a manifesto. In V. Lifschitz, editor, *Artificial Intelligence and Mathematical Theory of Computation: Papers in Honor of John McCarthy*, pages 151–176, San Diego, CA, 1991. Academic Press Professional, Inc.

[112] S.O. Hanson. Social choice with procedural preferences. *Social Choice and Welfare*, 13:215–230, 1996.

[113] G. Hardin. The tragedy of the commons. *Science*, 162:1243–48, 1968.

[114] D. Harel, D. Kozen, and J. Tiuryn. *Dynamic Logic*. The MIT Press, Cambridge, MA, 2000.

[115] P. Harrenstein. *Logic in Conflict*. PhD thesis, Department of Computer Science, University of Utrecht, 2004.

[116] J. Heal. Common knowledge. *The Philosophical Quarterly*, 28(111):116–131, 1978.

[117] P. Hedström. *Dissecting the Social: On the Principles of Analytical Sociology*. Cambridge University Press, 2005.

[118] P. Hedström and R. Swedberg. Social mechanisms: their theoretical status and use in sociology. Technical report, Department of Sociology, Stockholm University, 1995.

[119] M. van Hees and K. Dowding. In praise of manipulation. *British Journal of Political Science*, 38:1–15, 2008.

[120] A. Heyting. *Intuitionism: An Introduction*. Studies in Logic and the Foundations of Mathematics. North-Holland, 1956.

[121] W. van der Hoek, A.R. Lomuscio, and M.J. Wooldridge. On the complexity of practical ATL model checking. In H. Nakashima, M.P. Wellman, G. Weiss, and P. Stone, editors, *5th International Joint Conference on Autonomous Agents and Multiagent Systems (AAMAS 2006)*, pages 201–208. ACM, 2006.

[122] D.R. Hofstadter. *Gödel, Escher, Bach: An Eternal Golden Braid*. Basic Books, 1999.

[123] J. Horty. *Agency and Deontic Logic*. Oxford University Press, Oxford, 2001.

[124] D. Hume. *A Treatise of Human Nature*. Clarendon Press, Oxford, 2000.

[125] J. Illes, editor. *Neuroethics: Defining the Issues in Theory, Practice and Policy*. Oxford University Press, Oxford, 2005.

[126] N.R. Jennings and S. Bussmann. Agent-based control systems: Why are they suited to engineering complex systems? *IEEE Control Systems Magazine*, 23(3):61–74, 2003.

[127] M.L. Jones. A note on a cake cutting algorithm of Banach and Knaster. *The American Mathematical Monthly*, 104(4):353–355, 1997.

[128] D. Kahneman, P. Slovic, and A. Tversky, editors. *Judgment under Uncertainty: Heuristics and Biases*. Cambridge University Press, Cambridge and New York, NY, 1974.

[129] I. Kaul, P. Conceição, K. Le Gouven, and R.U. Mendoza. *Providing Global Public Goods*. Oxford University Press, 2003.

[130] I. Kaul, I. Grunberg, and M.A. Stern. *Global Public Goods*. Oxford University Press, 1999.

[131] D. Keown. *Buddhism: A Very Short Introduction*. Oxford University Press, Oxford, 1996.

[132] J.M. Keynes. *The General Theory of Employment, Interest and Money*. Macmillan and Cambridge University Press, 1936.

[133] B. Knaster. Un théorème sur les fonctions d'ensembles. *Ann. Soc. Polon. Math*, 6:133–134, 1928.

[134] H.W. Kuhn and S. Nasar, editors. *The Essential John Nash*. Princeton University Press, Princeton and Oxford, 2002.

[135] H. Labohm, S. Rozendaal, and D. Thoenes. *Man-Made Global Warming: Unravelling a Dogma*. Multi-Science Publishing, 2004.

[136] L. Lamport, R. Shostak, and M. Pease. The Byzantine generals problem. *ACM Transactions on Programming Languages and Systems*, 4(3):382–401, 1982.

[137] R. Layard. Happiness — has social science a clue? Lionel Robbins Memorial Lectures delivered at LSE: http://cep.lse.ac.uk/layard/, 3–5 March 2003.

[138] R. Layard. *Happiness — Lessons from a New Science*. The Penguin Press, 2005.

[139] H. Leitgeb and K. Segerberg. Dynamic doxastic logic: Why, how, and where to? *Synthese*, 155(2):167–190, 2007.

[140] D.K. Lewis. *Convention: A Philosophical Study*. Harvard University Press, Cambridge, MA, 1969.

[141] Richard S. Lindzen. Some coolness concerning global warming. *Bulletin of the American Meteorological Society*, 71(3):288–299, 1990.

[142] B. Lomborg. *The Skeptical Environmentalist: Measuring the Real State of the World*. Cambridge University Press, 2001.

[143] J. Lovelock. *The Revenge of Gaia*. Allen Lane, 2006.

[144] G. Lowe. Breaking and fixing the Needham-Schroeder public-key protocol using FDR. In T. Margaria and B. Steffen, editors, *Tools and Algorithms for Construction and Analysis of Systems, Second International Workshop, TACAS '96, Passau, Germany, March 27–29, 1996, Proceedings*, volume 1055 of *Lecture Notes in Computer Science*. Springer, 1996.

[145] R. Manning, M. Levine, and A. Collins. The Kitty Genovese murder and the social psychology of helping: The parable of the 38 witnesses. *American Psychologist*, 62:555–562, 2007.

[146] A. Mas-Collel, M. Whinston, and J. Green. *Microeconomic Theory*. Oxford University Press, 1995.

[147] M. Maslin. *Global Warming, a Very Short Introduction*. Oxford University Press, Oxford, 2004.

[148] J. Mayer. Outsourcing torture. *The New Yorker*, February 14th:106–123, 2005. Online version: http://www.newyorker.com/archive/2005/02/14/.

[149] J. Maynard Smith. *Evolution and the Theory of Games*. Cambridge University Press, 1973.

[150] J. Maynard Smith and G.R. Price. The logic of animal conflict. *Nature*, 246:15–18, 1973.

[151] J. McCarthy. Formalization of two puzzles involving knowledge. In V. Lifschitz, editor, *Formalizing Common Sense: Papers by John McCarthy*, Ablex Series in Artificial Intelligence. Ablex Publishing Corporation, Norwood, NJ, 1990. Original manuscript dated 1978–1981.

[152] R. McKelvey. Intransitivities in multi-dimensional voting models and some implications for agenda control. *Journal of Economic Theory*, 12:472–482, 1976.

[153] J.-J.Ch. Meyer and W. van der Hoek. *Epistemic Logic for AI and Computer Science*. Cambridge Tracts in Theoretical Computer Science 41. Cambridge University Press, Cambridge, 1995.

[154] G. Mobiot. *Heat*. Penguin Books, 2007.

[155] L. Mol, N. Taatgen, R. Verbrugge, and P. Hendriks. Reflective cognition as secondary task. In B.G. Bara, L. Barsalou, and M. Bucciarelli, editors, *Proceedings of Twenty-seventh Annual Meeting of the Cognitive Science Society*, pages 1925–1930. Erlbaum, 2005.

[156] P. Montague. A new disinformation campaign. *New York Times*, 29 April 1998.

[157] C. Mooney. *The Republican War on Science*. Perseus Books, New York, 2005.

[158] G.E. Moore. A reply to my critics. In P.A. Schilpp, editor, *The Philosophy of G.E. Moore*, volume 4 of *The Library of Living Philosophers*, pages 535–677. Northwestern University, Evanston, IL, 1942.

[159] J. Moore. Implementation, contracts, and renegotiation in environments with complete information. In J.-J. Laffont, editor, *Advances in Economic Theory — 6th World Congress*, volume I. Cambridge University Press, 1992.

[160] Y. Moses, D. Dolev, and J.Y. Halpern. Cheating husbands and other stories: A case study of knowledge, action, and communication. *Distributed Computing*, 1(3):167–176, September 1986.

[161] S. Nasar. *A Beautiful Mind*. Simon and Schuster, New York, 1998.

[162] R. Needham and M. Schroeder. Using encryption for authentication in large networks of computers. *Communications of the ACM*, 21(12), 1978.

[163] A. Newell and H.A Simon. *Human Problem Solving*. Prentice-Hall, Englewood Cliffs, NJ, 1972.

[164] BBC News. 'Maverick' risk to science debate, 30 November 2006. http://news.bbc.co.uk/2/hi/science/nature/6159371.stm.

[165] F. Nietzsche. *On the Genealogy of Morals: A Polemic: by Way of Clarification and Supplement to My Last Book, Beyond Good and Evil.* Oxford University Press, Oxford, 1998. Translated and annotated by D. Smith.

[166] NN. Klimaat: 'Kyoto is onzin'. *Elsevier*, Wednesday, June 20, 2007.

[167] M.A. Nowak and K. Sigmund. Evolution of indirect reciprocity. *Nature*, 437:1291–1298, 2005.

[168] M. Nussbaum and A.K. Sen, editors. *The Quality of Life.* Oxford University Press, Oxford, 1993.

[169] J. Oakman. The Camp David Accords: A case study on international negotiation. Technical report, Princeton University, Woodrow Wilson School of Public and International Affairs, 2002.

[170] M. Olson. *The Logic of Collective Action; Public Goods and the Theory of Groups.* Harvard University Press, Cambridge, MA, 1965.

[171] M.J. Osborne. *An Introduction to Game Theory.* Oxford University Press, 2004.

[172] E. Pacuit. *Topics in Social Software: Information in Strategic Situations.* PhD thesis, City University of New York, 2005.

[173] E. Pacuit, R. Parikh, and E. Cogan. The logic of knowledge based obligation. *Synthese*, 31:311–341, 2006.

[174] C.H. Papadimitriou. *Computational Complexity.* Addison-Wesley, 1994.

[175] R. Parikh. The logic of games and its applications. *Annals of Discrete Mathematics*, 24:111–140, 1985.

[176] R. Parikh. Language as social software. In J. Floyd and S. Shieh, editors, *Future Pasts: The Analytic Tradition in Twentieth-Century Philosophy*, pages 339–350. Oxford University Press, Oxford and New York, NY, 2001.

[177] R. Parikh. Social software. *Synthese*, 132:187–211, 2002.

[178] R. Parikh and P. Krasucki. Communication, consensus and knowledge. *Journal of Economic Theory*, 52:178–189, 1990.

[179] L.C. Paulson. Proving properties of security protocols by induction. In *10th Computer Security Foundations Workshop*, pages 70–83. IEEE Computer Society Press, 1997.

[180] M. Pauly. *Logic for Social Software*. PhD thesis, ILLC, University of Amsterdam, Amsterdam, The Netherlands, 2001. *ILLC Publications* DS-2001-10.

[181] M. Pauly. Changing the rules of play. *Topoi*, 24:209–220, 2005.

[182] M.S. Peck. *The Road Less Travelled*. Simon and Schuster, 1978.

[183] J. Peijnenburg. *Acting Against One's Best Judgement. An Enquiry into Practical Reasoning, Dispositions and Weakness of Will*. PhD thesis, University of Groningen, 1996.

[184] J.A. Plaza. Logics of public communications. In M.L. Emrich, M.S. Pfeifer, M. Hadzikadic, and Z.W. Ras, editors, *Proceedings of the 4th International Symposium on Methodologies for Intelligent Systems*, pages 201–216, 1989.

[185] V. Pratt. Semantical considerations on Floyd–Hoare logic. *Proceedings 17th IEEE Symposium on Foundations of Computer Science*, pages 109–121, 1976.

[186] A. Przeworski and P. Sprague. *Paper Stones: A History of Electoral Socialism*. Chicago University Press, Chicago, IL, 1986.

[187] H. Raiffa. *The Art and Science of Negotiation*. Harvard University Press, Cambridge, MA, 1982.

[188] R. Ramanujam and S.P. Suresh. Deciding knowledge properties of security protocols. In *TARK '05: Proceedings of the 10th Conference on Theoretical Aspects of Rationality and Knowledge*, pages 219–235. National University of Singapore, 2005.

[189] F.P. Ramsey. Truth and probability. In R.B. Braithwaite, editor, *The Foundations of Mathematics and other Logical Essays*, pages 156–198. Kegan, Paul, Trench, Trubner & Co, London, 1931.

[190] A.S. Rao and M.P. Georgeff. Modeling rational agents within a BDI-architecture. In J. Allen, R. Fikes, and E. Sandewall, editors, *Proceedings of the 2nd International Conference on Principles of Knowledge Representation and Reasoning (KR'91)*, pages 473–484. Morgan Kaufmann, 1991.

[191] A. Rapoport. Paradoxe der Entscheidungstheorie. In R. Martinsen, editor, *Das Auge der Wissenschaft. Zur Emergenz von Realität*, pages 57–73. Nomos, Baden-Baden, 1995.

[192] J. Raz. *The Morality of Freedom*. Oxford University Press, New York and Oxford, 1985.

[193] P.J. Reny. Arrow's theorem and the Gibbard-Satterthwaite theorem: A unified approach. *Economics Letters*, 70(1):99–105, 2001.

[194] P. Reps and N. Senzaki, editors. *Zen Flesh, Zen Bones*. Charles E. Tuttle, 1957 (many editions).

[195] Craig Reynolds. Boids: Background and update, 2007. http://www.red3d.com/cwr/boids/.

[196] W.R. Riker. Implications from the disequilibrium of majority rule for the study of institutions. *American Political Science Review*, 74:432–447, 1980.

[197] R. Rivest, A. Shamir, and L. Adleman. A method for obtaining digital signatures and public-key cryptosystems. *Communications of the ACM*, 21(2):120–126, February 1978.

[198] J. Robertson and W. Webb. *Cake-Cutting Algorithms: Be Fair If You Can*. A.K. Peters, 1998.

[199] H.-H. Rogner, R. Zhou, R. Bradley, P. Crabbé, O. Edenhofer, B. Hare, L. Kuijpers, and M. Yamaguchi. Introduction. In B. Metz, O.R. Davidson, P.R. Bosch, R. Dave, and L.A. Meyer, editors, *Climate Change 2007: Mitigation. Contribution of Working Group III to the Fourth Assessment Report of the Intergovernmental Panel on Climate Change*. Cambridge University Press, Cambridge, 2007.

[200] D.G. Saari. *Chaotic Elections*. American Mathematical Society, 2001.

[201] D.G. Saari. *Decisions and Elections: Explaining the Unexpected*. Cambridge University Press, 2001.

[202] T. Sandholm and V. Lesser. Issues in automated negotiation and electronic commerce: Extending the contract net framework. In V. Lesser, editor, *Proceedings of the First International Conference on Multi-Agent Systems (ICMAS'95)*, pages 328–335. The MIT Press, 1995.

[203] D. Sangiorgi. Bisimulation: from the origins to today. In *Proceedings of the 19th Symposium on Logic in Computer Science (LICS'04)*, pages 298–302. IEEE Computer Society, 2004.

[204] A. Sarin. *Akbar and Birbal*. Penguin India, 2005.

[205] M.A. Satterthwaite. Strategy-proofness and Arrow's conditions: Existence and correspondence theorems for voting procedures and social welfare functions. *Journal of Economic Theory*, 10:187–217, 1975.

[206] T.C. Schelling. *Micromotives and Macrobehavior*. W.W. Norton, New York, 1978.

[207] C.P. Schnorr. The black-box model for cryptographic primitives. *Journal of Cryptology*, 11(2):125–140, March 1998.

[208] N. Schofield. Instability of simple dynamic games. *Review of Economic Studies*, 45:575–594, 1978.

[209] A.B. Seligman. *The Problem of Trust*. Princeton University Press, 2000.

[210] A. Sen. *Collective Choice and Social Welfare*. Oliver and Boyd, Edinburgh, 1970.

[211] A.K. Sen, editor. *Commodities and Capabilities*. Clarendon Press, Oxford, 1985.

[212] J. Sgall and G.J. Woeginger. An approximation scheme for cake division with a linear number of cuts. *Combinatorica*, 27(2):205–211, 2007.

[213] K.C. Shepsle. Institutional arrangements and equilibrium in multidimensional voting models. *American Journal of Political Science*, 23:27–59, 1979.

[214] S. Simpson. *Subsystems of Second-order Arithmetic*. Perspectives in Mathematical Logic. Springer Verlag, Berlin, 1999.

[215] S.F. Singer. The scientific case against the global climate treaty. The Science & Environment Policy Project, 1999. http://www.sepp.org/publications/GWBooklet/GW.html.

[216] A. Smith. *An Inquiry into the Nature and Causes of the Wealth of Nations*. Liberty Fund, Indianapolis, 1982. First published 1776.

[217] A. Smith. *The Theory of Moral Sentiments*. Liberty Fund, Indianapolis, 1984. First published London and Edinburgh, 1759.

[218] R. Smullyan. *The Tao is Silent*. Harper and Row, 1977.

[219] E. Spaan. *Complexity of Modal Logics*. PhD thesis, Department of Mathematics and Computer Science, University of Amsterdam, 1993.

[220] D.O. Stahl and P.W. Wilson. On players' models of other players: Theory and experimental evidence. *Games and Economic Behavior*, 10:218–254, 1995.

[221] K. Stenning and M. van Lambalgen. Semantics as a foundation for psychology: A case study of Wason's selection task. *Journal of Logic, Language and Information*, 10:273–317, 2001.

[222] K. Stenning and M. van Lambalgen. A little logic goes a long way: Basing experiment on semantic theory in the cognitive science of conditional reasoning. *Cognitive Science*, 28(4):481–530, 2004.

[223] K. Stenning and M. van Lambalgen. *Human Reasoning and Cognitive Science*. MIT Press, Cambridge, MA, 2008.

[224] R.J. Sternberg. Why schools should teach for wisdom. the balance theory of wisdom in educational settings. *Educational Psychologist*, 36(4):227–245, 2001.

[225] P.D. Straffin. *Game Theory and Strategy*. The Mathematical Association of America, New Mathematical Library, 1993.

[226] W. Styron. *Sophie's Choice*. Random House, 1979.

[227] R. Sun, editor. *Cognition and Multi-Agent Interaction: From Cognitive Modeling to Social Simulation*. Cambridge University Press, New York, NY, 2006.

[228] A. de Swaan. Nood en deugd: over altruïsme en collectieve actie. *De Gids*, 147(3):139–151, 1984.

[229] B.Z. Tamanaha. *On the Rule of Law*. Cambridge University Press, 2004.

[230] A.D. Taylor. *Social Choice and the Mathematics of Manipulation*. Mathematical Association of America and Cambridge University Press, 2005.

[231] W. Teepe. *Reconciling Information Exchange and Confidentiality — A Formal Approach*. PhD thesis, Rijksuniversiteit Groningen, 2007.

[232] E. Tenner. *Why Things Bite Back; Technology and the Revenge Effect*. Fourth Estate, 1996.

[233] J. Tooby and L. Cosmides, editors. *Evolutionary Psychology: Foundational Papers*. MIT Press, Cambridge, MA, 2000.

[234] R.L. Trivers. The evolution of reciprocal altruism. *Quarterly Review of Biology*, 46:35–57, 1971.

[235] G.J. van Oldenburg. The mild winter of 2007: What were the causes?, 28 February 2007. Koninklijk Nederlands Meteorologisch Instituut. KNMI Kenniscentrum. http://www.knmi.nl/kenniscentrum/ zachte_winter_2007/index_en.html.

[236] T. Vanheste. De eenzame strijd van de broeikasongelovigen (the lonely struggle of the greenhouse-infidels). *Vrij Nederland*, 25 May 2005.

[237] R. Veenhoven. World database of happiness, distributional findings in nations. Technical report, Erasmus University, Rotterdam, Last revision: 2007. http://www.worlddatabaseofhappiness.eur.nl.

[238] R. Verbrugge and L. Mol. Learning to apply theory of mind. *Journal of Logic, Language and Information*, 17:489–511, 2008. Special issue on formal models for real people, edited by M. Counihan.

[239] F. de Waal. *Primates and Philosophers: How Morality Evolved.* Princeton University Press, 2006.

[240] B. Williams. *Ethics and the Limits of Philosophy.* Routledge, 2006.

[241] G.C. Williams. *Adaptation and Natural Selection: A Critique of Some Current Evolutionary Thought.* Princeton University Press, 1966.

[242] D.S. Wilson. *Darwin's Cathedral: Evolution, Religion, and the Nature of Society.* The University of Chicago Press, Chicago, 2002.

[243] H. Wimmer and J. Perner. Beliefs about beliefs: Representation and constraining function of wrong beliefs in young children's understanding of deception. *Cognition*, 13:103–128, 1983.

[244] G. Yule. *Pragmatics.* Oxford University Press, 1996.

Index